Contents

Preface

This book arose from the innovative and creative Qualitative Research Conferences held since 1984 at various universities in Southern Ontario. From more modest beginnings as an interdisciplinary conference with issues of deviance as its organizing theme, the "qualitatives" have grown in diversity and stature. Hosted over the years by the many folks at the University of Waterloo, University of Windsor, McMaster University, Carleton University, York University, and the University of Toronto, these meetings have become an important gathering place for those of us interested in the practical accomplishment of the social world.

This book is not, however, a collection of conference papers. Rather, the authors represented here quite willingly took up the project of asking, "What are some of the key research roblems in my field site and how have they been managed?" For the most part (with the exception of Chapters 7 and 12), these are original contributions. I remain deeply grateful for the willingness of the assembled authors to contribute to this project. The field research literature is better for their thoughtfulness and their candor.

With this book, I have tried to accomplish two goals. The first is to provide the relative newcomer to ethnography with a sense of ethnographic research as accomplished action. As the first tentative steps into the field are anticipated, it is important to remember that problems, ambivalences, uncertainties, and apprehensions are a part of the research process. The problems that you are facing are problems that others have likewise encountered. Some of those experiences are collected here. Although one needs to take into account the particular circumstances at hand, there is much to be learned by attending to how others have understood, managed, and responded to similar dynamics in their own work.

My second goal was to create an edited volume that would appeal to those of us who enjoy teaching field methods courses. By inviting something of an "ethnography of ethnography," the behind-the-scenes accounts offered provide some unique glimpses into the work of ethnography and accompanying theoretical concerns. I hope these papers find a productive place in your classroom. As I have used them in mine, I have found students quite willing to engage the similarities between their own projects and the problems recounted here in studies such as those of the marketplace, families, and survivalists. Not only do students learn about field methods as an accomplished activity but also they engage concepts more generically and appreciate firsthand how research in a substantive area quite distant from their own nevertheless holds an importance and a relevance to their own work.

Although the various issues in any one chapter may prove far ranging, I have ordered the papers in a loose natural history that follows the ethnographic project from more initial concerns to issues of presentation and representation. The book is organized into four major sections: Pursuing Intimate Familiarity and the Problem of Membership; Issues in Methodological Practice; Ethics, Intervention, and Emotionality; and Ethnographic Text and Ethnographic Voice. Although this ordering is intended to provide a framework for the reader, chapters are independent of one another and can be used in the classroom in any order desired.

Acknowledgments

Foremost, I recognize the contribution of each of the authors to this book, some of whom I have had the privilege to know and respect for many years. I also extend thanks to others. I appreciate the interest in and support of this project offered by Kieran Bonner, Carl Couch, Mary Lou Dietz, Skye Hughes, Peter Labella, Phil Merklinger, Chuck Tucker, Janet Wright, and the students in Fieldwork Methodology '97. I am also grateful for the financial assistance of Augustana University College. It is a lingering regret that the paper Carl Couch considered writing for this book was lost to his untimely death. He was looking forward to "giving us hell" for failing to study social process.

As a last word and a personal note, my deepest thanks go out to my friend, colleague, and wife, Sheilagh Grills. She has contributed to this project in so many ways. It would be poorer from beginning to end without her contribution.

From Albas, Dan and Cheryl Albas. Experience, Methodological Observation, and Theory: A Blumerian Excursion. *Canadian Journal of Higher Education*. Permission to reproduce.

From Mitchell, Richard and Kathy Charmaz. Telling Tales, Writing Stories: Postmodernist Visions and Realitist Images in Ethnographic Writing. *Journal of Contemporary Ethnography*. Permission to reproduce.

To Matthew, Samantha, and Nathan

A true question—a question seeking truth without expecting to find more than a fragment of it—will remain clear and unforgiving over hundreds of years.

—*John Ralston Saul*

PART I

Introduction

1

An Invitation to the Field

Fieldwork and the Pragmatists' Lesson

SCOTT GRILLS

Human society is to be seen as consisting of acting people, and the life of the society is to be seen as consisting of their actions.

—Blumer (1969, p. 85)

With this assertion, Blumer (1969) directs our attention to a rather basic question: What do we take to be the primary "units of analysis" in our research? The answer to this question is important because how we answer it influences what we study and what we can say about the social world as the result of our work. If we are studying people's responses to scripted questions (e.g., survey research and structured interviews), the products of human action (e.g., the content of the mass media and text analysis), or theories of theories (e.g., theoretical models constructed from prior theory), our sociology has little to do with the practical activities of everyday life. All these research questions serve to distance the researcher from the topic of study. For example, a survey of cult members, an analysis of how the evening news reports on cultic practice, or a theoretical distinction between "cult" and "sect" tell us nothing about what these people do as a part of a particular religious group. Such strategies keep the sociologist at arm's length from the people whose lives on which he or she is purporting to comment.

Field research, however, focuses on the interactive (e.g., processes, activities, and acts) and interpretive (e.g., definitions, perspectives, and meanings) aspects present within a particular setting.

3

By going to "where the action is," the field researcher pursues an intimate familiarity with the "world of the other," through getting close to the dilemmas, frustrations, routines, relationships, and risks that are a part of everyday life. This closeness to the social world is fieldwork's most profound strength as the researcher comes to know the world of the other through direct involvement within it. As Becker (1970) notes, being in a place allows our ideas of it to be resisted by the actions and words of those within the setting.

This is not, however, an entirely agreeable activity. In fact, "it is usually inconvenient, to say the least, sometimes physically uncomfortable, frequently embarrassing, and, to a degree, always tense" (Shaffir, Stebbins, & Turowetz, 1980, p. 3). Such qualities arise, in part, from the field researcher's commitment to asking questions of the social world that are infrequently raised by the participants. Quite irrespective of the field researcher's prior closeness to or distance from the activities he or she is attempting to understand more fully, it is perhaps a commitment to asking "how" questions that most clearly distances the field researcher from both the everyday members of the various settings under study and the other social scientists more generally. Although the chapters in this volume reflect some of the diversity to be found among field researchers (and as such represent some of the accompanying tensions), there is an underlying common interest in how people go about their lives and how they view the world. This rather broad interest often translates into a more detailed and dedicated understanding of questions presented in the following sections.[1]

How Do People Come to View the World as They Do?

Field researchers are often interested in developing an understanding of the perspective of the other. Because social objects (e.g., ideas, language, actions, symbols, physical objects, and identities) lack any inherent meaning, the researcher needs to understand how people view their world. Doing so helps us to make sense of the actions of others. For example, knowing something about how armed robbers think about their targets and themselves helps us to make sense of their willingness to "stick with stick-up" beyond what might seem reasonable to an outside observer (Katz, 1988). Objects may be viewed in a plurality of ways within a group: A gift may be simultaneously seen as beautiful, extravagant, divisive, or politically strategic. More collectively shared definitions may change over time: The music of a blues musician may at various points be defined as a race record, out of date, an influence on the next generation, and a national treasure. The problem of perspective, however, involves more than simply learning the worldview of the other. Taking this problem seriously means that the researcher develops an appreciation for the partial, situational, selective, and often inconsistent aspects of the perspectives that people utilize in their interactions with others (Berger & Luckmann, 1966; Schutz, 1967).

How Are Relationships With Others Created, Sustained, Reworked, or Sometimes Cast Aside?

Our relationships reflect the various "particularistic bonds" that people form with others (Prus, 1994). Unlike more fleeting and often impersonal encounters, relationships denote more enduring aspects of social life (Couch, 1989). Although the bonds we form with others vary greatly in their intensity, pervasiveness, duration, and relative importance, it is in the context of such relationships that the routine of everyday life is built up. To assert that human group life is relational is to attend to the various associations, collectives, partnerships, loyalties, and joint ventures that people undertake with one another.

Not unlike other strangers (Schutz, 1964), the field researcher who approaches a relatively unfamiliar research site does so in the context of preexisting relational dynamics—the content of which may be relatively unavailable to the newcomer. Nevertheless, the personal biographies that members may develop relative to one another denote elements of relational dynamics that may serve as interpersonal resources in subsequent interaction: People may be seen as trustworthy, loyal, like-minded, subversive, two-faced, or dishonest.

Relationships are to be profitably understood as dynamic features of everyday life. Despite the relatively enduring qualities of some patternings of human life, the relationships that mark these associations are themselves open to a continual "working out" as participants manage prior relationships in light of developing involvements, changing understandings of self, competing interests, and incompatible demands. As ethnographers interested in telling the story of a people, we are deeply interested in the relational claims that folks make relative to one another. For example, on university campuses people make a wide range of relational assertions identifying others as classmates, friends, professors, deans, fraternity members, roommates, lovers, and majors in a particular area (often with an implicit evaluative dynamic). An attentiveness to more enduring relational dynamics is essential to an analysis of community life.

How Are Activities Accomplished?

One of the striking shortcomings of more quantitative or causally oriented social science is that despite rather extensive study into a wide range of aspects of social life (e.g., voting behavior, consumer studies, and labor studies), we know surprisingly little about how people do politics, interact within the marketplace, or enter into occupational settings. The fundamental reason we know comparatively little about the practical accomplishment of intersubjectivity is that so little of our knowledge is grounded in or takes into account joint action—the coordinated activities of two or more actors.

As Couch (1995) has argued, the intertwining of social acts and social relations is a central problem in interactionist thought. For this intertwining to be made a real problem in our sociology, however, we need to go where the action is. Quite simply, there is no adequate substitute for the direct engagement of activities and acts of the other if we wish to understand the practical accomplishment of everyday life. We cannot manufacture social worlds out of bits of text, regression equations, or responses to questions that divorce the account of action from the action itself. Of course it is easier to do this, and it is less troublesome for the researcher. The result, however, is a sociology in which the people are hard to find. If we "go to the action," then, for example, we live the pain of chronic illness, the child's deep terror at her father's funeral, or the internal conflict in a labor movement. Although there is an emotive element present—which is enhanced as the vague distancing distinction between the researcher as a person and the "research instrument" is lost—this is not an emotive appeal. Actors can make a series of private indications, take others into account, and select from lines of action. It is in the context of the joint act, however, that the ethnographer engages the fully social. Here, I side more with Couch, Blumer, and Mead than with Weber and the German idealists who dance with a psychological reductionism. If our problem is understanding how we "do" family, justice, law, and religion, then the solution is to be found in research positions that move us toward activity and away from units of analysis.[2]

When we view action as, at least in part, joint action, we focus attention on the "doing" of activity. Terms that are often linguistically constructed as nouns are sociologically understood as verbs. Trade, religion, and kinship are "done." They are accomplished through the joint acts of barter and trade, worship and prayer, and naming and sharing, respectively. By attending to activity through the joint acts that are accomplished by actors, we bring life to otherwise lifeless conceptual structures and in the process "respect the nature of the empirical world" (Blumer, 1969, p. 60).

How Do People Become Involved in Various Groups or Activities?

Within the ethnographic tradition, concepts such as natural history, sequential involvements, and career point to a continuing interest in the uneven and uncertain path that people follow as they undertake an activity (e.g., Shaw, 1930, 1931). Whether it be involvement with biker gangs, 12-steps groups, choirs, university studies, or drug use, the various interests, concerns, allegiances, curiosities, and relationships that encourage initial participation may have little to do with continuing involvements. Likewise, activities previously defined as alluring, interesting, or otherwise enticing may subsequently come to be defined as risky, foolish, and otherwise misguided.

Therefore, understanding how people find themselves immersed in some activities rather than others requires us to take into account what Prus (1996) refers to as career contingencies: the dynamic ebb and flow of initial involvements, continuing involvements, disinvolvements, and reinvolvements. In many respects, more causally oriented questions concerning involvements are much less satisfying than their more processually oriented counterparts. Rather than generating a set of "in-order-to" or "because" accounts, the ethnographer who attends more fully to questions of involvement gains a richer and deeper sense of involvement as accomplished social activity. As a result, developed notions of career can be applied more generically to involvements in any activity.

How Are Identities Created, Managed, Embraced, Resisted, or Otherwise Presented to Others?

Who we are—who we think we are, how others see us, and how we think others see us—is social. Our sense of self, as various founding thinkers in pragmatism and interactionism have taught (e.g., James, Cooley, Mead, and Blumer), is established through our interactions with others. As children play, they gain a sense of self-other identities, learning, for example, how the "me" is situated relative to the "you," "we," and "they." The "self" is interactionally situated relative to others and therefore shares the qualities of social objects more generally. Claims as to who we are may be rather tenuous and are most certainly open to challenge on the part of others as well as ourselves.

It is this dynamic of the social self that makes questions surrounding the presentation, management, and negotiation of self ethnographically interesting. How, for example, do people encountering similar life events (e.g., chronic illness, religious conversion, the termination of employment, and homelessness) experience identity? How might peoples' identities change over time? What are the various dynamics at play that influence whether people are willing to share "who they are" with others? Although we might profitably ask such questions of virtually any setting, work in the area of the sociology of deviance has proven to be particularly attentive to such themes. Becker's (1963/1973) labeling theory locates questions of identity rather centrally in the understanding of the social production of deviance and the deviant.[3] The spoiling of identity involves the transformation of the public self, and also possibly the private self (Goffman, 1963; Karp, 1994; Lemert, 1962), as deviant identities are acquired, transformed, managed, embraced, or resisted. Although virtually any activity or set of ideas may be seen as troublesome or otherwise offensive by some audience (i.e., deviant), actors may quite willingly embrace and promote definitions of self that draw out or focus on aspects of deviance. Reflecting this theme, the identities that subcultural members develop may be reflected in the argot or special language found in some groups (e.g., "righteous bikers," "hardmen," or "rounders").

The interest in self that I have briefly described has produced a rich strain of sociological social psychology within the ethnographic literature.[4] By attending to the interactional, relational, and processual qualities of how people construct their identities, how others see them, and how the self is presented to various audiences, we add a richness and complexity to our understanding of the social world.

Problem Solving, Field Research, and the Pragmatists' Lesson

The questions discussed in the preceding sections are intended to provide an initial orientation to some of the more fundamental problems that have been a part of the ethnographic tradition. Researchers, however, may attend to one "set" of questions more fully than another (e.g., an anthropologist interested in kinship might devote the best part of a career to questions of relationship) or may treat such questions as useful only insofar as they produce some form of social change or desired political end (e.g., participatory action research combining more traditional scholarship with an interest in applied social science). Alternately, researchers may embrace ethnographic questioning as one aspect of other theoretical commitments (e.g., feminist scholarship or phenomenological analysis). Nevertheless, an interest in questions of process—how we perceive, accomplish, and construct the world we share with one another—remains central to the tradition of field research.

If the pragmatists are right—and I think that they are—that human group life is at least in part problem solving, then we can profitably think about field research as problem-solving activity. As

Rosaldo (1989) has argued, we are all "positioned subjects." That is, every social location that we occupy brings with it a mixture of insight and blindness. By being in one "place" (what phenomenologist Alfred Schutz would refer to as occupying a Here and Now), we gain a unique vantage point or sight line. That which allows us to see some things more clearly, however, also precludes other vantage points. It cannot be otherwise. We cannot be in two places at once. Although we can attempt to take multiple perspectives into account, and others can share their understanding of this or that aspect of social life, we always make sense of these representations through who we are.[5]

If the position that we occupy influences the range of interpretations available to us, then field research can be understood, in part, as an activity that repositions the social scientist in such a way as to allow for questioning that would be otherwise unavailable. As a pragmatic matter, this work of repositioning oneself involves gaining access to the lived experiences of others—their routines, concerns, activities, perspectives, and relationships. It is time-consuming, intensive, and exhausting work for which there is no substitute. We can imagine the world of the other and theorize about various aspects of the social world. Without an understanding of the perspectives and activities of those whose lives we claim to depict, however, our concepts can be nothing more than hollow reflections of the other—quite divorced from the worlds that we claim to know.

The field researcher's task of developing an intimate familiarity with the social world is, as Shaffir and Stebbins (1991) note, marked by the processes of getting in, learning the ropes, managing relations, and (possibly) leaving the field. Our attempts at such activities are littered with the various negotiations, false starts, misgivings, unfortunate alliances, performance anxieties, and other complications that reflect field research as an emergent and unpredictable practice. Reminiscent of themes that James (1893) struggled with more than a century ago, the various problems of ethnographic research always take place in the context of the particular settings. Although there are certainly more generic themes that reflect some of the frequently recurring issues faced by ethnographers, we confront these commonalities in the context of our own field sites. Reflecting the particularity of the setting, some issues will become much more pressing and some problems of research activities will impinge in more lively ways than others. For example, although the issue of identity and reputation of the researcher is a salient one for ethnographic work generally, it may be particularly relevant for some research projects and much less so for others.

This book developed from this interest in the problems of field research. I invited the ethnographers who have contributed to this volume to reflect on field research as problem-attentive action. I asked, "What are the central research problems to come out of your field sites and how have you managed them?" The answers presented in this book reflect the pragmatics of doing ethnographic work with groups such as Jewish communities, retailers, poachers, families, students, and members of a 12-step group. There is no attempt to provide a survey of various issues confronting ethnographers. Such a project in fact would be contrary to the editorial spirit of the book. Rather, I have encouraged the ethnographers represented here to draw out the themes that have proven to be most central to their own work and to utilize ethnographic resources where appropriate to take the reader into the field. As pleasing as it might be for a number of editorial reasons to attempt to compartmentalize chapters around a particular more narrowly defined theme, the problems that arise in the field rarely follow such neatly defined parameters. Problems of ethics merge with problems of membership, and struggles with researchers' identities may impinge on the research strategies that may be employed. Reflecting the emergent and negotiated quality of fieldwork, many of the chapters included here address several related themes. Some of the more recurring or generic issues are problems of (a) membership, (b) methodological practice, (c) competing obligations and intervention, and (d) voice.

Problems of Membership and Identity

Like other social activities that include elements of trust and developing relationships, field research includes a rather intense reputational dynamic. By placing themselves front and center in research activities, ethnographers' access to potential informants and their ability to "move" effectively within the field is influenced by how others understand their interests, intentions, and identities (e.g., see Chapter 2).

As Shaffir (Chapter 3) argues, field researchers have been somewhat remiss in the extent to which they have developed an appreciation of the role of "sociability" in sustaining field relations. As people go about their routines—within their families, workplaces, and places of worship—they may be much more attentive to the various qualities of the researcher (e.g., trustworthy, humorous, friendly, open, and nonjudgmental) than they are to the purpose of the research, consent forms, or credentials.

The various qualities of "who we are" are resources that we bring into the field. Stebbins' (Chapter 4) discussion of the vantage point of the ethnic outsider distanced by language or Grills' (Chapter 5) work on studying political parties while remaining nonpartisan illustrate how the various ways in which we work out our research relationships with others are influenced by such qualities of identity. Researchers, like any one else, may selectively disclose or may more actively conceal aspects of themselves, their activities, and their commitments (Chapter 9). How others construct the identity of the researcher, however, influences the overall depth and clarity of the larger project.

Choosing Between Methodological Strategies

Although not wishing to overwhelm the reader with a listing of the various practices engaged in by field researchers (the more central of which are participation, observation, and interview), the activities we undertake in the field may be problem solving in some ways but in turn may be accompanied by problematic dimensions (some of which are unanticipated). This should be neither surprising nor overly troubling. For if one is, as Prus (Chapter 2, p. 30) argues, pursuing intersubjectivity within a setting, then it is necessary to adopt methodological practices that allow for venturing "into the life-world of the other in a direct, interactive sense."

Within Albas and Albas' study of examinations and student life (Chapter 7) and Brymer's work on conflict gangs and hunting and poaching subcultures (Chapter 8), we find an argument presented for the relative benefits of utilizing multiple methodological strategies to overcome or compensate in some way for the limits of more narrowly conducted research. To borrow the analogy from Daly and Dienhart (Chapter 6), however, our methodological choices reflect something of a navigation of the field settings in which we find ourselves. As they point out, the particular dynamics of studying the "family domain" (e.g., entering family space, managing intimacy, and the dangers of alliances) are rather central considerations in choosing among various research strategies. Field research involves the ongoing work of coordinating lines of action as research activities are evaluated, challenged, and, at times, discarded.

Choosing Between Competing Obligations

The intimate involvements that are a part of field research mitigate against viewing those who share their worlds and their lives with us simply as respondents, informants, or case studies. Although ethnographers may use such terms to denote the particular relationship that develops in field settings, these same folks may also become our friends, business partners, sponsors, and coauthors. Such relational complexities may prove to be particularly troubling for some. For example, the perceived obligations of friendship may discourage otherwise helpful research activities.

Likewise, researchers' personal commitments to the groups and activities they study may contribute to a sense of competing obligations as the demands of the social scientist are understood in light of the obligations held as member. As Irvine's (Chapter 9) work draws out, we may come to see ourselves in the groups we study. Such challenges or modifications to identity may foster a series of ethical concerns as we attempt to balance our organizational commitments to our professional associations and particular institutional regulating bodies with the expectations of member participants.

At times, these perceived obligations may encourage ethnographers to become directly involved in their field sites as advocates for particular worldviews or members. Some would argue more generally that all fieldwork is "on someone's side" and is therefore political.[6] As a quality of lived experience, the decision to become more directly involved in a field site for purposes other than strictly research may be made in light of particular situational dynamics. Researchers may find certain situations in the field troubling or otherwise offensive and may choose to intervene on the basis of any number of interests and agendas. For example, Sanders (Chapter 10,

p. 193) argues that "should the ethnographer choose to intervene in situations that arise in the field, I maintain that these efforts are best focused on improving the lot of those with the least power." The distinction between those with power and those without, those who are in the right or wrong, and those with whom we side and those whom we oppose, however, tells us more about the commitments and the obligations held by the researcher than about some necessary qualities found in the field setting. The emotional involvement of field researchers with the social worlds they study provides a resource for understanding the social world that is relatively unavailable to other researchers.

Problems of Voice

How we talk about, write about, and present ethnographic research to others is a part of the extended research relationship we establish with respondents. What we are able to say about the lives of those who have given us access to their worlds reflects the various vantage points that have allowed us to intimately engage both processes and perspectives. In this sense, ethnographers are storytellers. How we see our tales and how we contextualize them relative to ways of telling stories (e.g., fictions, voices, truths, narratives, and versions), however, is a problematic feature of ethnography in postmodern times. If every claim becomes a fiction, then there is little reason to attend more closely to ethnographic research than to other stories of everyday life (e.g., journalistic accounts, novels, cinematic renditions, and diaries).

Blain (Chapter 11) addresses this general issue by examining the problems of utilizing more traditional (e.g., rationalistic) forms of social scientific presentation to convey the beliefs and practices of those who hold nonrationalistic worldviews. She asks, "How can we understand informants' constructions without granting validity to the premises on which these constructions are built?" (p. 204) The various assumptions and claims that we as ethnographers make about the social world may not be shared by others. In practice, those in various field settings may view the ethnographic interest as naive, irrelevant, or potentially dangerous. In such circumstances, the tensions between ones ethnographic voice, the ways in which it is experienced by members (e.g., in print, through interaction, and as students in our classes), and the general worldview held by the groups under study may present unresolvable conflicts or incongruities (see Chapter 5). However, as Silverman (1989) notes, quality ethnography does not substitute the members' accounts for theoretical analysis. Therefore, the problem of moving between members' stories and the ethnographer's vantage point is rather fundamental to ethnography and is a tension present in grounded theory more generally (Glaser & Strauss, 1967). As Mitchell and Charmaz (Chapter 12) affirm, however,

> Quibbles over the ontological status of the truly true and debates over the primacy of one discourse over another serve no useful purpose.... Our concern is finding ways for individual consciousness to join the intersubjective, ways to report experience to others and ourselves. (p. 243)

To write ethnographic stories is to engage in social action—to take multiple others into account, to manage impressions, to engage others, and to resist prior constructions. Our ethnographic "storytelling" begins with the most tentative and uncertain steps into the field, initial field notes that are disjointed and wandering, and first interviews dotted here and there with naive questions and our own, at times, careless responses. Irrespective of the various negotiations and dilemmas that arise in the course of our extended projects, the problem of moving from experience to text—from field setting to story—is one that binds ethnographers to the experiences of other writers. As Charmaz emphasizes (in Chapter 12), the work of "pulling the reader in," "re-creating experiential mood," "adding surprise," "reconstructing ethnographic experience," and "creating closure" are writing strategies that ethnographers may utilize to more effectively convey their stories—as provisional and situated as they are necessarily.

Conclusion

Sociology's history as a discipline is marked by a long and continuing relationship with field research. It is no accident that many of the best loved and most enduring essays and books in sociology are from this tradition.[7] These works have an ability to speak to the reader in a way that is unavailable to others. By "getting close," ethnographers provide a texture, an immediacy, and a depth of understanding that cannot be attained through research strategies that keep the social world at arm's length. This book is intended as an invitation to the work and pleasure of field research. By sharing some of the problems, frustrations, ethical dilemmas, and epistemological issues that arise from their work, the authors collected here are writing of lived research. This is different from the more inclusive term, lived experience. With lived experience, we draw from where and who we are to inform our sociology, and this may prove quite helpful along the way. Lived research, however, involves the disciplined and intentional attempt to engage the other and to learn their worlds, their ways of seeing, and their ways of doing and being. It is the pursuit of an intimate understanding of perspectives and activities that involves a series of practical accommodations oriented toward achieving intersubjectivity.

Although fieldwork may be an activity marked by awkwardness and populated by those who are on occasion taken for the fool (Wax, 1971), it also has the possibility to be one of the most rewarding learning experiences that social scientists will have. There is no substitute for the vantage point afforded those of us who conduct research in the field. What is learned where the action is cannot be acquired anywhere else. By engaging the field, our sociology takes into account the activities, perspectives, relationships, understandings of self, and involvements that mark the practical accomplishment of social life. Through field research, our literature comes to include the voices of those who would otherwise be silenced. Likewise, the distance between our concepts and the life that they are intended to "represent" is narrowed.

Some sociology is attentive to peoples' experiences and involvements, their conflicts and their alliances, their perspectives, and their beliefs. Other sociology is "peopled" by systems requirements, theories of theory, or postmodern self-congratulation. Given a choice between these two, I gladly choose the former. The commitment to the field is a commitment to the study of human life as it is "experienced and accomplished by the very people involved in its production" (Prus, 1996, p. 9).

Notes

1. Readers are directed to Prus (1996) for a more detailed discussion of these themes and for an overview of the ethnographic tradition.

2. Readers are encouraged to reflect on the place of survey research relative to this position. Despite the various ways in which survey research can be collected or presented, it inevitably reflects the responses of multiple individuals to a series of questions.

3. For example, Becker (1963/1973, p. 207) writes, "The interactionist approach shows sociologists that a major element in every aspect of the drama of deviance is the imposition of definitions—of situations, action and people—by those powerful enough or sufficiently legitimated to be able to do so."

4. Notable is Wiseman's (1991) study of the experiences of women married to alcoholics, Charmaz's (1991) study that explores the self in chronic illness, and Thumma's (1991) research on the experiences of gay males from evangelical backgrounds.

5. For example, my gender "places" me at a distance from women's experiences. To the extent that one is reflective, attentive, and analytical about such issues, however, living a life that is "gendered" also provides a vantage point from which to attend to the "gendering" of everyday life more generally.

6. For example, see Becker (1967). For a recent examination of related themes, see Gubrium (1989).

7. For recent accounts of the development of the ethnographic tradition, see Prus (1996) and Fine (1995).

References

Becker, H. (1967). Whose side are we on? *Social Problems, 14,* 239-247.

Becker, H. (1970). *Sociological work: Method and substance.* Chicago: Aldine.

Becker, H. (1973). *Outsiders.* New York: Free Press. (Original work published 1963)

Berger, P., & Luckmann, T. (1966). *The social construction of reality.* New York: Anchor.

Blumer, H. (1969). *Symbolic interactionism.* Englewood Cliffs, NJ: Prentice Hall.

Charmaz, K. (1991). *Good days, bad days: The self in chronic illness.* New Brunswick, NJ: Rutgers University Press.

Couch, C. (1989). *Social processes and social relationships.* Dix Hills, NY: General Hall.

Couch, C. (1995). Oh what webs those phantoms spin. *Symbolic Interaction, 18,* 229-245.

Fine, G. A. (1995). *A second Chicago School?: The development of a postwar American sociology.* Chicago: University of Chicago Press.

Glaser, B., & Strauss, A. (1967). *The discovery of grounded theory: Strategies for qualitative research.* Chicago: Aldine.

Goffman, E. (1963). *Stigma.* Englewood Cliffs, NJ: Spectrum.

Gubrium, J. (1989). *Politics of field research: Sociology beyond enlightenment.* London: Sage.

James, W. (1893). *Principles of psychology* (Vol. 1). New York: Holt.

Karp, D. A. (1994). The dialectics of depression. *Symbolic Interaction, 17,* 341-366.

Katz, J. (1988). *Seductions to crime: Moral and sensual attractions in doing evil.* New York: Basic Books.

Lemert, E. (1962). Paranoia and the dynamics of exclusion. *Sociometry, 25,* 2-25.

Prus, R. (1994). Generic social processes: Intersubjectivity and transcontextuality. In M. Lorenz Dietz, R. Prus, & W. Shaffir (Eds.), *Doing everyday life: Ethnography as human lived experience* (pp. 393-412). Mississauga, Ontario, Canada: Copp Clark Longman.

Prus, R. (1996). *Symbolic interaction and the ethnographic tradition.* Albany: State University of New York Press.

Rosaldo, R. (1989). *Culture and truth: The remaking of social analysis.* Boston: Beacon.

Schutz, A. (1964). *Collected papers, Vol. II: Studies in social theory* (A. Brodersen, Ed.). The Hague: Nijhoff.

Schutz, A. (1967). *The phenomenology of the social world* (G. Walsh & F. Lehnert, Trans.). Evanston, IL: Northwestern University Press.

Shaffir, W., & Stebbins, R. (Eds.). (1991). *Experiencing fieldwork: An inside view of qualitative methods.* Newbury Park: Sage.

Shaffir, W., Stebbins, R., & Turowetz, A. (1980). *Fieldwork experience.* New York: St. Martin's.

Shaw, C. (1930). *The jack-roller: A delinquent boy's own story.* Chicago: University of Chicago.

Shaw, C. (1931). *The natural history of a delinquent career.* Chicago: University of Chicago Press.

Silverman, D. (1989). Six rules of qualitative research: A post-romantic argument. *Symbolic Interaction, 12,* 215-230.

Thumma, S. (1991). Negotiating a religious identity: The case of the gay evangelical. *Sociological Analysis, 52,* 333-347.

Wax, R. (1971). *Doing fieldwork.* Chicago: University of Chicago Press.

Wiseman, J. P. (1991). *The other half: Wives of alcoholics and their social-psychological situation.* New York: Aldine.

PART II

Pursuing Intimate Familiarity and the Problem of Membership

Field researchers, whether their work involves observation, participation, interview, or all three have all "paid their dues" in the field. Unlike many of the other strategies social scientists may utilize to conduct research that may keep the world of everyday life at a distance, the ethnographer's experience places the self quite literally within the world of the other. Being there—whether "there" is with gang members, parents, or veterinarians—means that the researcher needs to find a place within the research setting. The ethnographer's proximity to the social world he or she wishes to learn more about is central to the success of the research enterprise. The practices of unstructured, in-depth interviewing and participant observation are contingent, in part, on the researcher's ability to gain access to those involved "in the life." If we cannot "connect" with a particular group or setting, or gain access to those who share particular experiences or involvements, then there is little basis for developing the familiarity with a life world required by the ethnographic enterprise.

The chapters in this part address the general problem of how ethnographers establish and maintain "viable working relationships" between themselves and others. The research setting influences how these relationships are negotiated and the various qualities that accompany them. The relationships established between

19

the researcher and the respondents portrayed in the following chapters reflect the field setting. Prus is the "student" of the marketplace, encouraging retailers to teach him about their worlds. Shaffir emphasizes the importance of being seen as decent, responsible, honorable—a "mentsh"—in his study of Orthodox Jewish communities. For my part, approaching more fundamentalist religious groups entailed managing the somewhat discredited identity of "sociologist" and utilizing the distance afforded through professionalism to establish a viable and rewarding research relationship with the group. Stebbins' chapter attends to the place that language and ethnicity may hold in establishing the researcher as an outsider and the pragmatic activities that may accompany the move from "outside" to, at least in part, "in."

All these "positions" are ways of managing the problem of membership. This problem is common to the ethnographic enterprise. If our research projects are to succeed, then we need to find a place for ourselves relative to the world of others. The research encounter involves a variety of negotiations, accommodations, and possible changes in membership roles over time. As readers work through the chapters in this section, the following themes deserve particular attention:

▓ The importance of a congruence between the understanding we develop of human action (our theory) and the activities we undertake to study group life (our method)

▓ The concept of intimate familiarity and the project of getting close to the topic of study

▓ The researcher as outsider or insider and the various practical strategies of managing closeness and distance

▓ The place of "sociability" specifically and the definition of the personal qualities of the researcher more generally

▓ Identity as changeable and fluid relative to various audiences and the accompanying problematics of self and other identities

▓ The ways in which researchers may modify the research role in light of the perspectives and relationships present within the group of study

2

Respecting the Human Condition

Pursuing Intersubjectivity in the Marketplace

ROBERT PRUS

While much overlooked as an arena of study by social scientists, the marketplace represents a setting rich in human dynamics (and contrasts). Marketplaces are often envisioned in terms of locations, structures, decor, and displays, and these elements are important in denoting "shells" of sorts or focal points around which a considerable amount of trade may take place. But it is not the location, the structure, the decor, or the displays that define the marketplace. . . . Particular locations may offer vendors and buyers certain conveniences, as may structures of various sorts, or various props and signs, but these elements are important only to the extent that people incorporate them into their selling and purchasing routines. . . . The marketplace is thoroughly and fundamentally social in its constitution. It involves preparation and adjustment, planning and uncertainty, persuasion and resistance, trust and skepticism, commitment and reservation, dreams and disappointments, frustration and excitement, as well as friendship and animosity. Marketplace activity reflects people's past experiences and their anticipations of the future, but it takes its shape in the "here and now" as people work out aspects of their lives in conjunction with the other people whose lives intersect with their own. (Prus, 1989a, p. 23)

In the course of drawing attention to the marketplace as an intriguing and instructive realm of inquiry for those in the human sciences, this chapter assumes three objectives: (a) outlining the basic assumptions undergirding the study of the human condition; (b) emphasizing the necessity of achieving intersubjectivity with (attending to the viewpoints of) those whose life-worlds that we, as social scientists, purport to study; and (c) indicating how the marketplace might be approached in ethnographic terms (i.e., as a realm of human lived experience). Because each of these topics is quite extensive on its own, it is possible to provide only a brief introduction to each. As will become quickly apparent, however, this chapter is about both the marketplace and the study of human group life more generally. The viewpoint taken here is that the study of the marketplace should be both informed by and used to inform scholarly endeavors in all realms of human activity.

A Realm of Intrigue

> When you're in business, you're dependent on all these other people. You may own the business, but they own you! Your fate is in their hands. Your customers, your suppliers, your staff, everyone you deal with. It's all part of the package. All these people, they're very important to whether you have a good day or a bad day in your business, or whether you survive or you don't [manufacture giftware]. (Prus, 1989b, p. 39)

> People [companions] try to talk you out of it even though you are so sure that you know what you've decided on, so it can help you and it can also confuse you while trying to be a smart shopper. . . . Everybody wants to go their own way. [m 30]l[1] (Prus, 1993b, p. 106)

Although very much neglected by sociologists and other social scientists, the marketplace offers a most intriguing arena for examining human interchanges. Reflecting contrasts of excitement and boredom, challenge and frustration, trust and deception, planning and ambiguity, solitary ventures and group endeavors, the marketplace denotes ongoing sets of enterprise, interchange, and adjustments. The objects (goods and services) of exchange range from the most basic of commodities required for human survival and all manners of work roles to vast realms of fashion, recreation, and entertainment. Included are things deemed legitimate and respectable as well as those defined as illegitimate and disrespectable.

The exchange of objects also assumes wide variations in form, ranging from the casual interchanges of items among acquaintances and occasional instances of bartering among strangers to people's involvements (as both buyers and sellers) in more sustained trading arenas such as outdoor markets, trade shows, stores, malls, coffee shops, bars, motels, concerts, commercial sports events, tourist attractions, advertising, catalog sales, and Internet shopping. Cutting across the arenas of construction, manufacturing, and transportation, the industries of clothing, food, accommodations, and entertainment, the print and electronic media, and the medical, legal, and other service sectors, as well as being extensively intertwined with the political and moral/religious realms of community life (including international relations), the marketplace is extensively interfused with virtually every aspect of our lives as urbanized denizens of this planet.

Furthermore, in addition to the many realms of ambiguity, challenge, and influence (and resistance) that research ventures into the marketplace may represent in more substantive (product focused) senses, studies of marketplace activity (on the part of both sellers and buyers) could enable researchers to develop more comprehensive understandings of basic or generic social processes of human association. By comparing (and contrasting) people's practices (and interchanges) in the marketplace with those occurring in other arenas of human endeavor (e.g., religion, family life, medical practice, and magic) along analytical themes, such as acquiring perspectives, developing relationships, achieving identity, doing activity, managing emotionality, and making commitments, one may develop a better understanding of several dimensions that cut across broad realms of human group life:[2]

> Sales is much like performing. I've worked on stage. . . . There's a lot of similarity between stand-up comedy and pleasing the client, bring a smile to their face and making a sale on a one-to-one basis [mixed sales]. (Prus, 1989a, p. 35)

As well, because our lives (and those of our associates) are so extensively interfused with objects obtained through marketplace ventures, the study of people's involvements in the marketplace should provide not only an important means of learning more about ourselves but also, and even more consequentially, an opportunity to learn more about the people with whom we attempt to relate on a day-to-day basis. The study of the marketplace thus provides an "open sesame" or "magic carpet" for learning about what Mead (1934) terms, "the generalized other":

> In sales, you see people at their worst when you're trying to sell them something. They're the most cynical. They want to establish dominance in the situation. There's the feeling that if you let the salesman get the upper hand in the situation that you're going to buy something you don't want. They're also parting with their money. I think we all have a little of the miser in us, and I'm not different from anyone else that way.... They put on a different kind of front [mixed clothing]. (Prus, 1989a, p. 287)

> I like going shopping with someone when I'm going with them for something they are going to buy.... I have always enjoyed window shopping. I enjoy spending money too, if there's lots of it and I don't have to worry or feel guilty about spending it. With someone else, I can have the vicarious fun through them and I'm not spending the money. So it's really fun to go with them and I don't feel any guilt, so I can push them to buy really expensive things. [f 30]m (Prus, 1989b, p. 102)

Respecting Our Human Subject Matter (Basic Assumptions)[3]

> I have a weakness for chocolate, and I know I shouldn't have bought it, because this was a fair bit of money and I'm trying to diet, right, but I stopped and it looked so good, and she was talking about it and how it melted in your mouth and all, and that was enough to convince me. [f 30]l (Prus, 1994, p. 256)

Despite the centrality of the marketplace for urban society, most social scientists have overlooked the rich diversity of human interchange that takes place in the arenas of trade and commerce. In a broader sense, most social scientists have failed to acknowledge the central and enduring human concern with [objects][4] and people's definitions of, modes of acquiring, and manners of dealing with objects.

To some extent, these approaches toward the marketplace are indicative of a more fundamental tendency on the part of many social scientists to disattend to the world of human lived experience and to disregard the ways in which people make sense of the world about them and accomplish their activities in the "here and now" circumstances in which they live.[5]

Although focusing on aspects of human behavior and community life for well over a century, most social scientists have attempted to impose (images of) theory and methods developed in the physical sciences on the study of the human condition. Following the models and methods proposed by John Stewart Mill and Wilhelm Wundt in psychology and Auguste Comte and Emile Durkheim in sociology, those in the social sciences have tended to view people's behaviors as the products of various forces (factors and variables) acting on them rather than examining the ways in which people meaningfully, actively, and interactively engage the world(s) in which they find themselves.[6]

The position taken here is quite different from that characterizing mainstream (positivist and quantitative) social science. If social scientists are sincere in their quest for a scientific appreciation of the human condition, they have an obligation to respect the nature of human group life and to develop theory and methodology that is attentive first and foremost to the human essence.

Although it would be a good start, this is not a simple matter of acknowledging human agency or people's capacities for intentionality. While people can act purposively or with intention, it should be recognized that human agency, itself, represents a process grounded in human interchange. Human behavior (and human agency) cannot be understood apart from an appreciation of ongoing community life:

> Well, it's their job in part to get you over the hurdles you may feel about buying something. Like maybe you're concerned about your budget, that it might be a little tight now. Well, they may help you get over that concern with a monthly payment plan. Or maybe you're not sure that your girlfriend will like it. Then they give you

all these reasons that she will. And it can sound good, it can make a lot of sense at the time. Later, you might regret getting it, and you think back to those doubts you had. . . . But here's someone who's going to help you get rid of certain doubts if they can, and maybe put things in ways you hadn't thought of. So, it's not just telling you how great something is, but this other thing too. [m 29]m (Prus, 1994, p. 254)

As Mead (1934) and Blumer (1969/1986) emphasize, society consists of people with selves in interaction, but people develop selves only through linguistic (or symbolic) interchange with those who have predated their presence within the human community. People's senses of reality (and self) are achieved most fundamentally through linguistic association, but human experiences with [the world] involve more than symbolic interchange. Because human experience also entails activity, intersubjectively acquired symbolic images become interfused with the activities through which people engage [the world] in some manner or other. What is required, therefore, is both a fuller recognition of the linguistically achieved intersubjectivity or sharedness of meanings within the human community and a more explicit appreciation of all the activities entailed in the human struggle for existence (and any other pursuits in which people may meaningfully engage).[7]

Thus, in contrast to scholars studying other objects (i.e., as in the physical sciences), those examining the human condition should explicitly (i.e., theoretically and methodologically) acknowledge that people have capacities to (a) use language (symbols) to communicate with others regarding [the world] around them; (b) assign differing meanings to [objects];[8] (c) take themselves and others into account in acting toward the world; (d) deliberately invoke specific behaviors in engaging the world; (e) influence and resist one another; (f) develop selective affiliations or associations with other people; and (g) attend to notions of emergence, sequence, or temporality. In other words, this requires that scholars of the human condition attend to the (a) intersubjective, (b) multiperspectival, (c) reflective, (d) action-oriented, (e) negotiable, (f) relational, and (g) processual dimensions of human community life.[9]

Rather than approach the study of human behavior (and community life) as if it were caused or produced by factors or variables acting on people, the approach adopted here assumes a socially constructed, linguistically enabled, and meaningfully enacted orientation to the study of human group life. Although focused on the marketplace (and people's activities and interchanges therein), this chapter addresses the broader topic of examining the ways in which people experience (and act toward) the day-to-day settings in which they find themselves. It is here that the matter of achieving intersubjectivity with the (ethnographic) other assumes such centrality.

Pursuing Intersubjectivity

> When you're selling, it's like you're putting on a show for the customer. . . . Sometimes I stutter, I get excited, but we've memorized our presentation, all our lines. And it is like being an actor, but you get tested more. And you have to give your version, but you have to watch it. It has to come out more naturally. Not like Sheila. She didn't last because of it [cosmetics]. (Prus, 1989a, p. 66)

Somewhat like salespeople trying to establish meaningful interchanges with prospective buyers, those engaged in ethnographic research also face the task of making contact and achieving viable working relations with those encountered in the field. Because I have written about the processes and problematics of doing field research in some detail elsewhere (Prus, 1980, 1991, 1996b, 1997b), I will mention only a few of the more basic themes here.[10]

First and foremost, however, I emphasize the necessity of researchers striving for sincere, open-ended understandings of the life worlds of the other—understandings that derive from sustained interaction with the other. For those embarking on field research, this means assuming the role of a highly motivated and curious researcher, someone who is there to learn as much as possible about the life-world of the other. In part, this requires putting one's presumptions, moralities, and wisdoms in suspension and attending in a very focused fashion to the experiences (viewpoints, activities, and adjustments) of the other. Researchers should be prepared both to learn about the world as *known to the other* and to represent it in a manner that is faithful to (and does not moralize about) the life-world experienced by the other. Those embarking on field research are also well advised to clarify in their own minds (and carefully attend to) the basic assumptions (see the earlier discussion) that they make in approaching the study of the human condition.

Whether one focuses on life-worlds in which one (a) is already a participant, (b) has preexisting contacts with the participants, (c) locates "sponsors" who introduce the researcher to others, or (d) engages in "cold calls" (approaching relative strangers on one's own), those embarking on ethnographic research typically face the task of encountering others in the field and presenting (explaining) one's project to these others in ways that they find comprehensible. It is essential that the researcher generate an openness with the (ethnographic) other that fosters both a tolerance of the researcher in the field and a willingness on the part of the other to share a wide range of materials (often personally unflattering) with the researcher. This seems most readily attained when researchers deal with others in straightforward, nonpretentious terms, indicating (and sustaining) an interest in carefully learning about the life world of the other as experienced by the other.

Although researchers sometimes feel awkward or experience "stage fright" (Lyman & Scott, 1970) when approaching and talking with others, it is much more important to ensure that others feel comfortable with researchers. Interestingly, in concentrating on the latter objective, researchers often find themselves feeling more relaxed with their respondents. Likewise, if one focuses on learning about the other (versus moralizing with or attempting to inform or reform), field research tends to be more productive.

Like most ethnographers, I encourage researchers to spend as much time in the field as possible, particularly talking in-depth with the participants about their experiences. Although most of my effort in the field is apt to be directed toward learning about the activities (and interchanges) that people do, I also studiously examine their viewpoints, identities, relationships, and anything else to which they seem to attend in the setting under consideration.

Part of the reason that it is advisable to be thorough when in the field (collecting and recording as much data as possible) is that the material is so important when embarking on a more extended analysis of a particular life-world. Focusing on the ways in which people manage various (activity) sectors of their lives in conjunction with others, one strives to articulate, in as much detail as possible, all the subthemes that particular lines of action entail and how, exactly, people work their ways (in process terms) through situations they face. Because the analysis is itself an emergent process in which one tries to comprehend (and convey) the viewpoints, practices, and adjustments of those in the setting, one is apt to appreciate having access to more data from the field when one embarks on the analysis. Still, as the analysis unfolds, other questions become apparent. This often means going back into the field to ask participants for more information about their experiences, but there is little doubt that those who have been more thorough at the outset are advantaged. The objective is to ensure that the manuscript being developed will be a more effective (accurate and comprehensive) conduit between those whose worlds one is trying to represent and prospective readers. Approached along these lines, ethnographic research is a very demanding, labor-intensive, and painstaking endeavor. It also represents the most effective means available for learning about the human condition, however.

Ethnographic inquiry is greatly facilitated by an almost endless curiosity, a tremendous amount of patience, a chameleon-like capacity for adaption (and composure), and an ability to deal with extended realms of ambiguity. Some people may be advantaged over others in certain respects at the outset, but most people can develop these capacities (adequately, if not sometimes surprisingly well) when they have sincere interests in learning about the human condition. Because human behavior has a situated or "here and now" quality to it, it is essential that researchers attend to the ways in which people accomplish their activities. This means focusing on the "how" as opposed to the "why" of group life. Novices may also be surprised to learn that the people they encounter in the field are apt to provide more extensive accounts (explanations, portrayals, and demonstrations) of their situations when asked *how* they do things. Asking people why they do things promotes "motive talk" or often results in people feeling obliged to justify their behavior in terms that might be deemed acceptable by the researcher.

It may also be useful to keep in mind that there is no such thing as "the perfect interview" or the "perfect researcher." Much more important than the specific questions one asks, for instance, is an ongoing receptivity to the viewpoints and practices of the other. As long as one gains material that further addresses the topic in some pertinent, open, and more sustained manner, then every encounter with the other can be productive in an overall sense. Most seasoned ethnographers will also observe that researchers typically are unable to recognize the value of the materials that they are collecting until they have developed more comprehensive appreciations of the life-world (or subtheme) under investigation. Minimally, like those venturing into the marketplace, every encounter with the other may be seen to contribute to one's stock of knowledge as an ethnographer. This includes any mistakes (and salvaging efforts) that might be made along the way.

It may be safer and easier to (a) bury oneself in the library, embarking on a comparative analysis or historical overview of existing materials, (b) embark on a "content analysis" of existing products (artifacts, events, or records), or (c) pursue knowledge about the other through experimental or survey research of some sort than to venture into the life-world of the other in a direct, interactive sense. Until social scientists put aside their hesitations of encountering the other in "the world out there," however, our theories (and other understandings) are apt to represent poor approximations of the human condition.

Studying the Marketplace Ethnographically

You have to have a liking and an understanding of people because, first and foremost, it's a people business! . . . If you can handle people, you can sell them anything. If you are an affable person, if you can talk to people, relate to kings or peasants, whether it's an upper-class person who wants to buy a top line or someone who is wanting to buy our least expensive model, that's a big part of your success [auto]. (Prus, 1989b, p. 62)

In pursuing the final objective of this chapter—that is, indicating how one might approach the study of the marketplace in ethnographic terms—I begin with a brief overview of my involvements in this arena. This may help readers put this entire chapter in a broader context, but more importantly this discussion may foster the realization that one would approach the study of the marketplace in the same way that one would approach the study of any other human subject matter. This means examining, in close detail, exactly what people do and how they develop their lines of activity in conjunction with others in the particular community (life-world) settings in which they find themselves.

Despite my own extended participation in the marketplace as a consumer (child, adolescent, and adult), long-term and ongoing contact with a variety of family members and friends who also actively participate in the marketplace, and some early "bit" part involvements in the retail sector, I did not engage the study of the marketplace in any direct sense. As someone trained primarily in quantitative methods in sociology (specializing in deviance and social psychology), my involvements in both ethnographic research and the study of marketplace activities have been rather circuitous. My first ethnographic ventures dealt with parole officers (Prus & Stratton, 1976) and the clergy (Prus, 1976). These graduate school undertakings were rather tentative and limited in cast, reflecting applications of what I had learned from some preliminary exposure to the interactionist literature (no courses on ethnographic research were available at the University of Iowa).

Rather fortuitously, I became involved in a study of confidence games (Prus & Sharper, 1977). Working with a former card and dice hustler, I found that I learned a great deal more about ethnographic research from C. R. D. Sharper (Prus, 1980) than from any of the literature I had read.[11] Subsequently, a chance contact with Styllianoss Irini presented an opportunity to engage in a field study of the people (hookers, strippers, bar staff, patrons, and others) who constituted "the hotel community" (Prus, 1983; Prus & Irini, 1980/1988).

As Irini and I were completing the hotel project, it became strikingly apparent that we also had been studying a number of businesses (albeit mostly illicit), and I began thinking about marketplace exchanges in a more explicit manner. Rather simultaneously (from this same study), I developed a profound realization that one could not comprehend the behavior of individuals without reference to the interchanges that they have with their associates and the particular subcultural contexts (involving activities, perspectives, identities, and relationships) in which they find themselves.

As an aside, it might be observed that I would have been quite interested in studying the marketplace as an undergraduate student, or later in graduate school, because I had become aware that it represented an important realm of influence work. Despite its apparent relevancy for social psychology and community life, however, the study of marketing or consumer behavior never seemed quite like something that one could viably pursue as a sociology student. At least, I did not see how one could formulate and academically justify a study of this type. On acquiring greater familiarity with field research years later, I began to realize that one not only could study any and all the activities in which people engage through ethnographic analysis but also could gain much insight into community life (and human lived experience) in the process.

Encountering the Literature

While I examined a great deal of published work on the marketplace, surprisingly little of this material focuses on people's experiences therein. Most of this literature (a) focuses on variables and factors that authors presume will account for successes and failures on the part of marketers or determine the shopping preferences of customers; (b) discusses particular companies and products (usually in more sweeping, sometimes trendy and sometimes historical, terms); (c) provides prescriptions and suggestions regarding procedures and practices that one should adopt to be more successful as a seller or buyer; or (d) addresses various problems or criticisms that particular authors associate with the marketplace. Remarkably little of this material attends to the ways in which people engage the marketplace in direct, experiential manners as either buyers or sellers.[12]

Envisioning Marketing and Sales in Process Terms

My first explicit venture into the marketplace was a study of vendor activity (Prus, 1989a, 1989b). Although I had never taken any university courses on marketing or consumer behavior (in retrospect, this may have been fortunate because it may have helped avoid the positivist frameworks and presuppositions that characterize most approaches within business schools), I did not enter the field as a complete novice. I did not know what I would find there, but I had fashioned an analytical tool kit that was to prove exceedingly valuable for undertaking the task of examining the market-place as a realm of human endeavor. Specifically, I benefited exten-sively from an attentiveness to an interactionist approach (Blumer, 1969/1986; Mead, 1934) to the study of human group life, an aware-ness of many of the ethnographic studies that had been accumulated in other areas of human interchange,[13] and earlier studies of the clergy, card and dice hustling, and the hotel community. Still, I had no idea how this project would turn out and kept expecting to find that the study was essentially redundant. Surely, I thought, some people in business schools must have studied the ways in which people engage in roles as vendors in direct, active fashions. Accord-ingly, I proceeded somewhat tentatively, but I took the viewpoint that minimally I was there to learn. My objective, most centrally, was to learn what people did in the process of attempting to sell things to others.

I began the marketing and sales study by talking with a few retailers at a neighboring shopping mall but soon expanded this to include a much broader assortment of merchants. The people with whom I spoke early on said that to understand them I would have to learn more about their suppliers and their relationships with their suppliers. They suggested that I attend some trade shows with them and talk to wholesalers, manufacturers, media representatives, and so on. I pursued this project as relentlessly as I could, using all sorts of contact occasions with those (broadly) "in the trade" to acquire more detailed information about, and a more intimate under-standing of, the ways in which people engaged in marketing and sales activities.

I told the people with whom I spoke that I was not interested in what people should or should not do but wanted to know what they did—all the things they did, enjoyable and otherwise, in the course of doing business. I also said that I needed all the help I could get and not to worry about boring me with the details. After that, I tried to be the best student they could have—endlessly attentive and inquisitive, nonmoralistic, and very concerned about learning all the ins and outs of their day-to-day activities—to develop a highly sustained awareness of the world as they envisioned it, engaged it, and adjusted to it.

In addition to the data obtained through interviews with people selling a wide variety of products and services (e.g., ice cream and candy, clothing, cosmetics, factory products, real estate, and advertising), I also attended a wide range of trade shows and participated for 3 years in a craft enterprise. These multiple realms of ethnographic involvement were highly instructive not only for the opportunities they represented for learning about the marketplace in themselves but also for providing comparison points and suggestions for subsequent inquiry in other contexts.

Once in the field, I also endeavored to find out where and how the activities of vendors might be similar to or different from those of people engaged in other (seemingly different) pursuits, such as managing illness (Roth, 1962), using marijuana (Becker, 1963), encountering religious cults (Lofland, 1966), or gambling (Lesieur, 1977). Thus, whereas my primary objective was to learn about people's activities in the marketplace, a related task was to compare what I found with other ethnographic studies of human behavior by using a set of (seemingly) basic or generic social processes as a reference point. In this way, I attempted to assess conceptual understandings that were grounded (Glaser & Strauss, 1967) more broadly in the accomplishment of everyday life and to develop (qualify, extend, or reject) these notions mindful of what I was encountering in the marketplace. In contrast to those who study the marketplace or other realms of human behavior in more singularistic or isolated terms, I found that this other literature enabled me to develop more sustained appreciations of the marketplace because of the great many conceptual comparison points that this more generic orientation afforded.

In the process of (a) attempting to comprehend the material being collected, (b) representing the viewpoints and experiences of those I had encountered, and (c) searching for a way of effectively and accurately conveying what I had learned about the marketplace to prospective readers, the material collected was eventually organized around 15 realms of activity.[14] As the project developed, the analysis became quite massive—too large to be conveniently presented within one book. Because of this, two separate volumes were developed around the topics of "pursuing customers" and "making sales."

The first volume, *Pursuing Customers* (Prus, 1989b), addresses the preparations that vendors make in anticipation of customer encounters. At one level, these "stage-setting" activities acknowledge vendor anticipations of both the interests of any customers with whom they expect to deal in the future and the practices of any competitors they envision on the horizon. The matter of pursuing customers encompasses the activities of setting up business (options, formats, and ownership dilemmas); doing management (responsibilities, staffing, and performance); purchasing products (concerns, gaming, and relationships); setting prices (price, value, and profit); using the media (tasks, formats, and dilemmas); working the field (prospecting, calls, and pressures); and exhibiting products (location, displays, and action).

Although one may pursue activities of these types in anticipation of customer contact, by no means are these realms of enterprise so limited in focus. Thus, for those already in business, activities along these lines also represent ongoing vendor adjustments to their experiences to date with both customers and competitors and their anticipations of the subsequent tendencies of these others. Thus, vendor stage-setting activities assume a dialectic or processually interconnected quality. Although merchants act in the present, they act mindfully of both their past experiences and their anticipations of the (rather unpredictable) future. Notably, too, vendors live in an interactive world; the outcomes that they experience not only reflect their own enterprises but also are collectively shaped by the activities of all those whose lives intersect with their own.

By virtue of their own consumer involvements, most readers are apt to be sensitive to the drama (i.e., dilemmas, sacrifices, and risks) entailed in shopper encounters with vendors, but merchants often experience intense dilemmas, major investments, and proportionately larger gambles as they set (and more or less continually reset) the stage for their encounters with "the generalized other" (Mead, 1934). This is not to imply that vendors do not experience interpersonal pressure or tactical dilemmas in dealing with the specific people that they meet in the course of doing business (or that these individual encounters are not consequential to the overall success of that business). It is in the activities involved in anticipating and preparing for these (ambiguous) encounters, however, that merchants tend to be more cognizant of the dramatic (and risky) nature of their undertakings.

Making Sales (Prus, 1989a) builds on vendors' ongoing background preparations (anticipations, gambles, and adjustments) but primarily deals with vendors' direct encounters with prospective buyers. The emphasis is on what is sometimes termed "eye-to-eye, belly-to-belly selling." By focusing on the ways in which interpersonal encounters are constituted, consideration is given to the tactics that vendors invoke in pursuing buyer commitments, the dilemmas and hesitations that vendors experience in situated interchanges, and vendor concerns with immediate sales and long-term buyer relations. *Making Sales* is organized around the activities involved in presenting products (approach, qualification, and interest); generating trust (integrity, quality, and obligations); neutralizing resistance (skepticism, price, and loyalties); obtaining commitments (closings, groups, and dilemmas); encountering troublesome customers (carelessness, rudeness, and returns); developing loyalty (service, signification, and contact); holding "Sales!" ("bargains," action, and dilemmas); and maintaining enthusiasm (pressures, slumps, and support).

Whereas the activities subsumed under the heading of pursuing customers are essentially directed toward vendor anticipations of, and ongoing adjustment to, a more amorphous generalized other, those depicted under the rubric of making sales are more explicitly focused on vendor encounters with the "interpersonal other." Taken together, these two larger sets of activities not only indicate the ways in which "organizational activities" and "interpersonal relations" are very much interconnected but also shed a great deal of light on people's involvements in influence work as both tacticians and targets.

Attending to Pricing (and Rationality) as a Social Process

Readers may find it surprising to learn that the very first realm of activity that I undertook to analyze was that of "price setting." Of all the activities in the marketplace, pricing seemed the realm least "social" in its essence—the set of practices least amenable to analysis as a social phenomenon. Because of this, I especially wanted to find out if and in what ways, if any, pricing reflected the same types of things we associate with other realms of group life or how it differed from (seemingly more socially entrenched) matters such as generating trust or developing customer loyalty in the marketplace. The result was quite (almost embarrassingly) surprising to me. I had no idea of just how thoroughly social price setting was in its constitution (anticipation, application, assessment, and adjustment). I had rather naively accepted a rational-economic image of pricing, and it was not until I had piled up many instances of price-setting practices from vendors that I began to see the practical, operational limitations of this model.

In short, although vendors typically attempt to operate "rationally," they act in a world in which reality is not theirs alone to determine (Prus, 1989b, pp. 133-200). Thus, their pricing practices reflect attempts to deal with amorphous target audiences (people working with diverse rationalities as well as shifting interests and object valuings), a potentially wide range of (direct and indirect) "competitors," a host of somewhat unpredictable supplier relationships, and their existing practices (and adjustments) in other aspects of their own (internal) marketing and sales programs. Vendors may invoke predetermined, rationally structured formulae in attempts to make "wise purchases" of stock and arrive at "the best prices," but because pricing is typically pitched to an amorphous generalized other, pricing is much more accurately envisioned as a socially constructed (and adjustive) process. The following extracts depict only some aspects of this larger process (Prus, 1989b):

> If something isn't moving, you've got to get rid of it! You've got to replace it with something that'll pay your bills. You can't tie up your display space with deadbeat merchandise. You're paying X dollars per square foot per month rent, and if you keep this around and that around, pretty soon you have no place to put your hotter items . . . storage, what's the point? It gets expensive. It eats up your profits. So reduce the price, keep knocking it down till somebody wants it. Let them [customers] store it. And you can't wait too long either, because if you don't catch something that's not moving soon enough, you're going to have to let it go for a lot less. . . . That's another problem too. How long do you wait [department store]? (p. 190)

> You can't sell some things very well at a 100% markup. The customers think that it's too cheap, that there must be something wrong with them. Some things, you mark up 150, 200%, and then the customers seem to think that they're getting a good bargain, then. It's funny, but I've seen that happen with some of my things

and some of the other people with similar lines have had similar experiences [jewelry]. (p. 184)

Attending to the Influence (and Resistance) Process

By focusing on the ways in which people engage the activities involved in "doing business," I not only became more acutely aware of the ambiguities, plans, excitements, frustrations, and competition that people experience as sellers (and their ongoing adjustments) but also developed a much fuller appreciation of influence (and resistance) work *in practice.* I ventured into the field fully anticipating that I would learn much about vendors as tacticians, but I also learned much about their experiences as *targets* (relative to their suppliers, their competitors, other staff, and those they encountered as customers). Along the way, I began to develop a much greater appreciation of the capacities of people to assume roles as both targets *and* tacticians on intermittent, sequential, and synonymous bases. This understanding would be informed further by a second venture into the marketplace—a project that considers people's experiences (and activities) as consumers (Prus, 1993a, 1993b, 1994, 1997a; Prus & Dawson, 1991; Prus & Frisby, 1990).

As with the study of marketing activity, the shopping study is very much an ethnographic venture. It is based on interviews with shoppers, observations of consumers in a wide range of settings, and my own long-term involvement and experiences in a vast array of marketplaces as a consumer.[15] Also, by teaching (for several years) a course on marketing and sales that requires students to keep journals on and write analyses of their experiences as shoppers, I have added to my stock of knowledge by attending to the consumptive practices of a significant segment of the "now" generation.[16]

Although the shopping project is only partially completed, it focuses on people's activities such as learning about products, judging shopping arenas and particular vendors, approaching shopping activity, shopping in groups, dealing with salespeople, defining quality, pursuing "good deals," shopping sales, becoming repeat customers, paying for purchases, and managing budgets.

While readers can presumably relate to these activities in direct experiential manners and may have taken many of these for granted because they seem so commonplace or mundane, once one begins to examine these undertakings in intimate detail by talking to others about their experiences (and practices) or even carefully reflecting on one's own experiences, these activities take on an entirely differ- ent cast. Not only is consumer behavior rife with images, dilemmas, negotiations, and the like but also it provides striking testimony to the ways in which people engage the world in meaningful, enter- prising terms. Focusing on group shopping, the following extracts provide glimpses into this broader phenomenon (Prus, 1993b):

> I think you're more careless to a certain point [when you shop with other people]. . . . I don't want the other guy to wait for me, so I'll go and make a quick, unprepared purchase to get finished my job. When I go alone, I can take my time and look around and then do my purchases. I won't look as much when I have friends. . . . I buy things that I'm not satisfied with. I just buy it because I want to get it over with because I don't want them to wait for me. [f 67]l (p. 101)

> I hate shopping with somebody who doesn't have any money and they're always saying "Oh, this is nice, but I can't afford it." That gets on my nerves after awhile. [f 23]m (p. 97)

Far from being the highly gullible (mindless) targets that they are sometimes portrayed to be, consumers assume a variety of target and tactician roles as they engage vendors, shopping companions, *and* other associates with respect to marketplace involvements. Clearly, customers do not always act "wisely" or in ways that may be seen to best reflect their interests, but much greater attention needs to be directed to the ways in which shoppers pursue products in the marketplace, interact with one another, and deal with vendors on a situated basis.

As well, much more sustained consideration should be directed to the ways in which shoppers make judgments of, and adjustments to, the *objects* (Belk, 1988; Prus, 1997b) that people obtain through their ventures into the marketplace. Beyond any interactions (per- taining to these objects) that they have with other people, this would require an attentiveness to people's subsequent uses of objects. The significance of object purchases does not end once people have made purchasing commitments (even of an irrevocable nature). Although detracting, in varying degrees, from a shopper's overall finances, each object purchase (including applications, maintenance, and object-related interchanges with others) typically adds to people's overall (and emergent) stocks of knowledge. Thus, people may (sometimes rather prominently) take earlier purchasing experiences into account when they venture into the marketplace for other objects. Research that focuses on these types of matters would not only generate more consequential understandings of consumer practices and marketplace exchanges specifically but also shed a great deal more light on human interchange and influence (and resistance) work more generally.

In the midst of the shopping study, I became involved in a study of business development (Prus & Fleras, 1996). I had encountered people promoting cities (as investment sites) at some of the trade shows I had attended while studying vendor activities, but I had never focused on these endeavors in any sustained manner. A colleague, Augie Fleras, had some time to devote to research, and as we talked about different things he might do, we became intrigued about the potential that an ethnographic study of economic development might have for the field. Minimally, it would be an opportunity to see if the things I had been finding in the marketplace (merchants and shoppers) were relevant to larger scale trade and the political dimensions associated with business locations.

Also some distance from being completed, this project examines the types of things that economic development officers working for cities (and states, provinces, and federal governments) do to attract and maintain businesses (and industries) in their areas. Pursuing this study has meant interviews with economic development officers, developers, and realtors, travel to various cities in Canada and the United States, and attendance at trade shows that feature (location) sites, industries, and representatives from a vast range of North American cities and regional governments as well as nations from around the globe. The study of economic development has also resulted in learning about some new playing fields (e.g., attending to local and regional promotional practices and related political interchanges, examining the activities of developers and realtors, and learning about international trade). It has provided an opportunity to explore and assess the applicability of the interactionist approach with respect to "macro" realms of human community life.

Although the contexts are substantively different, the preceding studies of marketing and consumer activity have provided valuable comparison points for this project. Indeed, it has become apparent that people sell investments, land, buildings, or workforces in ways that very much parallel the activities of others selling automobiles, shoes, candy, or lemonade. Matters of images, influence (and resistance) work, interpersonal relations, and so on appear to be central to all realms of trade (and investment). Conversely, it is important that social scientists not trivialize the selling of shoes or lemonade but rather attend to the images, enterprise, and interactions that enable humans to accomplish exchanges of all types.

Conclusion

Sometimes, when people learn that I have spent time studying the life-worlds of the people (hookers, strippers, hustlers, bar staff, drunks, and so on) who constitute the hotel community (Prus & Irini, 1980/1988), they say, "Wow that must be interesting!" The hotel project was interesting in many respects but it was also frustrating, difficult, and demanding. Much more importantly, though, studies of this type enable us to gain valuable insights into the human relations and enterprise that undergird community life. The research on the marketplace that I have discussed here is, likewise, frustrating, difficult, and demanding, but it is also very interesting and conceptually most intriguing.

Also, in part, because one does not have to more or less continually battle with the "deviant mystique" (Prus & Grills, 1996) associated with bar life and deviance, it has been possible to examine the influence process and human relations in more detail in the (legitimate) marketplace than in the hotel setting. As such, ethnographic examinations of the marketplace may present particularly valuable opportunities to develop fuller, more adequate conceptualizations of the human condition.[17]

In closing, it may be instructive to remind newcomers to the ethnographic enterprise of the importance of attending to people's life-world involvements as socially constructed, meaningfully enacted sets of activities. I mention this specifically because I have noticed how much difficulty many well-intentioned students have when embarking on and engaging in an analysis of ethnographic research. Because they have been so thoroughly exposed to the (positivist) idea that social science is to be achieved through "objective measurements" and the analysis of "outcomes" (dependent variables) and "factors" or "causes" (as independent variables), a great many have difficulty avoiding the tendency to impose notions of these types on both those they study and any ethnographic data with which they might work.

Ethnographic (interactionist) research, in which one attempts to develop an understanding of the life-world of the other, requires a radically different orientation. It is not a matter of being unscientific, however. To the contrary, the emphasis is very much on examining people's experiences and activities in a highly detailed, sustained, rigorous fashion. Although quantitative measures may be quite appropriate for the study of physical (nonlinguistic, nonminded, nonintending, and noninteracting) entities, the interactionists (Blumer, 1969/1986) contend that the study of human group life requires a rather different approach. Because "empirical reality" is bound up in the lived experience of people, empiricism (in the social sciences) may be achieved only through ongoing interchange with those (the people) involved in particular spheres of activity (i.e., the close, sustained examination of "group life in the making").

In contrast to those (positivists) who envision human behavior as caused or produced by the various factors or forces (internally or externally) that (they assume) impinge on humans to make them do this or that, the approach introduced here focuses centrally on the ways in which people experience and engage the world as (intersubjectively) minded, self-reflective, interacting, and acting entities.

Because people do not experience the marketplace (or other settings) in singular fashions, it is essential that those attempting to understand the behaviors of others be prepared to recognize the multiple definitions of objects with which people may work (i.e., encounter, create, acknowledge, sustain, invoke, adjust, and reject) as *they* go about their activities and attend to any variety of interests that they might deem appropriate.

From the objective of accomplishing social science, this means focusing on what people *do* in the course of engaging particular aspects of the situations in which they find themselves. It also means respecting the viewpoints and practices of those whose life-worlds are being studied (to avoid imposing one's own viewpoints, sensibilities, moralities, or other presuppositions on others). Likewise, those embarking on field research should be prepared to examine the data that they collect in great detail, attending to variants and commonalities across the instances they encounter. The objective is to use the data as a fundamental basis for learning what is going on and assessing existing conceptualizations rather than using data to illustrate (or prove) earlier formulations in the literature. Our conceptualizations of the human condition should be adjusted to accommodate the data we gather through sustained interchange with the other, not vice versa.

Thus, although encouraging students to envision the entire marketplace as an appropriate and highly fruitful setting for unlimited instances of ethnographic inquiry, I also emphasize the necessity of examining the production of all human activity in close, sustained, inquisitive, and reflective manners. Only in this way may we begin to build a social science that is grounded in human lived experience—one that is genuinely attentive to human lived experience.

Notes

1. To better enable readers to contextualize speakers, extracts from shoppers are affixed with symbols indicating [gender and age] class. The preceding speaker, therefore, is identified as a 30-year-old male of the lower class. Because identification tags of these types assume rather global, nebulous qualities, readers are explicitly discouraged from invoking causal assumptions (or presumptions) based on these categorical depictions.

2. For an elaboration of these notions and an ethnographic research agenda for pragmatizing the social sciences, see Prus (1997b).

3. This discussion of "respecting the subject matter we purport to study" derives much inspiration from Blumer (1969/1986) as does this chapter generally.

4. As with a more sustained discussion of human encounters with "objects" (Prus, 1997b), I have bracketed some terms (e.g., [objects] and [the world]) in this chapter to draw attention to the problematic and constructed nature of [reality] as it is humanly experienced (socially interpreted and meaningfully engaged in interactive terms). The critical point is that people do not experience [objects] in any pure, intrinsic, or objective way or even in consistently demarcated terms. Our experiences with objects, insofar as these can be seen to be meaningful or comprehensible, are intersubjectively (linguistically) mediated.

5. This critique is developed much more extensively in Blumer (1969/1986) and Prus (1996b, 1997b).

6. See Blumer (1969/1986) and Prus (1996b) for more extended considerations of positivist and interpretivist approaches to the study of the human condition.

Despite their extended criticisms of positivism (and modernity), the postmodernists (poststructuralists) have contributed little to the comprehension of human lived experience. Although drawing attention to some of the shortcomings of positivist social science, the lack of responsible scholarship (concepts, methods, and sincerity) on the part of those adopting the postmodernist mantle (e.g., Derrida, Foucault, Lyotard, and their followers) has resulted in subjective reductionism, expressive self-enchantments, and hidden (moralistic) agendas. For more sustained critiques of "postmodernist" ventures in the social sciences, see Dawson and Prus (1993a, 1993b, 1995), Best (1995), Charmaz (1995), Sanders (1995), Maines (1996), and Prus and Dawson (1996).

7. Somewhat similar appreciations of human agency, human enterprise, and human interchange can be found in other ethnographic inquiries, particularly studies developed within the Chicago school of symbolic interaction (see Prus, 1997b, for a review of the literature). Taken as a set, these materials challenge the viability of much of what passes as "social science." They also indicate that ethnography represents the pivotal or essential methodological foundation for comprehending the human condition. Profoundly relevant in this regard are the matters of social scientists achieving intersubjectivity with those about whose life worlds they purport to study and attending to the unique nature of the human condition.

8. It should be appreciated that people may not only define and act toward [things] in a great many ways but also vary greatly in the object distinctions with which they work. This is not to deny the existence of "things" but rather to point to the socially (intersubjectively defined and objectified) and situationally enacted essences of [objects]. For further elaboration on [objects] and the human condition, see Prus (1997b).

9. I can do little more than sketch the rudiments of a symbolic interactionist approach in this chapter. See Blumer (1969/1986), Strauss (1993), and Prus (1996b, 1997b) for more extended discussions of these and related theoretical and methodological matters.

10. Newcomers to the field are referred to other statements on field research (e.g., Becker, 1970; Bogdan & Taylor, 1975; Jorgensen, 1989; Lofland & Lofland, 1995) and encouraged to read as many (especially Chicago-style interactionist) ethnographies as they can locate on topics that are both related to and different from any substantive settings in which they may have particular interest.

As a class assignment, I sometimes ask students to pick three ethnographies in very different subject matters and compare (and contrast) these along a particular generic social process, such as achieving identity, acquiring perspectives, developing relationships, or engaging in influence work (Prus, 1996b, 1997b). Those who undertake this task are often surprised at the results but, more importantly, tend to develop greater appreciations of processual affinities characterizing the human condition.

11. Interestingly, on learning more about field research in practice, I began to develop a greater appreciation for the matters discussed in the ethnographic literature and especially of the importance of reading about ethnographic research in wide varieties of contexts—attending both to the conceptual comparisons (parallels and contrasts) that one might find and to the discussions of other researchers' experiences in the field. In the process, I became more aware of the holistic nature of interactionist enterprise. This reflects the importance of not only acknowledging the interrelatedness of theory, methods, and ongoing research but also of the necessity of "letting people [the data] talk back," of approaching the field with an openness to what-

ever one might encounter there, and of adjusting one's theory and methods to the instances of human behavior that one encounters in the field.

12. See Prus (1989a or 1989b) for an extended review of the literature on marketing and sales. Prus and Dawson (1991) provide a brief overview of the ethnographic literature on consumer behavior.

13. For an (inevitably incomplete) review of the ethnographic literature as this applies to community life more generally, see Prus (1997b). By focusing on generic or transcontextual concepts that may be applicable across multiple settings, one may not only arrive at more viable theoretical understandings of any particular situation at hand but also be in a better position to generate conceptual material that subsequently may be assessed in other (possibly quite different substantive) contexts.

14. Other researchers may have used more or fewer conceptual themes, possibly recasting these processes along somewhat different analytical lines. More important than the actual terms employed, though, is that one strives for concepts that comprehensively, openly, and sincerely attempt to capture the essence of the phenomenon at hand.

15. As an aside, I also note that I have benefited from being married to a "fantastic, foxy, and charming lady" who, as she has pointed out, has shown me "how to save and shop wisely." Without her (and our daughters), who knows where I would be! (Incidentally, anyone lacking a flexible sense of humor and a capacity for appreciating wide diversities of human expression is apt to encounter serious limitations as a field researcher more specifically, if not a social scientist more generally.)

16. Although university students generally prefer to envision themselves as "young adults," adolescents also tend to view themselves as a highly consequential part of the "now" generation. For an ethnographic research agenda that focuses on adolescent life worlds generally, see Prus (1996a).

17. More specifically, these research projects have provided valuable empirical and conceptual materials for embarking on critiques of positivist and postmodernist approaches to the social sciences (Prus, 1996b); elaborations of the roots, conceptual essences, and methodological practices of symbolic interaction (Prus, 1996b, 1997b); and the development of an ethnographic research agenda for pragmatizing the social sciences (Prus, 1997b). Also, the research on the marketplace discussed here (in conjunction with the broader ethnographic literature) has been most consequential for reconceptualizing "power" in ways that centrally acknowledge the definitional, situated, and enacted essence of human interchange (Prus, 1998).

References

Becker, H. S. (1963). *Outsiders*. New York: Free Press.

Becker, H. S. (1970). *Sociological work: Method and substance*. Chicago: Aldine.

Belk, R. (1988). Possessions and the extended self. *Journal of Consumer Research, 15,* 139-168.

Best, J. (1995). Lost in the ozone again: The postmodernist fad and interactionist foibles. In N. K. Denzin (Ed.), *Studies in symbolic interaction* (Vol. 17, pp. 125-130). Greenwich, CT: JAI.

Blumer, H. (1986). *Symbolic interactionism*. Berkeley: University of California Press. (Original work published 1969)

Bogdan, R., & Taylor, S. J. (1975). *Introduction to qualitative research methods.* New York: John Wiley.

Charmaz, K. C. (1995). Between positivism and postmodernism: Implications for methods. In N. K. Denzin (Ed.), *Studies in symbolic interaction* (Vol. 17, pp. 43-72). Greenwich, CT: JAI.

Dawson, L., & Prus, R. (1993a). Interactionist ethnography and postmodernist discourse: Affinities and disjunctures in approaching human lived experiences. In N. K. Denzin (Ed.), *Studies in symbolic interaction* (Vol. 15, pp. 147-177). Greenwich, CT: JAI.

Dawson, L., & Prus, R. (1993b). Human enterprise, intersubjectivity, and the ethnographic other: A reply to Denzin and Fontana. In N. K. Denzin (Ed.), *Studies in symbolic interaction* (Vol. 15, pp. 193-200). Greenwich, CT: JAI.

Dawson, L., & Prus, R. (1995). Postmodernism and linguistic reality versus symbolic interactionism and obdurate reality. In N. K. Denzin (Ed.), *Studies in symbolic interaction* (Vol. 17, pp. 105-124). Greenwich, CT: JAI Press.

Glaser, B., & Strauss, A. (1967). *The discovery of grounded theory: Strategies for qualitative research.* Chicago: Aldine.

Jorgensen, D. L. (1989). *Participant observation.* Newbury Park, CA: Sage.

Lesieur, H. (1977). *The chase.* New York: Anchor.

Lofland, J. (1966). *The doomsday cult.* Englewood Cliffs, NJ: Prentice Hall.

Lofland, J., & Lofland, L. (1995). *Analyzing social settings* (3rd ed.). Belmont, CA: Wadsworth.

Lyman, S., & Scott, M. (1970). *A sociology of the absurd.* New York: Appleton-Century-Crofts.

Maines, D. (1996). On postmodernism, pragmatism, and plasterers: Some interactionist thoughts and queries. *Symbolic Interaction, 19*(4), 323-340.

Mead, G. H. (1934). *Mind, self and society* (C. W. Morris, Ed.). Chicago: University of Chicago Press.

Prus, R. (1976). Religious recruitment and the management of dissonance: A sociological perspective. *Sociological Inquiry, 46,* 127-134.

Prus, R. (1980). Hustling the hustlers: The dynamics of acquiring information. In W. Shaffir, R. Stebbins, & A. Turowetz (Eds.), *The social experience of fieldwork* (pp. 132-145). New York: St. Martin's.

Prus, R. (1983). Drinking as activity: An interactionist analysis. *Journal of Studies on Alcohol, 44*(3), 460-475.

Prus, R. (1989a). *Making sales: Influence as interpersonal accomplishment.* Newbury Park, CA: Sage.

Prus, R. (1989b). *Pursuing customers: An ethnography of marketing activities.* Newbury Park, CA: Sage.

Prus, R. (1993a). *Encountering the mass media: Consumers as targets and tacticians.* Paper presented at Studying Human Lived Experience: Symbolic Interaction and Ethnographic Research '93, University of Waterloo, Waterloo, Ontario.

Prus, R. (1993b). Shopping with companions: Images, influences and interpersonal dilemmas. *Qualitative Sociology, 16,* 87-109.

Prus, R. (1994). Consumers as targets: Autonomy, accountability, and anticipation of the influence process. *Qualitative Sociology, 17*(3), 243-262.

Prus, R. (1996a). Adolescent life-worlds and deviant involvements: A research agenda for studying adolescence as lived experience. In G. O'Berick (Ed.), *Not a kid anymore: Canadian youth, crime, and subcultures* (pp. 7-69). Toronto: Nelson Canada.

Prus, R. (1996b). *Symbolic interaction and ethnographic research: Intersubjectivity and the study of human lived experience*. Albany, NY: SUNY Press.

Prus, R. (1997a). Shoppers as elusive targets: Reluctant involvements, evasive tactics, and the influence process. In N. Denzin (Ed.), *Studies in symbolic interaction* (Suppl. 3, pp. 221-246). Greenwich, CT: JAI.

Prus, R. (1997b). *Subcultural mosaics and intersubjective realities: An ethnographic research agenda for pragmatizing the social sciences*. Albany, NY: SUNY Press.

Prus, R. (1998). *Beyond the Power Mystique*. Albany, NY: SUNY Press.

Prus, R., & Dawson, L. (1991). Shop 'til you drop: Shopping as recreational and laborious activity. *Canadian Journal of Sociology, 16*, 145-164.

Prus, R., & Dawson, L. (1996). Obdurate reality and the intersubjective other: The problematics of representation and the privilege of presence. In R. Prus (Ed.), *Symbolic interaction and ethnographic research: Intersubjectivity and the study of human lived experience* (pp. 245-257). Albany, NY: SUNY Press.

Prus, R., & Fleras, A. (1996). 'Pitching' images to the generalized other: Promotional strategies of economic development officers. In H. Znaniecki Lopata (Ed.), *Current research on occupations and professions: Societal influences* (pp. 99-128). Greenwich, CT: JAI.

Prus, R., & Frisby, W. (1990). Persuasion as practical accomplishment: Tactical manoeuverings at home party plans. In H. Znaniecki Lopata (Ed.), *Current research on occupations and professions: Societal influences* (pp. 133-162). Greenwich, CT: JAI.

Prus, R., & Grills, S. (1996). Perpetuating "the deviant mystique": Fascination, indignation and the dramatization of evil. Paper presented at the Society for the Study of Symbolic Interaction, New York.

Prus, R., & Irini, S. (1988). *Hookers, rounders, and desk clerks: The social organization of the hotel community*. Salem, WI: Sheffield. (Original work published 1980)

Prus, R., & Sharper, C. R. D. (1977). *Road hustler: The career contingencies of professional card and dice hustlers*. Lexington, MA: Lexington Books.

Prus, R., & Sharper, C. R. D. (1991). *Road hustler: Hustlers, magic and the thief subculture*. New York: Kaufman & Greenberg.

Prus, R., & Stratton, J. (1976). Parole revocation related decision making: Private typings and official designations. *Federal Probation, 40*, 48-53.

Roth, J. A. (1962). The treatment of tuberculosis as a bargaining process. In A. Rose (Ed.), *Human behavior and social process* (pp. 575-588). Boston: Houghton Mifflin.

Sanders, C. R. (1995). Stranger than fiction: Insights and pitfalls in post-modern ethnography. In N. K. Denzin (Ed.), *Studies in symbolic interaction* (Vol. 17, pp. 89-104). Greenwich, CT: JAI.

Strauss, A. L. (1993). *Continual permutations of action*. New York: Aldine.

3

Doing Ethnographic Research in Jewish Orthodox Communities

The Neglected Role of Sociability

WILLIAM SHAFFIR

This chapter focuses on some of the generic problems that I encountered in my ethnographic studies of ultra-Orthodox Jewish groups including Hasidim, newly observant Jews or *baalei tshuvah*, and those who either left or disaffiliated from the *haredi* (ultra-Orthodox) fold. Ethnographers must generally overcome the problems of locating the subjects of the study, gaining access to settings, and securing cooperation for the research. Some groups, however, are more readily identifiable than others, and some settings more "open" than others.

Related to this problem are two aspects of my field experiences that, although they are likely shared by others, are somewhat neglected in the literature. The first is the extent to which the subjects of the research are knowledgeable about, and interested in, the researcher's objectives. The relationships that we may develop with respondents are limited, in part, by how the extended ethnographic project fits with the respondent's frame of reference. Second, this chapter addresses the importance of being seen as a *mentsh* (a Yiddish term denoting decency and responsibility). The extent to which we are seen as likeable, friendly, dependable, and honest bears directly on our ability to collect rich and deep data with which to better comprehend and analyze the social world under study.

The Three Projects:
Background

Hasidim

My most long-standing research began in the late 1960s and centers around Hasidic—ultra-Orthodox—Jews in Montreal and the social organization of their communities. My general interest has focused on matters of boundary maintenance and identity preservation (Shaffir, 1974, 1985, 1987, 1995b). Insulated from the mainstream culture that they identify as a threat to their distinctive lifestyle, the Hasidim have organized institutions and established interactional patterns to stave off assimilative threats from the outside. In effect, the research examines how these Jews have coordinated efforts to accomplish this goal.

The Montreal Hasidic community is actually divided into a number of distinct sects, each of which is organized around the leadership of a *Rebbe,* or charismatic religious figure. My original work focused mainly on the Lubavitch Hasidic sect, which is set off from the rest by virtue of its proselytizing and outreach work, as it endeavors to revitalize Judaism. From the early 1990s to the present, this sect has been featured prominently in the media because its followers believe that their Rebbe is the Messiah, and that the final redemption is imminent. As they desperately waited for him to be revealed as the Messiah, and mounted a successful publicity campaign, they suffered a powerful blow when, following a lengthy illness, he died in June 1994 (Shaffir, 1993, 1994, 1995a).

Recently, I have examined the Tasher community in Boisbriand, Quebec, a sect whose distinctiveness lies in its isolation from the urban center (Shaffir, in press). Although originally situated in the Mille End neighborhood of Montreal, which abuts Outremont and includes the majority of Hasidim in the city, it relocated in the 1960s to the rural municipality of Boisbriand, north of Montreal in the Laurentian mountains, to be more secluded from the assimilative influences of urban life. My involvement with the Hasidim for more than 25 years allows me to assess notable changes that this community has experienced during this period.

Baalei Tshuvah

Jews who have resocialized to Orthodox Judaism from a secular background are known as baalei tshuvah in Hebrew ("those who return"). Contemporary baalei tshuvah have grown up and lived outside the framework of traditional Jewish belief and practice. As such, their "return" is to a Judaism with which they have had little acquaintance.

This research was conducted in Jerusalem, Israel, in the late 1970s at a time when the city included over a dozen yeshivot that were established for recruiting and attracting students from abroad and that catered almost exclusively to these newly observant Jews. The majority of the students were from North America and mainly from the United States. These baalei tshuvah were not total strangers to Judaism, and a majority had received some Jewish education and came from families affiliated with conservative and reform synagogues. Nevertheless, the baalei tshuvah considered themselves secular and far removed from Judaism and Jewish concerns prior to tshuvah. I was interested in understanding the processes by which such individuals embarked on a path leading them to reorganize their lives around the laws and practices of Orthodox Judaism (Shaffir, 1983). These trajectories typically involved a radical transformation in their way of life and required considerable sacrifice, including the reevaluation of relationships with family members and friends. My attraction to this research derived from discussions with Lubavitcher Hasidim, years earlier, who had converted to Orthodox Judaism from their Jewish secular backgrounds.

Haredi Defectors

Although the term ultra-Orthodox still enjoys currency in North America, it has been replaced with haredi or in the plural haredim, a Hebrew term that is current in Israel and reserved for those religious persons who have not accommodated their religious beliefs to modern lifestyles. In this research, stumbled on by chance in 1986 when I lived in Israel, I have followed the trajectories of ultraobservant Jews who have bolted from that fold to become either totally secular or less fanatically observant (Shaffir, 1991; Shaffir & Rockaway, 1987). I have been interested in how such individuals reach the decision to defect and the manner in which they proceed to organize their activities once the decision is made. This research, too, became a study about conversion experiences. A term commonly used to identify those departing from the haredi fold is *chozrim beshe'aylah.* Guided by the initial hypothesis that chozrim beshe'alah's experiences were similar but the reverse to those encountered by newly observant Jews, the data have actually shown dramatic differences between these groups' socialization and resocialization trajectories.

Locating Respondents

Locating the subjects or the setting to be researched is an initial step confronting the researcher. The best intentioned project can be stymied if one is unable to identify the persons or setting from which the data will be gathered. This problem is minimized when the research population is confined to a particular setting, such as bingo players, prisoners, or undergraduate students, or situated within demarcated boundaries as in the case of slum dwellers, native band members, or the inhabitants of a certain census tract. Field researchers can rely on a variety of established practices, such as directories, guide books, and institutional listings, to seek out the research population. The "snowballing" technique, in which the researcher relies on respondents for introductions to others, constitutes a central approach for adding to the research sample.

My studies of Hasidic and newly observant Jews were relatively straightforward along this line. First, Hasidic Jews, in Montreal, live in a few select areas, and the researcher can easily pinpoint their whereabouts. Second, Hasidim can be identified through their institutions. All the Hasidic sects have their own house of worship that serves as a central meeting place. Also, although Montreal's Hasidic population is relatively small when compared to New York's, there are several commercial establishments that the researcher can frequent that are owned by and attract a Hasidic clientele. Furthermore, in the case of the Lubavitcher Hasidim, a sect distinguished by its aggressive proselytizing within the larger Jewish community, advertisements in a variety of media outlets inform the researcher of their whereabouts throughout the city. Finally, as any researcher quickly discovers, Hasidic Jews' distinctive dress and appearance renders them immediately recognizable: Men are bearded, have side curls and wear long black coats and occasionally fur-trimmed hats, whereas women wear high-necked, loose-fitting dresses, with kerchiefs or traditional wigs covering their hair. In short, the Hasidim are not hard to find.

Similarly, locating and identifying baalei tshuvah was quite straightforward. For a small fee, I purchased a booklet that listed the names, addresses, and telephone numbers of the yeshivot in Jerusalem catering to them. In fact, because several of the yeshivot were actively involved in recruiting newcomers, their witnessers, often baalei tshuvah themselves, were, at times, difficult to avoid, especially in Jerusalem's Jewish Quarter, a center for tourists, and at other popular meeting places in Jerusalem. Also, any observer would quickly discover that male baalei tshuvah, especially those new to the experience, could usually be identified by their somewhat disheveled appearance. Their attire was a blend of Western fashion along with accoutrements worn by observant Jews—a look they would even flaunt. For example, many of them ensured that their *tallit katan*, a rectangular garment of white cotton, linen, or wool with *tzitziyyot* ("fringes") on its four corners that is worn by strictly observant Jews under their upper garment the whole day, was visible to the eye or that, at least, the tzitziyyot hung freely. This appearance signaled their new status and identity. Also, baalei tshuvah wore a skullcap, and many grew a beard. As such, it was relatively simple to identify who they were and where they could be engaged.

Researchers are not always so fortunate in their searches, however. It is not unusual to discover that persons, though sharing similar life experiences, do not form a group or social relations on that basis. Instead, they organize their lives as individuals and fail to share their experiences with others like themselves. In addition, they may even be unaware that they are not alone. My research among the haredi defectors was such a case in point.

Ex-haredim who had recently severed their ties with their respective groups could not be identified through any institutional dress or affiliation. Although a newly established organization currently caters to former haredim, it was unavailable when I initiated the research. At that time, there was not any central office that could direct a researcher to their whereabouts. Nevertheless, on the basis of hearsay and occasional press reports, one knew that such persons existed. Because the circumstances surrounding their defection typically involved considerable deception and even intrigue, the media reported on them sensationally. They desperately attempted to assimilate into the mainstream, however, and left little trace of their former identities. In short, there was no obvious approach that I could rely on for locating ex-haredim. I was presented with a challenge that, I believe, added an adventurous and exciting dimension to the research and also helped sustain my interest.

With the exception of this latter project, the task of locating respondents was largely mechanical, requiring minimal skill and imagination. As field researchers know only too well, however, once the setting and its inhabitants are identified, the real challenge lies in gaining access and securing cooperation for the research. Herein lies the real art of field research: The investigator must marshall an appropriate self-presentation along with a convincing account to gain admission to a social circle or set of activities that may be sealed to outsiders.

Gaining Access

As is well documented, access to a setting can be supervised and controlled by gatekeepers (Burgess, 1991; Lofland & Lofland, 1995). Typically, either voluntarily or through some more formal process, researchers seek out gatekeepers for permission to conduct research. Both the nature of the research and the organization of the setting help shape such involvements with gatekeepers. My experiences in the field varied along these lines.

My outsider status among the Hasidim was strikingly evident. When I began conducting field research among the various sects, however, I did not seek out any identifiable leaders for their permission to hang around. Generally speaking, I visited the yeshivas, which are somewhat semipublic places at which religious services are held daily and that any Jew can attend. Although an outsider's presence attracts immediate attention, it is also explainable: Perhaps he or she is seeking spiritual direction but, more likely, has come to recite the kaddish, a prayer commemorating the dead that is recited in the presence of a *minyan* (a quorum of 10 adult males). Occasionally, strangers may also appear as the invited guests of members of the community, but this is more typical of Lubavitch than among the other sects. Although strangers are initially ignored, they are eventually approached to account for their presence.

Like all generalizations, this one fails to capture the flavor of how matters might evolve. The reception of Lubavitch, however, is likely to be qualitatively different than that among the other Hasidic sects. Because the Lubavitch movement is committed to proselytizing among uncommitted Jews, Lubavitcher are on the lookout for newcomers and have learned to welcome them warmly and engagingly. It does not follow, however, that the other Hasidic sects are unfriendly when accommodating strangers; they are simply disinterested. As a result, factors of chance play a decisive role in how an outsider is received. If fortune shines on him, he will be warmly greeted by a Hasid who may even invite him to his home for refreshments and perhaps extend an invitation for him to return on the Sabbath.

From the outset, I determined that the most sensible explanation for my presence was to claim an interest in Hasidic Jewry: Who they are and their customs and religious practices. Indeed, this claim seemed to make sense to them. Such curiosity was, to an extent, reciprocal: Why would an assimilated Jew like myself be interested in them? Nonetheless, they did not challenge me. At most, some inquired about my background and how I knew about them at all.

Although emphasizing my interests in Judaism and in their Jewishness, I also introduced Hasidim to my research agenda. I did so, for instance, by indicating that I was a graduate student in sociology at McGill University. Such information was usually meaningless to them, however: The concepts of "graduate student," "sociology," and "McGill University" were foreign to the majority of them. Although the Lubavitcher saw my presence as a confirmation of their successful outreach, the Hasidim tolerated me. To anyone who asked how I happened to come across their yeshiva, I answered that I was in the neighborhood and dropped in. Few even asked.

Although this general explanation was plausible in the city, it stretched the imagination in the case of the Tasher Hasidim, who lived in a community approximately 25 kilometers north of the city that was inaccessible through public transportation. Surrounded by farmers' fields, one reached this community only with the help of detailed directions. This community was not stumbled on in the course of a leisurely stroll in the neighborhood. As a result, access to this community required a more formalized accounting. In the end, I became an employee of the Tasher yeshiva, serving as a secretary, and in the process I was introduced to covert research.

Access to settings can be influenced by the researcher's decision to engage in overt or covert research (Goode, 1996; Van Maanen, 1988). The distinction between these approaches has engendered considerable debate among sociologists in relation to matters of ethics and deception. In contrast to overt research, in which investigators communicate their research interests to prospective gatekeepers and informants, such interests and intentions are hidden or carefully disguised in covert research. Although this poses a moral dilemma confronting all researchers, the debate seems especially directed toward field researchers.

I learned about the existence of the Tash community by chance. These Hasidim had formerly resided in Montreal, I would learn, but their Rebbe (charismatic religious leader), alarmed by the bustle of urban life, reestablished his community in an environment that was judged to be more conducive to the study of Torah. I visited one Hanukkah and concluded that any analysis of Hasidic life in Montreal must include them.

In contrast to Lubavitch, securing access to the Tasher community proved considerably more difficult. During my first visit, I was received politely but unenthusiastically. Therefore, I decided not to identify my research interests. The challenge was to devise a means of visiting the community fairly regularly without arousing strong suspicion. I seized the opportunity to become an office employee (Shaffir, 1985). Although the Tasher were unaware that I was collecting data about them, I did not hide the fact that I was studying sociology at McGill University. I hoped that would provide some understandable context for my interests about a Hasid's relationship with the Rebbe or the organization of secular and religious studies.

Whereas my position as an office employee enabled me to gather considerable data about the community's organization and financing—my work involved familiarizing myself with institutional files pertaining to fund-raising matters—my covert role con-

fined my movements within the community and severely constrained my data gathering initiatives. Defined as an office worker,
the two Tasher who supervised my work consistently discouraged
me from asking questions that appeared unrelated to my work or
from engaging students in conversation.

Although my research among baalei tshuvah could have been
pursued covertly, I elected to inform institutional officials of my
intentions. In retrospect, I believe that I adopted this approach
because of the aggravations that arose during my covert research
among the Tasher. The nature of the research population at hand,
however, was entirely different from the hasidim. The majority were
university educated, familiar with the concept of academic research,
and a few had even studied sociology. In addition, our Jewish
backgrounds were similar: We spoke a common language and, for
the most part, looked the same. Because outright subterfuge was
ruled out, I met with officials of these institutions to present my
credentials and research intentions. I was not entirely prepared for
what followed.

At the first yeshiva I visited, I was welcomed warmly and
invited to participate in any and all aspects of the program. "You
can eat with us, study with us, and we could even find you a place
to stay," said the rabbi with whom I met. What an auspicious
beginning! In the course of rehearsing the expected responses to my
request for access, I hardly anticipated such a welcome. How was I
to understand such immediate success? Simple, I thought: I presented the research convincingly. Buoyed by my success, I set off for
a nearby yeshiva expecting to score another triumph. The rabbi
listened to my spiel and promptly announced, "We don't need any
research. Please do me a favor and leave." I completed the research
in this institution without the rabbi's consent but with the full
knowledge of several of his most senior students who vouched for
me. To some extent, this situation curtailed my movements within
this institution's complex of buildings because I took pains to avoid
meeting the rabbi again. This experience, however, highlighted a
complexity of gaining entry: It may be partial rather than complete.
Although I was flatly rejected by one individual, others were forthcoming and cooperative. Gaining access, I discovered, is not fixed
at the outset but evolves over time and may be shaped by contingencies beyond the researcher's control.

My experience at a third yeshiva added yet another twist to the problem of access. There, my reception changed from an initial enthusiasm for the research to an invitation to abandon the research offered equally enthusiastically. I had agreed to the stipulation not to meet with students during scheduled lectures or study sessions and took elaborate pains to live up to this bargain. The rabbis soon concluded, however, that my research would inevitably sidetrack students. Permission to visit the yeshiva for research purposes was withdrawn: My research posed too great a threat. I subsequently learned that the rabbi who extended the initial invitation lacked the authority to do so, thus demonstrating another piece in the puzzle of gaining entry: Some persons enjoy greater authority than others to enable the researcher to overcome institutional resistance.

My research on ex-haredim presented a stumbling block that I had never previously encountered. I was frustrated for several months and then was introduced to the incalculable role played by chance in doing research. The snowball technique that proved so effective for meeting Hasidic and newly observant Jews was unhelpful. The precious few ex-haredim that I managed to meet suspected that there were others like themselves but claimed not to know their whereabouts. Although dubious of their claim at first, I gradually appreciated its veracity: Former haredim, as I was to discover, distanced themselves from their previous lifestyle and circle of friends and had little concrete knowledge of others who chose a similar path. A stroke of good fortune, however, changed the project's tedious trajectory. At the conclusion of a conversation with a former haredi, I routinely asked whether he knew of others whom I might contact. Both for personal and for professional reasons, he maintained a list of names of recent defectors. Their telephone numbers, along with some biographical notes about them, were listed in his address book, and he was kind enough to supply several names.

My experiences confirm what much of the research literature maintains: Access to settings may be mediated by circumstances beyond the researcher's control. Moreover, it is usually negotiated and renegotiated as the project unfolds and as relations are initiated with new casts of characters whom the researcher meets. Finally, I also discovered that the scientific merits of the research are more impressive to colleagues and peers than to those whose lives and activities we seek to understand.

Subjects' Understanding of the
Researcher's Objectives

The way we are perceived can greatly influence how others respond to our work (Anderson, 1978; Whyte, 1943; Wolf, 1991). The most critical response, I believe, is to the researcher's human qualities. Of course, the response is also shaped by how others define and interpret the researcher's objectives. At one extreme, the people we study are familiar with the nature of our work, having personally encountered similar experiences—they, too, for example, have conducted scientific research or have been the subjects of others' work (Maines, Shaffir, & Turowetz, 1980). In addition, expecting that our published work will make a difference in their lives, or in the lives of others, they are favorably disposed to our research-related activities (March, 1995; Miall, 1984). At the other extreme, however, are those who, although informed of the research, remain divorced from it because they are disinterested. Here, too, my experiences in the field have varied.

Admittedly, only a handful of baalei tshuvah and chozrim beshe'aylay directly expressed the hope that my published work might positively influence others in a particular direction. As a whole, however, neither group embraced the research because of any clearly articulated personal or institutional agenda they wished to advance. More generally, occasions to discuss their experiences were welcomed because these offered the opportunity to present their understanding of what happened to them; in short, to tell their story in a congenial context. By contrast, and with few exceptions, the Hasidim fit the second extreme.

We generally assume that the persons with whom we interact share our cultural universe of discourse. The researcher studying the Hasidim is confronted by a paradox. Although these Jews eschew contact with the larger society, they embrace modern technology, and although segregated from the mainstream, many display a sophisticated knowledge of economic and political concerns. At the very same time, however, and to the researcher's surprise, a range of experiences taken for granted in the mainstream culture are utterly foreign to them and beyond their grasp. I was unprepared for the chasm separating our respective universes of discourse.

With the exception of Lubavitcher Hasidim, particularly those who affiliated with this sect through proselytization, the vast number of Hasidim I encountered not only did not know about McGill University but also lacked any sense of what a university was in general. The concept of a university degree was entirely foreign to them. Explaining that I was a graduate student in sociology served little purpose because they knew neither about graduate studies nor about sociology; the mere mention of sociology resulted in a perplexed look. In fact, more often than not, my explanation about the research, which I eventually fine-tuned to deliver in a matter of seconds, was met with a quizzical look. To them, the purpose of life for a Jew was strictly defined by Jewish law, and my suspicion that they regarded my academic research as time misspent, if not entirely wasted, was confirmed in not so subtle ways as I came to know them better. More often than not, their nonverbal gestures, particularly their facial expressions, reflected their feelings: My research represented a colossal waste of time.

In terms of initial reception, my experiences among the Hasidim and former haredim reveal both a difference and a parallel. In contrast to the Hasidim, several ex-haredim could, indeed, understand why a researcher would be interested in their story. A few had already been contacted by the media, and the reports about them offered them a measure of celebrity status. In this regard, I was like other reporters who wished to hear their story. In addition, several had undertaken to fill their void in matters secular by reading voraciously and had developed an inchoate understanding of academic research. Others, however, precisely because of their highly sheltered background and meager base of secular knowledge, related only vaguely to my research interests. From their perspective, the secular world represented a very confused and confusing set of experiences whose logic they were grappling to comprehend. Meeting someone from Canada who was living in Israel and was conducting research on persons like themselves was not an easy picture to piece together. As it turned out, their interest in meeting me was to learn how they compared with other ex-haredim: To assess whether their experiences were typical and how their adjustment experiences compared to those of others with whom I had spoken.

My initial encounters with baalei tshuvah were significantly different from those of the two previously mentioned groups. The overwhelming majority were enrolled at university prior to visiting Israel. Indeed, several had completed their undergraduate studies and were pursuing graduate work or a professional degree. In addition, several had taken sociology courses and most were not unfamiliar with academic research. My presence and interests did not strain their frame of reference: They easily identified me as a Canadian professor who was on sabbatical and had received a research grant. My presence among them made sense and offered a reasonable context that could frame our relationship.

Subjects' Perception of the Researcher

Locating and gaining access to respondents, and negotiating a successful bargain with them, contribute vitally to the research enterprise. Practitioners of ethnographic research know only too well, however, both from published accounts and from personal experiences, that the venture's success rests less on the mechanical execution of a set of procedures than on the development and nurturing of relationships in the field (Harper, 1982; Horowitz, 1989). In other words, the art of gaining access and cooperation is largely determined by the display of interactional skills that set the stage for how the researcher is received. As Lofland and Lofland (1995) observe, although our proffered account of the proposed research may help gain initial access to the research site, "it would . . . be an error to attach too much importance to it" (p. 40). They cite Rosalie Wax (1971), who reminds us that

> Most sensible people do not believe what a stranger tells them. In the long run, [the investigator's] hosts will judge and trust him, not because of what he [initially] says about himself or about his research, but by the style in which he lives and acts, by the way he treats them. (p. 365)

The importance that we attach to our research is usually not matched by those we study. Persons cooperate less because of their evaluation of our work's scientific merits than their judgment of us as human beings. Do we laugh, show emotion, demonstrate concern, or offer a friendly smile? Are we cold, aloof, rigid, and present solely for purposes of gathering information? Although it is unlikely that people completely forget that we are present because of research interests, my experiences indicate that my researcher status is a secondary consideration in peoples' minds. In other words, the central yardstick is whether I am a mentsh—a term, which although uniquely Yiddish in its overtones, denotes decency, rectitude, and responsibility.

I have often asked myself why Hasidic Jews, committed as they are to curtailing unnecessary interaction with outsiders, are accepting of me. After all, I am not the bearer of gifts and, with few exceptions, have rarely been asked to do favors for them. I have spent countless hours with Hasidim of various sects discussing various topics that have interested me. They seem to enjoy our encounters, know that I am not an observant Jew, and that I visit to mainly collect materials for my research. I can also think of numerous occasions when I have greatly exceeded the amount of time that I asked people to set aside for our meeting. I am invariably left with a sense that they, too, enjoyed the conversation and are as sincere in thanking me as I am in expressing my gratitude.

As practitioners can attest, the craft of field research is largely acquired from experiences in the field rather than from formalized training in the classroom or laboratory. The importance of showing a human face in the field is rarely addressed in texts on field research. I was introduced to this significant dimension early on in the Hasidic project during one of my visits to the Lubavitcher yeshiva. My habit at the time—I thought that this was what I was supposed to do—was to sit at the very back of the synagogue to maximize my view of the goings-on in this large room. Surely this was the best and most effective way to collect objective data, I thought. An acquaintance from the community approached and offered the following advice: "You're making a mistake by sitting alone at the back. You make people feel uncomfortable. Sit with people, let them know you better and you'll learn a lot more." I could not have received better counsel.

Some of my richest data have come only after I have enabled people to learn about me. I make it a habit to provide informants with a biographical sketch of myself. I believe that they are entitled to this, especially because I occasionally question them about matters of a personal nature. In addition, I try to engage people in conversation rather than conducting a formal-type interview. Although I listen attentively, I feel free to inject my own views and even to challenge theirs. This usually makes for lively and interesting conversation and detracts from the sterile atmosphere surrounding a more formal encounter.

The significance of sociability resonates especially with researchers who acknowledge the distinction between how fieldwork is ideally practiced and how it is actually accomplished. Scientific canons of this methodology recede in importance as researchers attend to the exigencies of the fieldwork and even sacrifice objective data while attending to the human demands that shape our relationships with informants.

Conclusion

I wrote (Shaffir, 1990) the following:

> Cooperation depends less on the nature of the study than on the perception informants have of the field researcher as an ordinary human being who respects them, is kindly disposed toward them, and is willing to conform to their code of behavior when he or she is with them. In short, the skills in using commonplace sociability (friendliness, humor, sharing) are as much a prerequisite in conducting field research as they are in managing our affairs in other settings and situations unrelated to our professional work. (p. 80)

I am not the first to express this general idea. I am inclined to believe that in our haste to collect data quickly, or our obsession to follow scientific canons of objectivity and neutrality, we fail to attend adequately to commonsense sociability and, in the process, become unnecessarily anxious over collecting the right kinds of data. In our hurry to observe as much as possible, we neglect the importance of participating in rounds of activity in which such opportunities are available, thereby enabling persons to become familiar with a human side of ourselves. Just as we must instruct persons to become good respondents, we must also provide opportunities for others to relate to us out of our research self. Because we occupy several statuses simultaneously, we need not feel that the researcher role must always predominate (Kleinman, 1991). We must learn to share information about ourselves, just as we expect others to tell us about themselves. This is not to suggest that relations must be perfectly symmetrical—after all, we are there to conduct research—but that they should assume a better balance than, I suspect, is largely the case.

Is it possible to teach and instruct these affective components of field research? I think it is possible. We must learn to reclaim the virtue of patience. When we enhance the pace of doing the research, it is often at the expense of acquiring a deep appreciation of the research problem. As we sacrifice quality for quantity, we shortchange not only those persons whose perspectives we seek to understand but also an approach to studying social life that holds the greatest promise for acquiring the most credible understanding of the dynamics of social interaction.

References

Anderson, E. (1978). *A place on the corner.* Chicago: University of Chicago Press.

Burgess, R. G. (1991). Sponsors, gatekeepers, members, and friends: Access in educational settings. In W. Shaffir & R. Stebbins (Eds.), *Experiencing fieldwork: An inside view of qualitative research* (pp. 43-52). Newbury Park, CA: Sage.

Goode, E. (1996). The ethics of deception in social research: A case study. *Qualitative Sociology, 19*(1), 11-33.

Harper, D. (1982). *Good company.* Chicago: University of Chicago Press.

Horowitz, R. (1989). Getting in. In C. D. Smith & W. Kornblum (Eds.), *In the field: Readings on the field research experience* (pp. 45-54). New York: Praeger.

Kleinman, S. (1991). Field-workers' feelings: What we feel, who we are, how we analyze. In W. Shaffir & R. Stebbins (Eds.), *Experiencing fieldwork: An inside view of qualitative research* (pp. 184-195). Newbury Park, CA: Sage.

Lofland, J., & Lofland, L. H. (1995). *Analyzing social settings: A guide to qualitative observation and analysis* (3rd ed.). Belmont, CA: Wadsworth.

Maines, D., Shaffir, W., & Turowetz, A. (1980). Leaving the field in ethnographic research: Reflections on the entrance-exit hypothesis. In W. Shaffir, R. Stebbins, & A. Turowetz (Eds.), *Fieldwork experience: Qualitative approaches to social research* (pp. 261-281). New York: St. Martin's.

March, K. (1995). *The stranger who bore me: Adoptee-birth mother relationships.* Toronto: University of Toronto Press.

Miall, C. (1984). *Women and involuntary childlessness: Perceptions of stigma associated with infertility and adoption.* Unpublished doctoral dissertation, York University, Toronto.

Shaffir, W. (1974). *Life in a religious community: The Lubavitcher Chassidim in Montreal.* Toronto: Holt, Rinehart & Winston of Canada.

Shaffir, W. (1983). The recruitment of Baalei Tshuvah in a Jerusalem yeshiva. *Jewish Journal of Sociology, 25*(1), 33-46.

Shaffir, W. (1985). Some reflections on approaches to fieldwork in Hassidic communities. *Jewish Journal of Sociology, 27*(2), 115-134.

Shaffir, W. (1987). Separation from the mainstream in Canada: The Hassidic community of Tash. *Jewish Journal of Sociology, 29*(1), 19-35.

Shaffir, W. (1990). Managing a convincing self-presentation: Some personal reflections on entering the field. In W. Shaffir & R. Stebbins (Eds.), *Experiencing fieldwork: An inside view of qualitative research* (pp. 72-81). Newbury Park, CA: Sage.

Shaffir, W. (1991). Conversion experiences: Newcomers to and defectors from Orthodox Judaism (*hozrim betshuvah* and *hozrim beshe'elah*). In Z. Sobel & B. Beit-Hallahmi (Eds.), *Tradition, innovation, conflict: Jewishness and Judaism in contemporary Israel* (pp. 173-202). Albany: State University of New York Press.

Shaffir, W. (1993). Jewish messianism Lubavitch-style: An interim report. *Jewish Journal of Sociology, 35*(2), 115-128.

Shaffir, W. (1994). Interpreting adversity: Dynamics of commitment in a messianic redemption campaign. *Jewish Journal of Sociology, 36*(1), 43-53.

Shaffir, W. (1995a). When prophecy is not validated: Explaining the unexpected in a messianic campaign. *Jewish Journal of Sociology, 37*(2), 119-136.

Shaffir, W. (1995b). Boundaries as identity maintenance: Symbolic interaction as a framework for studying the Hasidim of Montreal. In J. Belcove-Shalin (Ed.), *Hasidic ethnography today* (pp. 31-68). New York: State University of New York Press.

Shaffir, W. (in press). Still separated from the mainstream: A Hassidic community revisited. *Jewish Journal of Sociology.*

Shaffir, W., & Rockaway, R. (1987). Leaving the ultra-Orthodox fold: The defection of Haredi Jews. *Jewish Journal of Sociology, 29*(2), 97-114.

Van Maanen, J. (1988). *Tales of the field.* Chicago: University of Chicago Press.

Wax, R. H. (1971). *Doing fieldwork: Warnings and advice.* Chicago: University of Chicago Press.

Whyte, W. F. (1943). *Street corner society.* Chicago: University of Chicago Press.

Wolf, D. (1991). High-risk methodology: Reflections on leaving an outlaw society. In W. Shaffir & R. Stebbins (Eds.), *Experiencing fieldwork: An inside view of qualitative research* (pp. 211-223). Newbury Park, CA: Sage.

4

The Ethnic Outsider

The Hurdles of Anglophone Field Research on North American Francophones

ROBERT A. STEBBINS

The history of my passion for the French language is too complex to recount here, but readers interested in learning more about this part of my professional life can read the preface of my book *The Franco-Calgarians* (Stebbins, 1994). What cannot be left unsaid in this chapter, however, is that this passion, when joined with my growing participation in the francophone subcommunity of Calgary, possibly the most thoroughly anglophone of Canada's large cities, led me to carry out an ethnography consisting of systematic observation from 1987 to 1993 and 85 semistructured interviews from January through June of 1992. The principal research question in this study–one gained from my ever deeper involvement in the community–was, How do urban francophone communities outside Quebec survive and even flourish in the overwhelmingly Canadian–American anglophone environment that envelops them? Particularly, what features of everyday francophone life in minority circumstances (*la vie en milieu minoritaire*) contribute to this survival and development?

In the course of this project, the results of which are reported in Stebbins (1994), I made the decision to continue my interest in the aforementioned research problem by executing a series of "concatenated" qualitative and exploratory investigations of urban Francophones living outside Quebec in Canada and the United States. Stebbins (1992) notes, "concatenated exploration refers at once to a research process and the resulting set of field studies that are linked together, as it were in a chain, leading to cumulative grounded, or inductively generated, theory" (p. 435). To this end, I have recently completed the second phase of this series, an interview study of francophone volunteers in Calgary and Edmonton. The third phase will be devoted to exploring a number of smaller urban francophone communities in Atlantic Canada and some of the New England states. The final phase of field research will take place in New Orleans, where, according to the 1990 U.S. Census, more than 25,000 people living in its Standard Metropolitan Statistical Area said they occasionally or always speak French at home (Bureau of the Census, 1992). A side trip to Miami is also being considered during that period, the purpose of which would be to examine "Floribec," a French Canadian suburb composed chiefly of Francophones from Quebec.

I faced three major hurdles in the first two studies, and it is now clear that I will have to face and surmount all three in each future study if they are to end in success. These hurdles are mastering the French language, becoming an insider in the target subcommunity, and becoming an insider in the intellectual circle bent on studying it. While attempting to clear the three hurdles, I was pleasantly surprised to learn that I had also acquired some significant personal advantages, which will certainly continue to help me as I work through the series of projects. These advantages are my anglophone background, my commitment to French, and my theoretical and empirical work in the fields of leisure science and lifestyle studies. The remainder of this chapter describes the three hurdles and how they are interwoven with these advantages.

Mastering French

Mastering the foreign language to be used in a research project is more problematic than would first appear. First, mastery, which refers to developing an acceptable grasp of the language's grammar, syntax, pronunciation, vocabulary, and the like, is, in reality, a matter of degree. Particularly, the level of mastery needed depends greatly on how the researcher intends to use his or her new language. For example, does the researcher need only a tourist's knowledge of it, or does he or she need the significantly greater competence of a casual conversationalist? Second, I discovered that, in my investigations, the idea of mastery also includes knowing a great deal about French Canadian culture, consisting as it does of a variety of distinctive values, practices, attitudes, and expectations as well as a very special historical background. Third, I further discovered, as I approached an acceptable level of spoken French, that because I am an intellectual, my francophone respondents often assumed I had already mastered written French, both as a reader and, far more challenging, as a writer.

My conversational French was sufficiently well developed by early 1992 to conduct in that language the interviews for the Calgary study. In other words, I had surmounted this hurdle, albeit rather minimally because, as I write 4 years later, I am still improving in this respect and will surely continue to do so far into the future. As a result, my respondents' reception and evaluation of me as a researcher is sure to improve as well because it will become increasingly apparent to them that I fully comprehend what they are saying. Additionally, my ability to express myself orally will continue to grow, becoming a substantial asset for interviewing and for presenting my research both to the local community and to my francophone colleagues around the world. Finally, I will understand more completely what is happening at the various meetings, events, and get-togethers that I attend.

Learning about French Canadian culture was the least difficult part of this hurdle. Like most people studying French in Canada, I was instructed by French Canadian teachers using French Canadian educational materials, both of which are major channels for transmitting the allied culture. I also encountered numerous expressions of it while systematically observing the Calgary francophone community; they served well as background for interpreting the interviews that I conducted subsequently with its members.

For me, reaching a passable level of writing in French has been by far the most difficult linguistic hurdle, where the level in question is one befitting a university professor. I have faced the requirement of writing in several ways. For instance, I have found it necessary to write letters to many of my respondents setting out the nature of my research and asking their consent to be interviewed. Furthermore, because I am a professor and speak French reasonably well, members of the local community have occasionally assumed that, with ease and expedition, I can intelligibly record the minutes of a meeting, write a memorandum to someone, or summarize in a note to the local francophone press what happened at an event. Writing French, however, is by far the most exacting of the four principal avenues of linguistic communication, the other three being listening, speaking, and reading. Indeed, the difficulty of written French is well-known and widely discussed in many parts of the world (Ager, 1996, p. 181).

It has been 13 years since I started formal lessons in conversational French. Even after considerable reading in French during this period and consultation with experts on how to write it, however, I am only now beginning to feel that I can communicate acceptably in this mode. True, I have written a number of journal articles and book chapters in French (e.g., Stebbins, 1995), but I have always done so with the aid of, first, my own hired editor and, second, the house editor of the publishers of these works. Today, I am comfortable writing letters in French, for which the expectation of stylistic excellence is generally lower when compared with scholarly writing and its uncompromisingly high standards. I even considered writing in French the book that will report the main findings of the volunteer study mentioned earlier, but I decided in the end that I could not afford the cost of editorial assistance. In short, even this far into the concatenation of this project, writing in French remains a significant hurdle, partly because this form of communication signifies for my respondents and my colleagues in this area the deepest commitment anyone can make to the French language and its various cultures.

Gaining Insider Community Status

Becoming an insider in the Roman Catholic francophone community of Calgary turned out to be easier than I expected. At the outset, I worried about my status as a (nominal) Protestant raised with English as my first language—two demographics that clearly identify me as a member of the dominant linguistic group now threatening to assimilate Francophones in many parts of the world. Moreover, my family name originates in England, which until well into the 20th century was the chief military and political rival of both France and Quebec. Nonetheless, a mastery of the language of the type described in the preceding section, a profound interest in and respect for francophone culture, and an unmistakable desire to help the local community survive and flourish by volunteering (I discuss my participation in decision-making bodies later) have been the main conditions for my success in this regard. It seems that, once these three conditions were met, being a mother-tongue Anglophone of English stock became largely irrelevant.

What does insider status mean in practical terms? In my case, it has been expressed in the willingness, indeed, in many instances the eagerness, of my respondents and other francophone acquaintances to talk freely about their feelings toward Anglophones, people with whom they are in continual contact in all kinds of ways. In these conversations, they discuss abrogations of language rights in Canada, an officially bilingual French-English country. They also discuss the stereotypes that many English Canadians hold about French Canadians, with the first using these images from time to time to shape and justify their social and political treatment of the second. Furthermore, they occasionally tell jokes about Anglophones, although this practice seems to be declining, possibly due to the influence of the principle of political correctness and certainly due to a growing confidence in their own competence and legitimacy.

Being invited in some instances and elected in others to serve on the decision-making bodies of various francophone organizations is the second indicator of insider status. Thus, for awhile, I was treasurer of the Calgary branch of the Association Canadienne Française de l'Alberta, the largest francophone organization in that city and the main conduit for conveying information about local Francophones to the larger anglophone community. I also served for 2 years as the speaker coordinator for one of their largest social clubs, although I declined an invitation to run for its presidency, a post that would have required more time than I had to give. Finally, I am currently part of a five-person, provincewide committee established to evaluate the contents of the provincial francophone weekly, *Le Franco*. With these involvements and others, I genuinely feel I have become part of the local francophone community.

A third sign is my favorable reception throughout the community. Were I an outsider, this reception would be cool and guarded.

Instead, however, for many years, I have been warmly greeted wherever I go, invited to join conversations, introduced to others (including numerous dignitaries), and often acknowledged at formal functions.

It could be argued, nevertheless, that this favorable reception rests primarily on my dual roles of university professor and sociological researcher inquiring into francophone life outside Quebec. These are relatively high-status roles, and anyone filling them can enhance the dignity of many a community's groups merely by becoming a member. Along these same lines, I am also the author of a book on Calgary's Francophones. This book was the first ever published on this subject and contains a great deal of information of considerable interest to many Francophones. Still, my favorable reception predates by several years the publication of that book. Furthermore, I know of French-speaking professors at the University of Calgary and some other Canadian universities who are not generally welcome in local francophone circles.

It is critical that researchers of closed ethnic groups gain insider status if they are going to effectively explore the everyday lives of these people, their attitudes toward survival and development, as well as the strategies they adopt to reach these two goals. Although some sociologists and anthropologists have found this hurdle nearly insurmountable (e.g., Briggs, 1986; Wolf, 1991), given the specifics of my field site I found it relatively easy to get around. My "secrets of success" seem to be my willingness to learn French, to help the community by volunteering there, and to respect its culture and values.

I also had additional advantages peculiar to North America's French communities outside Quebec, however. One of these is that, because the vast majority of the members of these communities also strive to speak English well and, with it, to operate effectively in certain sectors of the anglophone world (Stebbins, 1996), I represent something that they are hoping to become. I have joined them, publicly counting myself as one of them while, however, having neither a cultural nor a linguistic need to do so. In this fashion, I am viewed as complimenting them and their language and culture.

Nevertheless, I have been somewhat less successful in gaining the other kind of insider status considered in this chapter: insider status in the intellectual circle composed of those who study Francophones outside Quebec.

Insider Status in Intellectual Community

The intellectual community to which a field researcher aspires to gain acceptance as an insider consists of the other social scientists working in the same area. In most areas of research, these scholars appear to make up a rather demographically heterogeneous set, in which the principal requirement for intellectual recognition and acceptance is to publish theory or research in refereed outlets. By contrast, in the sociological study of ethnic groups, important exceptions occasionally contravene this general tendency toward heterogeneity. Here it is relatively uncommon, for example, for a Protestant to study Jews, a white to study blacks, or an Anglophone to study people who speak Chinese. This is also the case for those who do sociological research on Francophones living outside Quebec; very few Anglophones are found in their ranks and most of them speak little or no French, and even fewer of them write in that language.

How does becoming an insider in the appropriate intellectual community constitute a research hurdle if, as is generally true, other scholars cannot, and indeed seldom have a desire to, prevent an outsider from entering the group he or she intends to study? The answer to this question lies in the observation, stated first in its most general terms, that considerable time must pass before ethnic acceptability is achieved, as manifested in the researcher's grasp of the language and its culture and his or her unambiguous intention to make an intellectual career of studying the collectivity in question. Particularly, even though the outsider manages to gain access to the group for research purposes, invitations to contribute in the future to one or more of the intellectual forums controlled from the inside by the ethnic scholars (e.g., conferences, anthologies, and special issues of journals) will come slowly and cautiously at first. This, in turn, retards public dissemination of the outsider's data and ideas, thus amounting to a potentially discouraging impediment to that person's further research in the area.

For their part, these insiders, acting as gatekeepers, may be justifiably put off by the outsider's comparatively weak writing or speaking skills in their language, nearly always their mother tongue and principal language of scientific communication in that field of research. Consequently, outsiders have little choice but to wait until they have matured in this regard, eventually reaching a point at which the majority of insiders will accept them. Moreover, unless the outsider arranges for an extended linguistic immersion somewhere, this kind of personal development takes many years, although it is possible to expedite the process by conducting another study or two in the second language in question.

Less excusable, however, is the questionable attitude held by some insiders that only they can properly understand their own people. The logical impasse encountered in following this line of reasoning has been examined by Robert Merton (1972, p. 22), who points out that any researcher embracing it inevitably winds up being excluded from a number of important subgroups and subcategories for the simple reason that no one can be an insider in them all. Far more tenable is his counterargument that, because of their substantially different social vantage points, insiders and outsiders are able to contribute sets of observations about group life generally unavailable to each other. Furthermore, both sets are valid because outsiders can see aspects of social life that insiders often take for granted and are therefore usually unable to report and because insiders feel the full poignancy of their ethnic involvements, a sentiment that most outsiders have trouble appreciating at its deepest and most touching levels.

To illustrate how insider and outsider viewpoints can diverge, I present one of my key observations about the institutional basis of francophone communities outside Quebec. Over the years, my participant observation revealed more clearly that these communities revolve primarily around the institutions of education, religion, family, and leisure, especially the latter because leisure activities are often conducted in educational, familial, and religious circles. When invited to talk about them, few Francophones deny the centrality in their everyday lives of the family, the school, and, for some of them, the church. Very few, however, point to leisure activities, preferring instead to underscore the importance of work. Historically, many Francophones outside Quebec did not work in French, doing so to such an extent that it became ingrained in local culture as an ideal. Today, even though most of these Francophones admit they have no choice but to work in English, they continue to talk about the importance of francophone employment while overlooking the far greater centrality of leisure in their contemporary lives.

Notwithstanding the convincing case to be made against the claim that only insiders can scientifically know their group, however, the claim is still invoked by some of them to justify their efforts at gatekeeping, much to the disadvantage of would-be researchers coming from the outside. For the latter, their only recourse at this point is to parade their credentials as qualified and committed students of the group in question to try to impress the other insiders who reject this claim. It is clear that linguistic competence, both oral and written, extensive knowledge of the group's history and culture, and participation in at least some of its routine affairs can help an outsider gain the confidence of many insiders, possibly even some who hold that, for the most part, outsiders can never really know them.

I have traveled many miles down the road to insider status within the intellectual community studying Francophones outside Quebec. Although I have yet to complete my voyage, I sense that its end is near, which is unqualified recognition as a researcher in this circle. This has taken several years, however, because I first presented research data in public in this area in 1991. At that time, I spoke French with a noticeable English accent, and I had only begun to try to write in it. In fact, that initial presentation would have been impossible had I not collaborated with a francophone colleague in making it and in gathering the data we reported. Fortunately, my speaking ability subsequently improved, and able coaching from local francophone educators and translators has brought my writing to the point at which discerning readers no longer wince and sometimes even lightly compliment what they read. As for spoken French, my accent, grammar, syntax, and vocabulary are now sufficiently well developed to enable me to pass as a mother-tongue Francophone—sometimes for several minutes and sometimes for an entire conversation.

Proof of my identity as an insider came in May 1996 in the form of an invitation to chair a committee established to organize for the next year the national colloquium on francophone communities outside Quebec. At about the same time, I was also asked to join two Francophones in writing a book in French on bilingual education. My linguistic development, my handful of French book chapters and journal articles, and my steady participation over the years in the various conferences have all been instrumental in generating these invitations. Still, I strongly suspect that, whether I write it alone or with someone else, a book in French will be needed to firmly anchor my status as an insider—to complete my voyage of acceptance. Throughout this journey, my research interests in leisure and lifestyle have turned out to be solid assets because no one among the researchers on the inside has systematically explored these facets of francophone life in minority circumstances. Therefore, I have brought a couple of new perspectives to the scene, which only now are beginning to attract serious attention.

Conclusion

As stated at the outset, the hurdles never fully disappear in concatenated research. Instead, they reappear with each project. With an English name, it will never be presumed among each new sample of respondents that I speak and write French. In each new community that I enter, I will have to live down this presupposition, which, however, should take significantly less time than it did initially. Also, it is perhaps patent to say that, in every local francophone community, I will need to prove again my qualifications for insider status according to the criteria mentioned earlier. Finally, as I begin work on the American francophone communities, I will encounter other circles of intellectuals whose reception of me and my work will most likely be guarded until I can demonstrate that both are worthy of their attention. I expect to jump these hurdles with greater ease than in the past.

In closing, I hypothesize that outsiders who qualitatively examine ethnic groups and therefore encounter these three hurdles along the way are unique in the larger and highly diverse world of social science research. Whereas other researchers sometimes have to learn a technical language, they seldom have to learn another group's mother tongue, an essential building block in the personalities of its members and the subcommunity to which they belong. Nor do other researchers normally have to gain insider status to the point where they are considered full members of the subcommunities they are studying. Of course, some of them do penetrate deeply into such formations as juvenile gangs, sports teams, and work organizations, but even as they do this they commonly retain their status as researchers; they are not usually also seen as adolescents, basketball players, or coworkers. Finally, although other researchers also face the hurdle of establishing their intellectual credibility among their colleagues working in the same area, as a rule they do not also have to prove their ethnic credibility with those same people.

All in all, qualitative research in ethnic studies, when conducted by ethnic outsiders, is no easy task. It is hardly surprising, then, that few of them take it up even once and that still fewer of them continue on to execute a series of concatenated investigations from which they would learn, however, that the hurdles gradually become lower and easier to jump.

References

Ager, D. (1996). *Francophonie in the 1990s: Problems and opportunities.* Clevedon, UK: Multilingual Matters.

Briggs, J. L. (1986). Kapluna daughter. In P. Golde (Ed.), *Women in the field* (2nd ed., pp. 19-46). Berkeley: University of California Press.

Bureau of the Census. (1992). *Census of population and housing, 1990* (Summary Tape File 3 on ED-TOM [Louisiana]). Washington, DC: Author.

Merton, R. K. (1972). Insiders and outsiders: A chapter in the sociology of knowledge. *American Journal of Sociology, 78,* 9-47.

Stebbins, R. A. (1992). Concatenated exploration: Notes on a neglected type of longitudinal research. *Quality & Quantity, 26,* 435-442.

Stebbins, R. A. (1994). *The Franco-Calgarians: French language, leisure, and linguistic lifestyle in an anglophone city.* Toronto: University of Toronto Press.

Stebbins, R. A. (1995). Famille, loisir, bilinguisme et style de vie Francophone en milieu minoritaire. *Recherches Sociographiques, 36,* 265-278.

Stebbins, R. A. (1996, October). *La sociologie des Francophones hors Québec: Des nouveaux concepts pour L'analyse du milieu urbain.* Paper presented at the Annual Colloquium of the Centre d'Étude Franco-Canadien de l'Ouest, Winnipeg, Manitoba, Canada.

Wolf, D. R. (1991). *The rebels: A brotherhood of outlaw bikers.* Toronto: University of Toronto Press.

5

On Being Nonpartisan in
Partisan Settings

Field Research Among the
Politically Committed

SCOTT GRILLS

As a part of its history and practice, the extended ethnographic tradition has developed a series of general rules and expectations of its practitioners. The practical constraints of being in the field, however, mean that "the formal rules and canons of research must be bent, twisted, or otherwise abandoned to accommodate the demands of the specific field research situation and the personal characteristics of the investigator" (Shaffir & Stebbins, 1991, p. xi). In this chapter, I examine such "bending" and "twisting" during 4½ years of field research with two ideologically desperate political parties—the Communist Party of Canada (Marxist-Leninist) and the Christian Heritage Party of Canada. Specifically, I address the problem of managing the identity of participant observer as an interested but nonpartisan actor in the context of the committed and often emotionally charged partisan activities of others. Recognizing the necessary tension between these positions, I argue that we can nevertheless effectively manage the research role and develop the trust of others.

The Nonpartisan Ethnographer

Early on in my own personal "conversion" to field research, I had concluded that if only I were a good enough field researcher

I could gain access to almost any setting. The classics and soon to be classics in ethnography do little to dispel this. If ethnography's "stars" can crack taxi-dance halls (Cressey, 1932), gain the confidence of jack-rollers (Shaw, 1930), socially construct "doing death" (Sudnow, 1967), enter cults (Lofland, 1977), ride with a biker gang (Wolf, 1991), and endure the pain of chronic illness (Charmaz, 1991), then there seems to be no social arena that is unavailable to the skilled ethnographer. If we are effective enough researchers, then we will get in, learn the ropes, and adequately manage our relations with others in the field.

It is such an image that is implied through the portrayal of the ethnographer as a nonjudgmental "chameleon-like" inquirer who is able to elicit depth and clarity of response in interview settings (Prus & Sharper, 1991). This ideal posits a particular relationship of the researcher to community. Here, the field researcher utilizes the distance afforded by remaining nonjudgmental to interpersonal advantage—as an interactional strategy that allows for access to the relations, negotiations, perspectives, and processes found within any particular research setting.

The researcher I am describing is a committed actor. This, however, is a commitment directed more toward producing a detailed rendering of the social world than toward becoming directly involved as an advocate for particular worldviews or groups. Ethnographic research and partisan involvement are not mutually incompatible. For example, someone may be a member of a moral crusade and also undertake a sociological analysis of the group. Sharing a certain like-mindedness with others may provide some degree of comfort, familiarity, or sense of additional purpose for the researcher (e.g., to be doing some "good" in the course of research). We do not only study those groups for which we have some sympathy or affinity, however.

In my work on two of Canada's smaller and more marginal political parties, the Communist Party of Canada (Marxist-Leninist) (CPC-ML) and the Christian Heritage Party (CHP), it was necessary to manage research relationships with folks who held widely divergent views. By developing the research relationship around the more nonpartisan position of nonjudgmental student of social life, I was afforded the freedom to move within each group without having aligned myself with one or the other. As initially desirable as this may seem, however, the claim of being nonpartisan may, in and of itself, be defined as troublesome.

Here lies the heart of the problem for more traditional field research in highly politicized settings. How does the researcher sustain and negotiate a nonpartisan identity in partisan settings? If participants have constructed and maintained a worldview that is demarcated by moral absolutes and dichotomies, there may be little flexibility to allow for the more neutral status of sociologist and participant observer. There is little middle ground in the world of us and them, right and wrong, and the chosen and the damned. In such a context, any claim of neutrality can become highly problematic. The researcher may become the target of a series of deviance designations. In the context of a local culture in which "you are either with us or you're against us," any claim of neutrality or appeal to the ideals of social science has the potential to be cast as opposition. Therefore, field research in politicized settings involves more than managing relations. It may also include the work of accommodating a "spoiled" or "discreditable" identity (Goffman, 1963).

Stigma Management

As Adler and Adler (1994) note, designations of deviance can occur in bureaucratic settings as well as in encounters that are more or less limited to interpersonal situations. Although each may be discrediting, the controls and sanctions available to those moral entrepreneurs within bureaucracies are substantively distinct from those available to others (Becker, 1963). Members of bureaucracies may be able to impose a series of sanctions, penalties, and reprimands that are unavailable in a variety of other settings. For those who choose to do research in more formally organized groups, the successful challenge of a denouncer may allow for similar institutional sanctions to be levied on the researcher. Depending on the nature of such measures, the researcher may find the continuation of the project unmanageable.

In the course of my research, I have not been so successfully denounced as to be cast from the field. I have, however, endured (because these were not particularly pleasant experiences, the term endured seems appropriate) the anger, disappointment, and, at time, outright hostility of those involved in political campaigns and crusades. These challenges have tended to focus on three of the more generic aspects of field research relations: (a) managing multiple audiences, (b) living up to the research bargain, and (c) the absence of adherence.

Managing Multiple Audiences

In my research, I adopted what Douglas (1976) refers to as the classical or cooperative paradigm of field research. Within this tradition, the story I can tell is limited by what participants are willing to share. For the most part, members knew of my interests, had consented to my presence, and had established some understanding as to the tolerable range of my access to information and settings. This type of research relationship is intended to be a consensual one, free of coercion, deception, and usury.

Having said this, extended research in politicized settings is likely to place demands on the researcher such that at least a portion of the work be carried out in a covert fashion. For example, as I came to be accepted by party promoters, my ability to disclose my purpose was restricted lest party efforts at recruitment and persuasion be put in jeopardy. Members of the CPC-ML were routinely involved in organizing demonstrations or otherwise promoting a variety of social justice issues. The role of the CPC-ML in the event, however, would be intentionally concealed from the casual participant. Therefore, in much the same fashion as Prus and Sharper (1991) were required to conceal their research interests from the targets of card and dice hustlers, the student of political process must similarly be willing to not "give up the game" to obtain access to it.

Political activity is, to borrow from Goffman (1959), work that is accomplished through coordinating the activities of team members. As policies are constructed, concealed, and then strategically revealed, strategies are formulated, informants are "placed" in competing "camps," and key financial donors are identified, team members may be particularly attentive to the relative advantages of concealing information from competing interests. As my research relationship developed, levels of intimacy and familiarity were enhanced between myself and various team members. I was increasingly likely to have access to elements of the backstage preparations and planning that are a part of various political activities. As I was accepted, others gradually shared with me various secrets of the group (Grills, 1988).

The shared secret, as Simmel (1950) notes, establishes a rather unique relationship between the parties involved. The power of the secret lies in the telling; in its telling, however, the power held in the secret is lost. Where the confidentiality of the respondent is at stake, the fact that one has a secret itself can become a secret. As some members become more involved with the research enterprise, they may facilitate access to a variety of settings by aiding the researcher in "passing" in such roles as member, friend, party official, potential candidate, and employee. What constitutes a covert performance to some audiences (e.g., journalists, audience members, and demonstration participants) is, from another vantage point, sponsored research. A CHP party promoter discussing my attendance at recruitment meetings explained:

> I don't mind you coming along. We don't mind you coming along. We just don't want you going around and telling everybody what you are doing. When we get there help us set things up and take them down when we are done. If people want to know where you are from and what you are doing just tell them you came with us.

Regardless of who "gets us in," the inability of the researcher to disclose the research project to all present means that there is a secret available to be revealed. Its reevaluation may hold risks for the researcher, his or her sponsors, and the research project.

A "Secret" Revealed

In the summer of 1985, I was teaching a social problems course at a southern Ontario university. Most evenings, as I made my way to class, I would pass a man in his early 20s who was, to all appearances, homeless. The irony of talking about social problems in a university classroom while a homeless person was sleeping in a university lounge was too rich for me to ignore. I began talking to "Mark," and I eventually invited him to join our class. All in all, he was the type of "student" whom I value in the classroom. When the course ended, so did our relationship.

In late 1986 and early 1987, I was undertaking a study of a local cell of the CPC-ML.[1] After nearly 6 months in the field, planning was under way for a public demonstration that was to include acts of civil disobedience. Strategies were cast and recast, allegiances were confirmed, and transportation was coordinated. The arrival of a representative of a similar group from another community was somewhat impatiently awaited. Members of the group I was studying decided that no account of my research would be offered to their visitor. All things considered, they concluded they would rather not let other party members and adherents know that they had consented to my access. This strategy likely would have worked had Mark not been the contact for the adjacent community.

When Mark entered the small, smoke-filled bookshop, he immediately recognized me from our previous meetings approximately 2 years earlier. Beginning from the assumptions that those gathered were unaware that I was a sociologist and that I was undertaking covert research, he attempted to reveal my identity as an ethnographer and expose the accompanying risk that he believed I represented to all gathered. One of my sponsors, a regular volunteer at the local communist bookstore, responded, "We know. He has told us all about it and he has been around for a while. He's okay. So what have you got for us?"

The potential threat to the project was mitigated by the overt and cooperative nature of my research. Had I attempted some form of infiltration, the outcome of this encounter would have been quite different. Likewise, had a member of the group not been willing to speak up for me, my options would have been reduced because I would have been unwilling to violate the confidentiality of my respondents. Mark's attempt at degradation hinged on the sharing of a secret—on revealing a hidden research agenda. His ability to "see through" the setting was facilitated by our prior relationship. It does, however, stand as an exemplar of complex and at times competing obligations that field researchers must manage.

Living up to the Research Bargain

The research bargain reflects shared understandings of the general terms and conditions for research activities. When researchers are dealing with groups with relatively clear and stable boundaries and understandings of the research project, the research bargain may prove to be relatively nonproblematic. In my projects, however, gaining access to the back rooms of politics required extended and ongoing work relative to the definition of boundaries. Questions continually arose regarding which internal documents, meetings, membership information, and individuals I might access and in what circumstances.

This process of negotiating the research bargain and defining boundaries may involve a reevaluation of access to information. The bargain that seemed reasonable to participants in the first year of the study may seem untenable at a later date. Likewise, previous concerns may fall by the wayside. Therefore, the researcher must attempt to conduct the study within the context of a research bargain that is emergent and open to continual renegotiation. This uncertainty is compounded by the pragmatic reality that research in politicized settings may involve multiple agreements. The organizational dynamics of political parties (national executive, provincial wings, and riding associations) increases the number of gatekeepers whom the researcher must take into account. As a result, my study of political action is in practice derived from a series of smaller studies, each marked by its own problems of access. For example, to gain information about the operation of local ridings, I in effect conducted a series of smaller research projects on particular riding associations, each with its own research bargain.

Herein lies the problem of maintaining the perception that the research bargains are being honored. Different agreements may provide different avenues of access. What one campaign manager defines as confidential another may readily make available, access denied at the provincial level may be granted at the national level, and so on. Such diversity in the field holds direct implications for the perceived trustworthiness of the researcher. Information declared off limits in one setting may be acquired through the support and interest of another situated elsewhere. To possess such information leaves the researcher open to charges of impropriety that may be difficult to deflect while maintaining the confidentiality of re-spondents.

The Absence of Adherence

During the more than 4 years I spent in the field studying political parties, I never thought of myself as a member of any one them. Although participants have at various times indicated that they have taken my research interests as an implicit endorsement of their views (e.g., I have been asked to take organizational roles or to run as a candidate), I have quite openly and continuingly identified my primary commitment in these settings as being a student of social life. The researcher who chooses to maintain the distance afforded by rejecting political party membership must develop strategies for managing the overtures of recruiters and the potential skepticism of "true believers" (Hoffer, 1951). For some, the absence of committed involvement to an enterprise that they have endowed with sacred or near-sacred qualities is in and of itself enough to undermine the research project and question the integrity of the researcher. For example, a CHP member stated,

> I don't know how you can do this without joining us. . . . All I know is there are two forces in this world. The saving blood of Jesus Christ and the hand of Satan. If after hearing the word of the Lord here tonight you can still hide behind the lies you have learned in those universities, then you have declared yourself very clearly. I just hope that when people hear what you write, that they hear the evil you represent.

As the previous quotation illustrates, the absence of adherence can be defined as such a fatal flaw of the person that no amount of "cooling out the mark" can overcome concerns (Goffman, 1959). My claim to be nonpartisan reflected, for some, a position that does not and could not exist. If the participant's worldview is divided into "those who are for us and those who are against us" and the researcher claims a more neutral ground as his or her own, then the interaction sequence itself has the potential of disintegrating. If neutral ground is defined away, then the claim of nonpartisanship can be cast as a cleverly veiled way for the opposition (however "they" are defined) to cause harm. Because other members of the political organization may have accepted the researcher's tale of neutrality, some may undertake the task of collecting evidence to reveal the researcher (here I borrow qualities attributed during my experiences with both groups) as evil, satanist, feminist, humanist, infiltrator, police officer, or university spy.

In much the same fashion as those who impute deviance relative to sexual orientation (Kitsuse, 1962), those who seek out direct and indirect evidence of the deviant status of the researcher may attend to any aspect of everyday life. Routine ethnographic tools, such as notepads, tape recorders, and research notes, may create suspicion in that they violate more commonly held assumptions of the "sociologist as survey researcher." Reading material, hairstyles, and style of clothes may be interpreted as sign indicators of those who hold particular worldviews. The presentation of self remains problematic, yet the strategies of impression management allow for some personal control over the identity kit adopted by the researcher. Imputations of deviance, however, may also be based on indirect evidence drawn from the actions of others.

Sometimes Your Colleagues Can Get You Into Trouble

During research at a national convention of the Christian Heritage Party, I had been "working the floor" soliciting interviews and discussing proceedings. On the second night of the convention, a faculty member in my department was interviewed on the local nightly news and apparently associated the growth of the CHP with the rise of fascism in Europe during the 1930s. Having not seen the broadcast, I arrived on the convention floor on the third day to a series of misinterpretations and hostile responses:

Delegate: How could you do that to us?

Scott: Do what?

Delegate: Say those horrible, mean things on the news last night.

Scott: I really don't know what you are talking about.

Delegate: Last night, a sociologist from McMaster [University] was on the news. I didn't see it, but I assumed it was you. They said he really ran us down.

Scott: I was asked to do an interview by Channel 11 and 13 but I refused them. I really don't know who they talked to.

This was my first encounter of the day. Although I made no representations to the media, the comments of another faculty member did have a lasting impact. This group was continually looking for attention from the media, and what was received was pondered, magnified, and rehashed. During the course of that day, delegates discussed "what the sociologist said" and "what the guy from McMaster [University] said." For those who were less than pleased with my presence, my colleague's comments legitimized their concerns and fears. One CHP member who had been aware of my project for more than 6 months observed the following:

> That professor in your department didn't do you any favors. Does he not like you or what? All he did was reinforce what people here think about university people: That they are all Marxists—that they spout off on things that they don't know anything about. If I was you I'd keep a pretty low profile for the next little while. But don't worry, I've been telling people that it wasn't you.

The Problem of Trust: Toward the Professional Researcher

Gordon (1987) emphasizes the relative benefits to a researcher studying proselytizing groups of removing himself or herself as a target of recruitment efforts. This provides the researcher with some latitude of movement and distances him or her from the particular struggles of their respondents. Many of the difficulties I have recounted arise from the respondents' awareness (if at times misguided) of my research intent. When political parties are promoting commitments, constructing a worldview, overcoming opposition, managing relations with the media—in short, "doing politics"—the researcher is not particularly important. As Becker (1970) makes clear, the practical constraints of accomplishing action take precedence over attending to the inquisitive other. Although this is a quality of participant observation more generally, once access is gained specifically to larger scale settings (e.g., a leadership convention or a policy discussion group), the dynamics are not altered appreciably by the presence of an observer.

One of the advantages of establishing a clearly defined research presence in the field is that the researcher can demonstrate a commitment to his or her role. I suggest that openly embracing the identity of field researcher is of particular value in the study of proselytizing groups that view themselves as sharing in some level of risk. Reflecting a wide range of member concerns, the identity claims made by those seeking direct involvement with party organizations may be questioned. Newcomers may be defined by some as potential police informants, members of competing organizations, or party moles. If accused of these types of involvements, those potentially discredited may find such accusations of deviant behavior difficult to resist. In encounters not dissimilar from those recounted by Erikson (1966), the accused's denial of deception may be taken as further evidence of wrongdoing because "that is just what you would expect from these kind of people." My field experience suggests that although disproving these allegations may be difficult, adopting the membership role of professional researcher allows for some concerns to be diffused.

By professionalism, I mean to denote the process by which respondents may come to view the participant observer as a serious, committed, and relatively competent performer of the research role. We can demonstrate this to our respondents over time and through a range of strategies. A research partnership may be developed and nurtured by activities such as demonstrating a willingness to be inconvenienced to gather data, emphasizing a desire to learn, keeping confidences, and making ourselves available to respondents.

Essential to one's status as the professional researcher is the development of trust and the interpersonal work required to sustain it. Some researchers may utilize prior relationships and the trust established within them as a point of departure for their research. This may include the posture of "complete member researcher," wherein the trust that facilitates research is bound to the membership status of the researcher (Adler & Adler, 1987; Dilorio &

Nusbaumer, 1993; Wolf, 1991). In addition, the researcher may choose to pass as a member, concealing his or her research intentions while being afforded the trust offered to group members. A third strategy is to gain the trust of respondents through the performance of the research role and the accompanying demands of participant observation. Here, the position of full membership is rejected in favor of the role of interested other in our midst.

These strategies are not mutually exclusive. In practice, more than one may be utilized in the completion of an extended research project. Given the reference points of perspective, all three may be present in an interactional encounter. That is, the trust necessary for research may be facilitated by prior relations, overt research, and covert dimensions simultaneously. Reflecting the earlier discussion, the researcher may benefit from the trust of a sponsor, the trust of other team members through the adequate performance of the research role, and the trust of the targets of the performance through passing as a team member (Goffman, 1963; Prus & Sharper, 1991).

Trust has an elusive quality. It is held up by field researchers as a desirable or indispensable quality of the research enterprise (e.g., Shaffir, 1991). The trust of the other facilitates candor and increased access. How do we know that we have it? The problematic nature of trust may serve as an analytical resource in much the same way as the field researchers' emotional experiences of the field (Kleinman, 1991). We cannot easily demonstrate levels of trust afforded to our research projects. We can, however, examine the process of gaining access and the accompanying relational dynamics within a natural history framework. This involves the reflective work of the ethnography of the ethnography—a willingness to examine the joint action required to accomplish field research. The extent to which participants are willing to place their trust in the researcher is a part of the narrative and influences the story we choose to tell.

To place one's trust in another is to anticipate the outcome of future action. As I have argued elsewhere, trust is somewhat of an interpersonal gamble (Grills, 1994). Although the stakes vary considerably, trusting another imputes qualities to actions not yet performed. To trust is to anticipate that others will, for example, maintain discretion, resist self-interest, and maintain prior commitments. By reflecting on our experiences in the field, we can identify "trust markers"—significant indicators of access, of confidence in the researcher, and of a willingness to endure a certain level of risk. To illustrate, I comment briefly on two important trust markers in my work with the CHP.

The Founding Convention

The first major trust marker that indicated a change in my research posture came in the sixth month of fieldwork. During this time, local organizers were making plans for the founding convention of the party. At these meetings, the party constitution would be ratified, party policy would be established, and the party executive would be elected by delegates from across Canada gathering for the first time. At the national level, the interim executive had made a decision that I initially feared would have a detrimental effect on my research. In an effort to limit potential negative exposure, it was decided to bar the media and all nonregistered convention attenders from policy and debate sessions.

The one loophole from this banning was to register for the convention as an "observer." This registration category had been created to allow for access to the proceedings to interested representatives from complementary associations. After first airing my desire to attend the convention before members of the national and Ontario executive, I formally submitted my registration documents and was granted access to the convention. In conjunction with my request, I was asked to volunteer to serve as the leader's press secretary for the week prior to the convention. The task involved little more than driving the party leader to and from previously established appointments with the national and local media. My modest volunteer contribution as a glorified "driver" and the accompanying access to the convention proved invaluable to my research, however. During my week as press secretary, I gathered almost 20 hours of interview material and had the opportunity to observe the interviews conducted by the press. The founding convention, attended by more than 500 delegates, enabled me to witness the formal ratification of the party's constitution and policy statements. I gained access to the internal debates that delayed procedure and to the points of unanimity around which the collective rallied.

In addition, the convention marked the point at which I perceived that my credentials as a professional researcher had been established and confirmed by the key gatekeepers within the organization. I was allowed access to meeting halls from which the media were prohibited entry, and this access added a legitimacy to my efforts. Although some still questioned the hidden intent of my "snooping," the period following my participation at the founding convention was a time in which my movements within the party were facilitated rather than hindered, and my opportunities for data collection widened.

Candidate Training Sessions

Sanctioned access to closed settings indicates the implicit support of gatekeepers and may serve as a valuable resource in resisting subsequent challenges. Those suspicious or otherwise uneasy with a particular aspect of the project may themselves attend to the levels of trust afforded the researcher by others and may correspondingly reevaluate some of their prior concerns. At times, the trust afforded researchers may be public and biography altering.

With an established research presence in the field came access to previously closed meetings.[2] As a result of the helpfulness of those in the field, I was a participant in meetings and seminars that the general membership were unaware existed. I was subsequently allowed access to organizers' conferences, a cabinet meeting of the key officers of the national executive, and candidate training sessions. One CHP member of the provincial executive remarked:

> I thought we were taking a pretty big risk letting you into the organizer's conference. But I figured you had been around for a while and no harm had come of it so far, so we might as well take the chance.

The candidate training sessions were perhaps the most helpful and the most sensitive of the meetings I attended. At these sessions, potential candidates tried to come together with a unified voice on policy and election strategies. The process entailed a fair amount of debate and apprehension that was not intended for the electorate.

This was backstage work to give the party and its promoters an election-ready public face.

I was also asked to participate as a guest speaker in a candidate training session. An organizer for the event asked if I would be willing to speak about how the CHP could sell their message to the public. I declined. I explained that I was unwilling to take such a direct personal hand in establishing agendas and priorities. As Adler and Adler (1987) note, however, the exchange relationship in the field is often uneven. In a compromise intended, in some direct way, to redress my level of indebtedness, I agreed to present the draft of a paper to their meeting of candidates and organizers (Grills, 1997).

The transition from questioning the appropriateness of my presence in the room at the start of the project to being the dinner speaker a little more than a year later is similar to that of other researchers' findings. As Haas (1977) came to be trusted by his high iron workers, they approached him with their fears. As Leibow (1967) came to develop an empathetic understanding with juvenile delinquents, they shared their "family" secrets with him. Similarly, as members of the CHP came to see me as less of a threat, doors opened, my judgment as "their sociologist" was taken into account, and the distinction between my interests as a researcher and their political ambitions was developed and clarified.

My claim to the role of researcher allowed me access to a series of meetings that were, to some extent, restricted. This same research status, however, also led my respondents to conclude that they could expect something from me in terms of the product of the research enterprise. By sharing a conference paper, I was able to help clarify my research role. With this paper and presentation, a select group of respondents were given some insight into the sociological use of their words, accounts, and actions. It allowed me to provide further evidence that I was living up to my end of the research bargain. In addition, and perhaps of most value, it provided an opportunity for my respondents to comment on the extent to which I was coming to understand their worlds in a meaningful way. One provincial organizer stated, "I won't say I actually liked everything you have found out about us. But I think you have pretty well got us the way we are, warts, halos, and all."

Conclusion

In some ways, I am quite fond of the phrase "warts, halos, and all." It reflects the group and their struggles with moving from the religious life (halos) to the activities of electoral politics (warts). The ability of others to see themselves in our work addresses the pursuit of Blumer's (1969) elusive intimate familiarity.

Achieving a research presence among those who are committed to political action is a highly problematic endeavor. The highly politicized worldview of participants, quite unlike that which is found in many other groups, may challenge the legitimacy of the research enterprise and the integrity of the researcher. By retaining a distance from the various causes and campaigns embraced by party members, the more nonpartisan researcher may become the target of some who equate such a position with opposition, apathy, or a lack of personal integrity—with deviance.

Successful field research among such groups requires researchers to resist designations of deviance. Establishing trust through adopting the role of the professional researcher is one interactional strategy by which this may be accomplished. Such a research posture challenges designations of deviance without neutralizing the denouncers' claim. We should not underplay the importance of attending to the reception, depiction, and ongoing relations between the researcher and others, however, because attempts to discredit the research or the researcher are a part of the total culture that is the topic of our analysis. By reflecting on how group members make sense of researcher interest, strategies that are utilized to discredit the project, and the various ways in which some may take on advocacy roles on behalf of the researcher and his or her project, access is gained to some useful and important ethnographic resources.

Notes

1. The members of the CPC-ML who were a part of this study considered themselves to be involved in an organization that was at risk. Some were considerably more concerned about the potential for possible arrest, police infiltration and surveillance,

loss of employment, or the harassment of their children than were others. Reflecting generalized concerns, the group was organized into locals or "cells" with limited formal contact (in terms of record keeping and membership lists) with other CPC-ML groups in other cities. Although some participants publicly embraced CPC-ML affiliations, the group was organized to allow for relatively anonymous involvements as well.

2. As people became more comfortable with my research, party affiliates would point out events that I attend. Sometimes respondents have a clearer sense of where "answers" are to be found than does the researcher.

References

Adler, P., & Adler. P. (1987). *Membership roles in field research.* Newbury Park, CA: Sage.

Adler, P., & Adler. P. (1994). *Constructions of deviance: Social power, context, and interaction.* Belmont, CA: Wadsworth.

Becker, H. S. (1963). *Outsiders: Studies in the sociology of deviance.* New York: Free Press.

Becker, H. S. (1970). *Sociological work: Method and substance.* Chicago: Aldine.

Blumer, H. (1969). *Symbolic interactionism: Perspective and method.* Englewood Cliffs, NJ: Prentice Hall.

Charmaz, K. (1991). *Good days, bad days: The self in chronic illness and time.* New Brunswick, NJ: Rutgers University Press.

Cressey, P. (1932). *The taxi-dance hall.* Chicago: University of Chicago Press.

Dilorio, J. A., & Nusbaumer, M. R. (1993). Securing our sanity: Anger management among abortion escorts. *Journal of Contemporary Ethnography, 21*(4), 411-438.

Douglas, J. (1976). *Investigative social research: Individual and team research.* London: Sage.

Erikson, K. (1966). *Wayward puritans.* New York: John Wiley.

Goffman, E. (1959). *Presentation of self in everyday life.* New York: Anchor.

Goffman, E. (1963). *Stigma: Notes on the management of a spoiled identity.* Englewood Cliffs, NJ: Prentice Hall.

Gordon, D. F. (1987). Getting close by staying distant: Fieldwork with proselytizing groups. *Qualitative Sociology, 10*(3), 267-287.

Grills, S. (1988, June 4-7). *Secrecy as accomplished activity: The problematics of "doing good" within the Canadian radical Left.* Paper presented at Canadian Sociology and Anthropology Association Meetings, University of Windsor, Windsor, Ontario, Canada.

Grills, S. (1994). Recruitment practices of the Christian Heritage Party. In M. L. Deitz, W. Shaffir, & R. Prus (Eds.), *Doing everyday life: Ethnography as human lived experience* (pp. 96-108). Mississauga, Ontario, Canada: Copp Clark Longman.

Grills, S. (1997). Tomorrow for sale: Politics and religious fundamentalism. In L. Tepperman, J. Curtis, S. J. Wilson, & A. Wain (Eds.), *Small world: Readings in sociology* (2nd ed., pp. 262-271). Scarborough, Ontario: Prentice Hall.

Haas, J. (1977). Learning real feelings: A study of high iron steel workers. *Sociology of Work and Occupations, 4*(2), 147-170.

Hoffer, E. (1951). *The true believer.* New York: Harper & Row.

Kitsuse, J. (1962). Societal reaction to deviant behaviour: Problems of theory and method. *Social Problems, 9*(3), 247-256.

Kleinman, S. (1991). Field-workers' feelings. In W. Shaffir & R. Stebbins (Eds.), *Experiencing fieldwork* (pp. 184-195). Newbury Park, CA: Sage.

Leibow, E. (1967). *Tally's corner.* Boston: Little, Brown.

Lofland, J. (1977). *The doomsday cult: A study on conversion, proselytization and maintenance of faith.* New York: Irvington.

Prus, R., & Sharper, C. R. D. (1991). *Road hustler: Grifting, magic and the thief subculture.* New York: Kaufman & Greenberg.

Shaffir, W. (1991). Managing a convincing self-presentation. In W. Shaffir & R. Stebbins (Eds.), *Experiencing fieldwork* (pp. 72-81). Newbury Park, CA: Sage.

Shaffir, W., & Stebbins, R. (1991). Introduction. In W. Shaffir & R. Stebbins (Eds.), *Experiencing fieldwork* (pp. 1-24). Newbury Park, CA: Sage.

Shaw, C. (1930). *The jack-roller: A delinquent boy's own story.* Chicago: University of Chicago Press.

Simmel, G. (1950). *The sociology of Georg Simmel* (K. H. Wolff, Trans. & Ed.). New York: Free Press.

Sudnow, D. (1967). *Passing on: The social organization of dying.* Englewood Cliffs, NJ: Prentice Hall.

Wolf, D. (1991). *The rebels: A brotherhood of outlaw bikers.* Toronto: University of Toronto Press.

PART III

Issues in Methodological Practice

This part deals with some of the problems that accompany various methodological strategies. Although field research is often cast relative to the practices of observation, participation, and interview, what we actually do in the field may look much more like "hanging out," conversation, or engaging in whatever it is we are "supposed" to be studying. Because field research is accomplished with the help of others, it is not surprising that field research involves a series of accommodations, redirections, backtracking, trying things out, and discarding earlier strategies. The research project is marked by various activities that are directed toward navigating the field site—gaining access, respecting the other, maintaining the ethnographic gaze, and evaluating impressions.

Field research is joint action in the full Blumerian sense of the term. It requires the "fitting together" of various lines of action—the actions of the participants with those of the researcher. Although, as is illustrated in the chapters in this part, the distinction between participant and researcher is often less than clear, there remains the pragmatic problem of accomplishing research in the context of ongoing action. Social life does not pause to allow for the ethnographic project. As the substantive areas discussed in this part illustrate, the hunt goes on, the exam is written, and family life continues in the presence of the ethnographer. It is into the confusing and emergent world of everyday life that the ethnographer is immersed.

The three chapters that comprise this part offer a diverse collection representing divergent traditions within the larger ethnographic project. Readers are encouraged to attend to differences between Albas and Albas's focus on "data collection," Daly and Dienhart's more phenomenologically influenced interests, and Brymer's representation of the full member as researcher. Students may find the following common themes particularly helpful as they attend to related issues between field settings:

▓ Entering various "spaces": private space, family space, occupational space, and subcultural space

▓ Penetrating the "taken for granted" and making the "obvious"—what "everyone here knows"—interesting and problematic

▓ Attending to the "politics of fieldwork" by being aware of the problematics of forming alliances, cultivating identities, and being associated with authority

▓ Managing intimacy as one becomes (or is) a member, friend, advocate, or invited guest

▓ Deciding who we talk to, whose perspectives dominate our work, and who is, by comparison, relatively silenced

▓ Utilizing various methodological strategies in the field to allow access to otherwise unavailable aspects of social life

▓ The importance of the distinction between exceptional events and routine events and the methodological problem of establishing the difference

▓ The commitment to the field, embodied in the willingness to "pay one's dues," endure the inconvenience, and commit to the breadth of the project

6

Navigating the Family Domain

Qualitative Field Dilemmas

KERRY DALY

ANNA DIENHART

This chapter is based on our experience as qualitative researchers interested in studying families. We present some of the more salient challenges we have encountered in carrying out family research. Specifically, we examine these challenges on two levels. First, there is a critical exploration of what it means to do family research. We scrutinize the term family and, by direct implication, we open for critique our efforts to understand and know the family. These are ontological and epistemological field dilemmas. Second, we discuss a range of practical field dilemmas that we have encountered in our own work of observing and interviewing individuals, couples, and families. Kerry has had experience as a participant observer in an infertility support group setting, has interviewed couples about the transition to adoptive parenthood, and has interviewed men about their experience as fathers. Anna has interviewed men and women about the patterns and practices associated with their declared commitment to "shared parenthood." She has extensively interviewed couples about their family life and relationships in her work as a couple and family therapist. In keeping with the movement in qualitative work to keep the voice of the writer present in the text (e.g., Daly, 1997), we have chosen a style that allows for the expression of both shared and individual ideas. To this end, we have adopted a kind of narrative style that identifies which author is speaking throughout the chapter.

Ontological and Epistemological Field Dilemmas

Is It Family Research at All?

Studying families is a problematic endeavor. One of the main reasons for this is that it is increasingly difficult to determine what is a family or family experience.

> **Kerry:** A valued colleague of mine recently approached me at the National Council of Family Relations conference and, with a sense of indignation, pointed to a number of papers on the program that were not "family" papers. He said, "Don't you get annoyed that there are so many papers on this program that don't deal with families? This is supposed to be a conference on research about families!" He pointed to a paper on unplanned pregnancy and another on a feminist analysis of aging. Initially, I was not sure how to respond because he had pierced my complacency about what family is or can be. What this experience highlighted for me is that for qualitative researchers who are interested in studying families, determining what constitutes family experience is not an unproblematic endeavor. Where once the term family was definable with some distinct parameters, it has now broadened to mean many things.

It is in this regard that qualitative family researchers must first ask whether it is family research at all. Cohen and Katzenstein (1988), for example, suggest that many research questions that present family as the primary focus are really studies of gender practices. In other research, responsibilities such as housework, caregiving, and child care are routinely viewed as occupational, organizational, and economic phenomena that are only incidentally associated with family. Additionally, when we focus on individual member perceptions of their family experience, more often than not our questions cross many domains. For example, we found we could not talk about fatherhood without talking about work. We could not talk about fatherhood without understanding the way in which men establish and maintain a variety of relationships—some of which are family (e.g., partner, wife, or children) and others that clearly are not (e.g., friends and coworkers). As this suggests, the study of family experience is not a tightly boundaried domain but rather is one that intersects with many other domains and involves regular forays into arenas of meaning that are in some ways quite distant from what we have traditionally thought of as family.

In recent years, the conceptual parameters that were traditionally used to define families have been losing their privileged and unquestioned status. Families can no longer be seen as monolithic structures with a uniformity of experience and a universality of structure and functions (Eichler, 1988). There have been a variety of forces that have contributed to the dethroning of "the family" (Coontz, 1992). Increased labor force participation of women, divorce, violence, the women's movement, changes in the economy, and individualism have been identified as major forces in the "erosion" of the traditional family structure of our nostalgic past. In the face of these changes, efforts to define the family as a unique domain with rigid boundaries have met with strong resistance. As a consequence, any effort to qualitatively study families must in some way attend to these diffuse definitions and elusive boundaries.

The ways families have changed in recent years, and how we study them, have become an important focus in the modernist-postmodernist debate. Whereas the modernist position holds to the family as a uniform and monolithic structure, a postmodernist view sees families as varied and diverse (Cheal, 1991). Postmodernism, with its focus on "pluralism, disorder, and fragmentation" (Cheal, 1993, p. 9), not only views the structure of families as diverse but also views the ways that families are defined and interpreted as pluralistic. The diverse empirical reality of families is now generally accepted among researchers. This diversity, however, finds expression in many other forms in families, including family structure, language usage, power relationships, and expectations (Gubrium, 1993).

Postmodern ideas play an important role in dereifying the family. To speak of a reified family is to make reference to family as some kind of unchanging, identifiable family form. From this perspective, the family can no longer be seen as a thing or an ideological representation but must be viewed as a diverse and changing set of everyday practices (Gubrium & Holstein, 1990). The challenge for qualitative researchers who study families is to confront, represent, or accommodate diverse family realities. Rather than artificially dividing the social world into heuristically convenient categories such as the family, it is important to examine the complex unity of people's lives (Bernardes, 1986) as they are experienced across a variety of categories, including work, media, education, commerce, class, race, and gender.

Ways of Knowing Families

Family experience plays an important role in shaping the course of everyday experience. Family continues to have remarkable power over the way that people experience their lives: "Family ideology is so deeply integrated into our consciousness that most people cannot support the idea that the family does not exist for any length of time" (Bernardes, 1993, p. 40). Whether we think of family as ideology, experience, process, or structure, it continues to reflect a sphere of meaning that is part of the everyday life world. Our efforts to understand this sphere of meaning through qualitative methods must be attentive to the limitations of knowledge. As Lather (1990) has suggested, all knowledge is social, partial, local, and critical. From this standpoint, the knowledge that we can expect to garner from family spheres of meaning involves an attentiveness to the way in which meanings are produced through interaction (social); the changing and incomplete view of those meanings (partial); how they are located in a specific space, time, and a cultural and ideological context (local); and the manner in which values are produced, maintained, or constrained in the production of that knowledge (critical).

These epistemological questions present the qualitative researcher with some of the most fundamental field problems. First, because families represent particular structures, practices, forms of consciousness, traditions, ideals, discourses, and interactions, any effort to define family as a category must be based on the emergent meanings and experiences of family members. In keeping with this, research about or with families must be attentive to the conceptual boundaries associated with the family that have real meaning for individuals who are a part of diverse families. At the same time, there must be an attentiveness to the unboundaried flow of experience that is multifaceted and that may include dimensions of family roles or practices in tandem with other "outside the family" practices and experiences. In addition, researchers have an experience of family and this affects values, priorities, and interpretations in the research endeavor. Researchers need to be clear about their own family politics in relation to how, what, and why they study what they do in families. How does their positioning within their own families affect what they study and how they report the results? What is the goal of the research? Is the purpose to reflect "the way things are in families" or to bring about social change in the way that power, responsibilities, and activities are distributed in families? Does the research support current family ideologies or challenge them? What are the "ideological codes" that "infect" (Smith, 1993, p. 62) interpretations? Finally, researchers must deal with continuous change and temporal complexity within families. Individual development, family development, and historical time intersect to create unending configurations of new meaning. As a consequence, ontological questions arise with respect to the form that knowledge about families can take. Do we believe that there are nomothetic patterns of family experience that can be generated? Is idiographic, thick description the best approach for studying postmodern families? If we believe that patterns are identifiable, how far do we go with this? That is, are they generalizable to larger populations? Do these reflect "generic processes"? Can we theorize about families?

These are broad, foundational field dilemmas that require qualitative researchers to adopt a reflexive and critical stance toward the study of families. Specifically, it means maintaining a diligence to question what families are and how we can know them. It means we must be explicit about our theoretical perspective on studying families, our hidden assumptions about family experience and meanings, our blind spots in understanding diverse family experiences, and the values that underlie our personal and theoretical interpretive perspectives.

Practical Field Dilemmas

The family domain is typically associated with the private and personal parts of our lives. Although feminist thinkers have challenged the rigorous separation of the public and private spheres (Feree, 1990), for most people the deep and intricate texture of the family domain continues to be experienced as a separate and unique space that is backstage from their public presentation of self (Goffman, 1959). In this regard, families are a distinctive focus of study characterized by privacy; shared meanings that are not readily available to nonfamily members; relationships with an intended permanency that are rooted in kinship, blood ties, adoption, or marriage; shared traditions; intensity of involvement that ranges from the most loving to the most violent; and a collage of individual interests, experiences, and qualities. The field researcher who studies families faces the challenge of entering and managing an intimate space. In each of the following sections, we first set out some of the recurring problematics we have faced as field researchers and then provide some suggested practices we have found useful in managing these problematics in the research endeavor.

Entering Family Space

A challenge for qualitative researchers is to enter the relatively closed and highly protected boundaries of families' experiences. Although families vary with respect to the permeability of their boundaries, they typically are thought of as being one of the most closed and private of all social groups. Family members coalesce in the processes of preserving and protecting their traditions, habits, and secrets. Keeping conflictual, dysfunctional, or sexual behaviors from the purview of outsiders is a key mechanism by which families construct and maintain their unique self-definitions.

> **Kerry:** One of my interviewing "epiphanies" serves as an important reminder of the power of these boundaries. In my study of infertile couples who were considering adoption, I recruited couples through a fertility clinic at a large teaching hospital. I met them, explained the study, and if they agreed to participate I set up a time to meet them in their home. With one particular couple, I set up an evening interview. I drove 90 minutes to their home only to be greeted by an enormous barking dog and a wife at the door who had forgotten about our appointment. She excused herself to discuss this with her husband, leaving me just inside the door with the dog. The dog was apparently uneasy with my presence and proceeded to snarl and jump on me. After

what seemed like an eternity, the wife returned and indicated that this was just not a good time to talk. The dog, keeping guard of me at the door, serves as a powerful metaphor for me regarding the importance of family boundaries.

Anna: One of my experiences of waiting for an invitation "in" involved a 7-year-old boy (son of one of the couples I was trying to recruit into my research) greeting me at the door and grilling me about what I wanted to speak to his mother or father about. Finally, after what seemed like an endless barrage of questions and the passage of a considerable amount of time, he went to tell his parents that someone was at the door. He certainly was curious about me, but I had the impression he had been taught to not let "salespeople" into the house.

Although each of us has had several experiences in which we have been unable to get beyond the family's threshold, for the most part, families have welcomed us into their home. In some ways, doing interviews within the home is facilitated by norms of hospitality. Although they may be unclear as to your purpose as a researcher, they usually welcome you in because that is what "you are supposed to do with invited strangers." In this regard, qualitative research, in comparison with more remote methods of data collection, allows for the construction of relationships with participants that gradually can build trust and rapport. By offering to enter participants' life worlds, rather than imposing the formality of a survey or an experiment, qualitative researchers are in a good position to better understand the private meanings of families. For example, the use of unstructured interviews, observations, or diaries and letters allows participants to discuss their experiences in their own language, in their own natural setting, and according to their own comfort in disclosing.

Of course, the process of entering family space is not simply a matter of getting beyond the physical threshold: It also involves a challenge of entering the social psychological space. This space is characterized by family loyalties, secrets, values, and practices. Stepping over this threshold can be considerably more challenging than even getting past the dog. Few researchers acknowledge their limitations in crossing this threshold. Making these limitations obvious in the research can provide insight into the ways in which boundaries are defined and maintained in families. These limitations are apparent when participants avoid sensitive topics or request that the tape recorder be shut off to reveal something "off the record." Rather than seeing these as barriers to accessibility, they can serve as rich data in themselves. Although researchers have ethical obligations to honor participants' requests that some statements not be included as data, these moments can provide the researcher with insight into disclosure limits and the norms of social acceptability. Moreover, the face-to-face intimacy of interviews or observation allows the researcher to observe these processes firsthand. These are opportunities to understand private-public boundaries as well as processes by which these boundaries are presented and maintained.

Practices to Ease Entering Family Space

Anna: How a field researcher interacts with barking dogs, curious children, and those first awkward social moments at the door may ultimately determine not only the access to data but also the quality of the data accessed. As a field researcher, you are something of an "invited intruder" in their private world of family. As Kerry suggests, social norms typically carry you through those first few moments of being welcomed into their physical space. I believe, however, that at a deeper level of interactional expectations, the researcher has both an opportunity and a responsibility to influence the "welcoming" ritual in ways that can facilitate maximal access to high-quality "data." Upon crossing the threshold of their home, you have the implicit contract of their participation in your research, but you do not have a contract on what they will tell you, how they will tell you, and how much of a view they allow into their everyday interactional patterns. What you do and how you interact in those opening moments will convey important information about your trustworthiness. I believe establishing trustworthiness is not just a matter of offering reassuring words about confidentiality and the researcher's interest and intents. I believe it is important for field researchers to consider explicitly what they want to convey about their trustworthiness in those first few moments and then specifically adopt practices that will subtly demonstrate genuine openness and interest in receiving the family's stories.

For example, in my research about "shared parenthood" experiences of men and women, I usually arranged my meetings with these people during a part of the day when their young children would be present (at least initially). When I entered their home, I made a point of getting down to the children's level (physically crouching so they could speak to me face-to-face) and engaging the child in some talk about themselves. I then proceeded to show the children my recording equipment and let them talk into the tape, then rewound the tape so they could hear themselves as recorded. In deciding to begin with this procedure, I was aware that the parents would be watching my interaction and likely would be making initial judgments about my trustworthiness. I believed I could begin to establish that trustworthiness by interacting with their children in a respectful, interested, playful manner that involved their whole family in my research and provided a relatively nonthreatening introduction to the recording equipment. I took as long as seemed necessary for the children to satisfy their curiosity about me and waited for the children and parents to signal each other that they were ready to move on to the interview. I remember in at least one family, I took the time to accompany the children down to the basement to see and briefly play with some of their favorite toys. In effect, I engaged their curiosity and entered their world—a style I believed I needed later when I began to interview the parents.

Something to Talk About: Getting Beyond the Taken for Granted

Although some aspects of family experience are deliberately hidden from researchers, some aspects of family reality are hidden simply because of their apparent mundaneness. Often aspects of family roles and relationships are so routine and repetitive that they are taken for granted and not considered to be important by participants. This was particularly the case in both of our fatherhood projects. As a way of finishing each interview, we both adopted the practice of asking these men whether there were any other things that they wanted to tell us. We also asked them whether the interview was what they expected. In response, many of these fathers indicated to us that they were very puzzled about what to expect coming into the interview. Even though we each had communicated the purpose of the research in an introductory letter to them, many had a hard time imagining what we could ever talk about for a whole hour and a half on the topic of fatherhood. In retrospect, we each arrived at the plausible interpretation that fatherhood was such a "natural" and routine part of their everyday world that they truly believed that there could not possibly be much to discuss.

In the research literature, housework serves as an interesting parallel. It was Betty Friedan (1963) who referred to housework as "the problem with no name." Prior to housework being politicized and understood as part of a broader ideological structure, it was so mired in the mundaneness of everyday life that we could not even articulate it as a legitimate focus of study. Qualitative scholars, such as Anne Oakley (1974) and Helena Lopata (1971), successfully excavated this taken-for-granted domestic site and, in so doing, brought about a whole new consciousness of gender practices in the home. Families have many problems with no names that need to be examined. For the qualitative researcher, the invitation is to question the taken for granted so that he or she might have a more focused view of family meanings and interactions.

> **Kerry:** Of course, the taken-for-granted family meanings are made even more understandable when we study the problematics, the disruptions, or the nonnormative transitions in family experience. These are family crisis points or "epiphanies" (Denzin, 1989) that make their realities manifest and apparent to researchers. For example, my own study of infertility provided considerable insight into the taken-for-granted meaning of parenthood. When people are unable to have children when they desperately want them, they are in a very good position to articulate what they are missing. For example, they talked about the value and importance of parenthood for legitimating marriage and the family, the cultural pressures that are brought to bear on couples who do not have children, and the impact of childlessness on adult development and identity.

Practices to Get Beyond the Taken for Granted

At the concrete level of what may transpire in the research interview, persons may discount the importance of their experience or withhold information that they see as too obvious or because they view the researcher as an "expert."

Kerry: In one instance in my research, a woman began to talk about her experience of going to the gynecologist for infertility investigation and having to sit in a waiting room full of pregnant women. She said, "Its not fun going to these things . . . but well, you know." In this situation, it was necessary to establish a "pretense awareness context" (Glaser & Strauss, 1967) that conveyed a message of my own ignorance. Therefore, regardless of whether or not I could anticipate what informants were going to say, I encouraged them to continue by saying something such as, "No, I'm not really sure what you mean. Could you explain?" or "No, I've not had that kind of experience. Please go on."

Maintaining a pretense awareness context may be particularly challenging when there is a gender match, or other particularly salient experiential match, between the researcher and the research informant.

Anna: In my research with couples, I found it more challenging to maintain this position when I was exploring women's experience than when I was excavating men's experience. When talking with women, I found that the times a woman would easily move over territory of great complexity were full of "knowing" glances that I surely understood the deep texture of what she experienced. I often felt quite awkward asking her to tell me more or suggesting I had not had that particular experience and wanted to hear the details. For me, it often became a dilemma of balancing a pretense awareness context with maintaining a believable rapport between myself and the woman. One practice I use to sustain rapport that conveys respect, openness, and believability while maintaining the necessary pretense of ignorance to obtain a full and specific description is to say, "I know something of what you are saying, but I would like to hear more about your particular experience."

When I interviewed men, I found that maintaining the pretense awareness context, or a "not knowing curiosity," was not so challenging. I was more concerned that men may not tell me things that they thought I would not be able to understand because, as a woman, I could never share their experience. As such, I worried I might diminish my credibility regarding understanding a man's experience if I did not intermittently convey some connection to what he was relating. I found the practice of saying, "other men have mentioned similar things, but I would like to hear more about how you experienced . . ." seemed to facilitate further exploration of the taken for granted. I also made a point to ask men if there were some things in their experience that they thought I may not be interested in or able to understand because I was a woman. If so, I would then ask them what those experiences, ideas, feelings, or all three might be and would they help me gain an appreciation for their male experience and perspective.

Managing Intimate Space

When researchers enter into the family domain, they temporarily become part of the family system. They are typically welcomed into the home, and although they may be treated with caution, they nevertheless become part of the network of interacting personalities. (Researchers must decide what stance they will take to the interaction and then develop clear guiding principles for themselves to maintain that stance in the midst of the family. Choosing a stance falls on a spectrum of possibilities spanning passive observer, interactive inquirer, friend, detached inquirer, or, in some instances, an unwitting participant in the sharing of family stories and experiences. The stance that we adopt is a function of both our research interest and personal abilities that shape the course of our position as it changes and evolves in the research context. Being attentive to stance means being reflexive about our role as we attempt to manage the flow of information within the family system. Although the traditional norms of question and answer typically guide the course of our focused research conversations, there are occasions when the unpredictable happens and we are called on to delicately manage our role in the family. We focus on two issues in particular: unanticipated disclosures and the dangers of being co-opted or triangulated in the family.

Unanticipated Disclosures

Within our culture, a family's business is by nature considered private. Family members are generally discouraged from hanging out their dirty laundry in public. Despite this, many families are willing to talk to researchers about some of the most intimate and private aspects of their lives. Perhaps Simmel's (1950) discussion of the "stranger" comes closest to accounting for these intimate disclosures. For Simmel (1950, p. 404), the perceived "objectivity" of the stranger may give rise to "the most surprising openness—confidences which sometimes have the character of a confessional and which would be carefully withheld from a more closely related person." In our own research with families, it seems that we play the role of the stranger who invites personal disclosures of many types. This is the basis on which we can begin to understand the meanings and processes that occur within families. For example, we have noticed that at the end of most of our interviews, when the tape recorder has been shut off, participants routinely tell us that they had never talked about some of these things either between themselves or with close friends or family members. In such instances, our impression is that the interview experience is viewed positively and, in some cases, as a kind of catharsis. At the same time, however, there are occasions when we have been aware that we have heard too much.

> **Kerry:** For example, in an interview with an infertile couple, I was left feeling some awkwardness for how to respond to the husband's unanticipated disclosure:
>
> > HUSBAND: Everyone believes that "it [i.e., infertility] will not happen to us," and until it does, I don't think that they will ever understand. When I realized that the only way we were going to have our own children was through adoption— even to the day that we picked up our little girl, I was really very tentative. I really wanted to—but I think I went along with it because it meant a lot to her.
> >
> > WIFE: That's a terrible thing to say! (nervously laughing)
> >
> > HUSBAND: Well . . . I was in agreement but I was in all honesty very tentative about the whole thing. (uncomfortable silence)

Unanticipated disclosures may be associated with the inherent power imbalance between researchers and participants. This imbalance may result in participants feeling obligated to respond to questions that they might otherwise not answer. The potential power imbalances may be further compounded when interviewing more than one family member, where disclosures by one can be considered to be a violation of privacy by others. For others, the informal atmosphere of an unstructured interview in the home may lead them to disclose more than they had originally planned. This possibility may also be related to the potential of an outsider's (i.e., the researcher's) interest to invite perspective taking that had not been anticipated or perhaps even considered when the individual or couple or both privately worked to understand their experiences.

Dangers of Alliances or Triangulation in the Family

The inherent power imbalances between researchers and participants may also underlie our vulnerability to participate in alliances or triangulation. It seems quite understandable that people who are being interviewed may invite some subtle acknowledgment or affirmation or both of their experiences, life meaning, feelings, or all three. Such invitations may be subtle ways people naturally move to redress the implicit power imbalance between the researcher and themselves. Researchers, too, may intentionally or unintentionally move to minimize that imbalance. When we choose to move intentionally to minimize the power imbalance, we may enhance the quality of the data we generate with the participants, but we may also be in danger of forming an alliance or being co-opted into a triangle. This danger is especially present when we interview more than one member of a family, particularly in a group (family or couple) interview.

A complicating variable associated with alliances and triangles in family research is that you, the researcher, may be the only one unaware of the implicit, and perhaps extremely subtle, power structures in the family that may be playing out in the interview itself. In addition, the researcher may find that family members may subtly beckon support for their viewpoints or feelings from researchers. Through our reactions of agreement, support, and interest, on the one hand, or indifference, on the other hand, we give our participants relationship cues that communicate acceptance or rejection, withdrawal, and support.

Anna: For example, during a couple interview, I was following some back and forth dialogue between the couple. When I reread the transcript and referred back to my field notes, I noticed I had redirected the flow of conversation between the father and mother and in the process had inadvertently favored the wife's view. They were talking about issues that each may choose to tackle with their child. The dialogue is as follows:

WIFE: Jason chooses thumb sucking. (laughter)

HUSBAND: I choose that he has to wear a seat belt in the car.

WIFE: Well that's shared. That's strange. I don't understand that one.

HUSBAND: We share that one.

INTERVIEWER: Thumb sucking is one of yours?

HUSBAND: Yeah. On his 5-year-old checkup, we decided that we would talk to the doctor about it.

WIFE: No, no, no!

HUSBAND: I decided that we would talk about it. . . . Hillary was on the bandwagon as well, trying to convince Mike (son) not to and I've stayed on.

WIFE: Well I was not willing to do it in that way. I felt like it's making this big issue about something. Things were going all right and you hit with this issue.

HUSBAND: I thought I saw you going along with the program for a while.

WIFE: No, I don't think I went along with that program.

As the conversation proceeded, it became obvious to me that the wife had very different views on this issue, and it seemed to give her a platform to air those views. I felt the tension between them fill the room, and a few moments later, just as the wife gave a clear justification of her position, I asked them if they were ready to shift to another question. On reflection, I thought that my eagerness to shift to another question likely gave a cue that I thought her explanation was a good one, perhaps inadvertently discounting his concern over this issue.

Practices for Managing Intimate Space

In dealing with unanticipated disclosures, sometimes the nature and timing of these disclosures may be beyond the control of researchers. Nevertheless, always maintaining a respectful stance to informants' privacy is a useful ethical guideline. Among other things, this involves periodically checking in with participants regarding their comfort levels and, if necessary, withdrawing segments of data from the record. Researchers may actively discourage informants from talking about certain topics when they see an unwelcome level of anxiety and stress.

> **Kerry:** In my interviews with infertile couples, I occasionally found myself in the midst of a potentially dangerous alliance that was difficult to avoid. For example, a husband and wife were having widely different experiences in the way in which they were coping with infertility and were having difficulty understanding each other's experience. As a result, the wife turned to me to try to understand:
>
>> WIFE: He doesn't know exactly how I feel and I find that hard to understand, because he is my husband and this is his problem too. He wants a child too. He just seems to be able to accept it so much easier without asking questions.
>>
>> HUSBAND: Well you just have to accept it, no?
>>
>> WIFE: Well I agree with him, you have to accept it because I have no choice. Like what am I going to do? I can't go on crying all my life. But what I can't understand is, how can it be so much easier for him to accept than me? How? (turning to me inquisitively)
>
> For me to provide an answer to this question would be to form an alliance with the wife. By providing advice or an explanation, I would be working with her to explain him. After some initial squirming, I avoided being placed in the role of being both the expert and her ally by simply reflecting the same question back to her. In other words, I asked her why she thought it was easier for him to accept it, to which she responded with a long explanation about his family background. This technique was effective insofar as it served the respondent's need to understand her husband's behavior. More important, from my standpoint, it allowed me to manage the intimate space in a way that kept me in a more neutral role and kept the husband engaged in the interview.

Anna: Similar to Kerry's example, I am aware of the complications associated with the gender match or mismatch between the researcher and the participant. The way that gender is aligned in the interview may inherently contribute to the formation of alliances and the possibilities of triangulation. I wondered how it might have been for the woman in the previously discussed couple to be sitting there with two men, one of whom was the researcher or expert. I wondered if the inherent power imbalance was more pronounced in this situation and how that may have influenced the flow of the interview. I wondered if Kerry's initial squirming, when experienced by the male researcher, suggests that he was tempted to move to an "expert" position and explain a "male's perspective," or if he was tempted to "protect the man" from further pressure to discuss or disclose, or if he was just painfully aware of the tension between these spouses as they lived through their different experiences of infertility. I also wondered how the interview might have unfolded from here if he had moved from his squirming to invite the husband to explain himself further. I was left wondering whether Kerry indeed avoided a dangerous alliance or became involved in an even more subtle alliance. Finally, I was painfully aware of how I, as a woman with some experience of infertility, would likely have squirmed too and been painfully aware that no matter which direction I went in this situation, I had the potential to inadvertently form an alliance. I am aware I might take the same position as a male researcher in this situation, perhaps even ask the same question, but the perceived potential to form an alliance could have a different impact.

In conclusion, we recommend a basic practice: We believe researchers must remain keenly aware of the complexities of gender mixed with the inherent power of being in the position of researcher. In the intricate interview space, relying on the simple notion of maintaining researcher neutrality may not be a neutral position, especially in the context of family research. We encourage researchers to make decisions that move them closest to a position that generates information about the participants' experiences. Remember, however, that the "issue" will need to be examined with all the involved family members to obtain the multiple perspectives needed for a holistic understanding of collective family experiences.

Whom Do We Talk To? Issues of Voice

Families also present a challenge in terms of the "unit" of analysis. Most survey research focuses on the individual as the unit and focuses on that individual's characteristics, attitudes, and behaviors. By contrast, qualitative research can accommodate multiple perspectives and can better deal with families, couple relationships, or sibling relationships as units. Such units, composed of more than one member, can provide richer accounts and closer approximations of lived family experiences. Although the practical limitations of an observation or interview segment or the nature of some research questions or both may lead researchers to focus on one family member at a time, the composite family picture, with all its inherent corroborations and contradictions, is a strength of qualitative research.

As researchers, we also need to be attentive to the fact that families may have spokespersons who present the family to the outside world. As Saffilios-Rothschild (1969) warned, women often are sources for explaining families' realities. Although these spokespersons can serve as key informants, they also can act as a kind of gatekeeper in the presentation of family images. Research questions will determine with whom we speak in the family. The value of multiple-member perspectives, however, may be paramount in many types of family research. For example, when the focus of investigation is parent-child relationships, data minimally would be gathered from mothers, fathers, and children.

A particular challenge in this regard is to access men's perspectives of family experience because men typically have been seen as difficult to recruit in qualitative family research. As researchers interested in men's experiences of fatherhood, we have had different experiences of such difficulties. We first look at the more typical difficulties Kerry had in recruiting men and then explore Anna's experience of recruiting couples to interview for her fatherhood research.

> **Kerry:** In my research with fathers, I learned how difficult recruiting male participants can be. My first strategy of recruitment in-

volved approaching a YMCA and asking them to send out a letter of invitation to families who had young children involved in recreational programs. The organization insisted on controlling the distribution of the letter because they did not wish to have the researcher present at the programs (too much interference) and they did not wish to release the names of the parents. The agency distributed approximately 80 letters on my behalf to families. From this effort, only three fathers agreed to participate! This traditional recruitment method proved to be an unwelcome reminder of the way not to engage men in the process of research.

After I regained my composure, I approached the vice president of human relations at a large corporation with a request to interview some of the employees about their family experience as fathers. He agreed to do this, and the Employee Assistance Program staff assisted me by inviting all eligible fathers to an introductory meeting during company time. During this meeting, I explained the purpose of the research, the kinds of questions that I was interested in asking, and invited them to sign up for an interview. All who were present agreed to participate. Using this approach, 29 men were eligible and interviews were completed with 27. The 2 who were not interviewed did not show up for the information session and no reason was given. It appears that having sponsored, face-to-face contact between the researcher and eligible participants as part of the recruitment is critical for recruiting men. This approach appears to have lessened the anxiety felt by these men in response to the invitation. Not only did the company encourage their participation in a letter but also it provided time during working hours for the researcher to do a "sales pitch." This provided an opportunity for me to raise their curiosity, to give them some reasons to participate, and to establish a relationship with them before they had to commit themselves. These efforts appeared to be important in light of the fact that fatherhood is not a topic that men have traditionally spoken about and face-to-face interviews may have appeared to be intimidating and time-consuming.

Anna: Given Kerry's previous experience, I was quite aware of the potential difficulties I might encounter in recruiting men for my study. At the same time, I was interested in recruiting couples to talk about fatherhood in the context of sharing parenthood. I made the decision to adopt a combination sampling strategy starting with convenience referrals (from my social network) and then moving to a purposive, snowball recruitment strategy because I wanted to be quite deliberate in my selection of study participants. Because I was aware of Kerry's success with using direct contact and sponsorship, I adopted those strategies and added explicit information on taking a "not-knowing" (nonexpert) stance to exploring the subject. I believe the not-knowing perspective conveyed in my informational packets served to assure the men that I was interested in their expertise, suggesting that they would be invited to share what works for them rather than focus on the problems or failures. As a result, all the men who were recruited or referred engaged as participants in the study.

My research challenge regarding representing voice came to the fore when interpreting and analyzing the information generated in my interviews with the men, the women, and together as couples. Certainly, I had gained multiple perspectives on their family experience of parenting, but how was I to focus on fatherhood without unduly privileging the man's experience and obscuring the woman's experience. Ethically, I believed that because I had explored multiple perspectives, I must somehow mediate the multiple views into a richly textured collage of a family picture without falling prey to the pitfall of telling "his story" and then "her story." I was reminded that people's experiences in family are intricately linked but simultaneously distinctive.

Practices for Deciding Who to Talk to and Representing Voice

The question of deciding who to talk to is intricately linked to the research question and who we believe can best inform us about the phenomenon in question. At the same time, these considerations must stay with the researcher throughout the difficult interpretative and analytical process. Making decisions about what excerpt to use to illustrate your analytical frame is not simple, even when you have interviewed individuals, but it becomes even more complex when you have tapped the multiple perspectives of various family members.

As the researcher, you have been a part of the "observing system" (Hoffman, 1990). Your analytical frame has been heavily influenced by following intricate conversational transitions and the working out of the individual and collective experience in your presence, all while you as the researcher are being subtly influenced by the tone and texture of the verbal and nonverbal cues.

Anna: In my decision to hear both the father's and mother's perspective on how shared parenthood shaped fatherhood, I later experienced the elusive process of trying to make sense of how men and women both experience intricately interwoven and changing demands on their individual pattern of parenting. I worked on understanding their patterns, but I could not find any particular excerpts that clearly illustrated the concepts I came to understand in the course of my long and repeated conversations with them. I was struggling to clarify the concepts of men claiming aspects of parenthood as part of their parenting repertoire and what challenges they faced in making these claims. I decided the concept of men exerting their right to parent in certain situations was not to be found in the man's explanation, nor the woman's explanation, but rather somewhere in between their experiences.

For example, I identified an intricately woven pattern of men intentionally taking responsibility to experiment in new parenting situations and to learn adequate (and flexible) parenting skills, whereas women struggled to step back and let go of domains of parenting that the culture sanctions as their right, responsibility, burden, or all three. The women talked about feeling displaced, whereas the men talked about hesitating to encroach on the woman's domain. Eventually, in fitting these pieces together, I arrived at complementary explanations rooted in cultural traditions. I understood some of the struggles men and women encounter as men become more involved fathers to be complementary "acculturation holdovers" rather than individual resistances by both the man and the woman.

I knew I was dealing more with impressionistic data than with the research evidence I could provide in the tapes and transcripts. Ultimately, the impressionistic data I brought to the analytical framework were of several types: observing the man, the woman, and their children interacting in their home environment; segments of the conversation when I was talking to both the man and the woman in which I observed and felt the flow of ideas between them; listening for affective information behind their descriptions by tuning into the expressive tones men and women used to convey their sense of living in this family; and reviewing the tapes and transcripts repeatedly to hear the grand story as well as the fragmented stories presented in the analytical bytes.

A few very important practices allowed me to navigate this extremely tricky data analysis territory. Most important, making detailed field notes, especially with attention paid to the researcher's own affective experience of the interview, is recommended. I found it critical to make notes about interactional processes that I noticed but that would not show up in the transcripts. It seems important to have the interviewers intimately involved in the analysis of the findings because I often wondered how a researcher would piece the findings together if he or she had not sat with these people but had used interviewer assistants who would not be analyzing the data. I found it crucial to listen to the audiotapes repeatedly, listening for the affective cues in people's voices and the flow of conversation between them. I noticed I experienced an intuitive leap of understanding when I had immersed myself in the stories repeatedly. That leap seemed to allow me to craft a research picture that captured something of each individual's experience and something of the story that existed between the interwoven individual stories. I had to trust my own intuition, but only after I had taken care to raise my consciousness about my own interpretive framework (informed by analyzing personal family experiences and examining my theoretical perspectives). In this endeavor to know my analytical framework, I enlisted several consultants who had their own experiences of working out shared parenthood but were not participants in my study to check and clarify the meanings I was making of the findings. Finally, I found it extremely beneficial to submit my version of the research to the participant families (at least a selection of the sample) for verification.

Conclusion

To successfully navigate our way through a seemingly endless array of methodological puzzles, obstacles, and questions, we need to attend to our motives, stances, and values as we develop relationships with our research participants. When the focus of our attention is families, we argue that this reflexive process occurs at two levels. The first of these concerns the way in which we think about what is the family and what the participant members are telling us about family experience. Although we have argued that the boundaries around family experience are changeable and diffuse, our task is, nevertheless, to examine the many meanings that our participants create for family. Our challenge, as family researchers, is not to examine families in isolation from other institutional or relational domains but rather to explore the emergent constructions of family meanings across many domains. At an epistemological level, the qualitative family researcher is faced with the dilemma of elaborating the many forms that these constructions take, including the ideological, discursive, structural, and phenomenological.

On a more pragmatic level, a reflexive posture serves as an important tool for working through the practical dilemmas associated with researching families. The practices we have suggested may facilitate the researcher's ability to maintain a reflexive posture in the research endeavor. A reflexive posture in itself is seen as made up of practices that support the researcher's documentation of the meaning construction process. These reflexive practices must incorporate the circular process of examining our own ideas and perspectives that will initially focus our view and later reexamining those ideas and perspectives in light of what the research experience has begun to reveal. As researchers, we argue that we need to maintain a reflexive posture in several core arenas: theoretical and ideological perspective, bias that may be associated with a gendered experience, blind spots that may be inherent in the influence of our personal and familial histories, and the tendency to believe that we can maintain a stance of neutrality. We suggest researchers adopt purposeful and specific practices to establish trustworthiness with research participants to enhance their ability to access high-quality data and then submit their analysis to scrutiny by those participants for verification.

We suggest that reflexive practices are particularly important in managing the challenges of crossing the physical and psychological threshold of family space, getting beyond the hidden, taken-for-granted familiarity of everyday family life, managing unanticipated disclosures and unexpected alliances, and making decisions about whose voice to solicit and represent in the research. Although these field dilemmas are a predictable part of researching families, they are ones that can be expected in research with many other kinds of groups.

References

Bernardes, J. (1986). Multidimensional developmental pathways: A proposal to facilitate the conceptualisation of "family diversity." *Sociological Review, 34*, 590-610.

Bernardes, J. (1993). Responsibilities in studying postmodern families. *Journal of Family Issues, 14*, 35-49.

Cheal, D. (1991). *Family and the state of theory.* Toronto: University of Toronto Press.

Cheal, D. (1993). Unity and difference in postmodern families. *Journal of Family Issues, 14*, 5-19.

Cohen, S., & Katzenstein, M. F. (1988). The war over the family is not over the family. In S. M. Dornbusch & M. H. Stroker (Eds.), *Feminism, children, and the new families* (pp. 25-46). New York: Guilford.

Coontz, S. (1992). *The way we never were: American families and the nostalgia trap.* New York: Basic Books.

Daly, K. J. (1997). Re-placing theory in ethnography: A postmodern view. *Qualitative Inquiry, 3*, 343-365.

Denzin, N. K. (1989). *Interpretive interactionism.* Newbury Park, CA: Sage.

Eichler, M. (1988). *Families in Canada today.* Toronto: Gage.

Feree, M. M. (1990). Beyond separate spheres: Feminism and family research. *Journal of Marriage and the Family, 52*, 866-884.

Friedan, B. (1963). *The feminine mystique.* New York: Dell.

Glaser, B., & Strauss, A. L. (1967). Awareness contexts and social interaction. *American Sociological Review, 29*, 669-679.

Goffman, E. (1959). *The presentation of self in everyday life.* Garden City, NY: Doubleday Anchor.

Gubrium, J. (1993). Introduction: Rethinking family as a social form. *Journal of Family Issues, 14*, 3-4.

Gubrium, J., & Holstein, J. (1990). *What is family?* Mountain View, CA: Mayfield.

Hoffman, L. (1990). Constructing realities: An art of lenses. *Family Process, 29*, 1-12.

Lather, P. (1990). Reinscribing otherwise: The play of values in the practices of the human sciences. In E. Guba (Ed.), *The paradigm dialog* (pp. 315-332). Newbury Park, CA: Sage.

Lopata, H. (1971). *Occupation: Housewife.* New York: Oxford University Press.

Oakley, A. (1974). *The sociology of housework.* London: Martin Robinson.

Saffilios-Rothschild, C. (1969). Family sociology or wives' family sociology? A cross-cultural examination of decision making. *Journal of Marriage and the Family, 31*, 290-301.

Simmel, G. (1950). *The sociology of Georg Simmel* (K. H. Wolff, Trans. & Ed.). New York: Free Press.

Smith, D. (1993). The standard North American family: SNAF as an ideological code. *Journal of Family Issues, 14*, 50-65.

7

Experience, Methodological Observation, and Theory[1]

A Blumerian Excursion

DAN ALBAS

CHERYL ALBAS

Herbert Blumer (1931, 1954), in his epic articles "Science Without Concepts" and "What Is Wrong With Social Theory?" stresses the importance of the proper playback between theory, observation, empirical facts, and the reinterpretation of theory to make it more consistent with actuality. In this playback, he emphasizes the importance of rigor in the construction of concepts (the tools of theory) derived from perception (felt experience); the molding of concepts into the formulation of explanation (theory) and constant reformulation toward greater congruence with actuality as a result of further observation and experience. For example, Blumer (1931, p. 527) quotes Charles Darwin's account of his excursion with another scientist into a valley in Wales where both of them completely failed to see traces of glaciation that "were as distinct as when the glaciers were actually there." The point Blumer stressed was that, without conceptualization, perception is blind. At another point, he quotes Kant: "Perception without conception is blind, conception without perception is empty" (Blumer, 1931, p. 531). Blumer shows us how

AUTHORS' NOTE: This chapter is a revised version of *An Invitation to the Ethnographic Study of University Examination Behaviour: Concepts, Methodology and Implications*, which originally appeared in the Canadian Journal of Higher Education XXVI(3): 1-26, and is used with permission. The authors thank D. L. Rennie for his contribution.

perception results from experience and also demonstrates that conception, in turn, is an attempt at a new view of what was previously perceived. For example, a child burnt by the flame of a match perceives pain, which is an outcome to be avoided by staying away from flames. The same child touches the side of a hot stove (where there is no flame) and is burnt again. From these and other painful experiences, the child comes to a wider conception of heat as existing not only in flames but also in a wide variety of observable objects. The wider conceptualization permits more effective problem solving and avoidance of error.

In these articles dealing with concepts, variables, and generalizations, Blumer also stresses the importance and utility of appropriate definitions and rigorous analysis of relationships under a wide variety of social situations. He notes that the main areas of malaise in sociological theory are (a) its divorce from the empirical world, (b) its failure to guide research effectively because it is so maladapted to operationalization, and (c) the marginal benefits derived from a poor fit between the huge accumulation of facts and the existing conceptualizations of them.

The present work is focused with Blumer's strictures regarding the proper relationship between theory and research in mind. A review of the literature on student life reveals a dearth of studies of a qualitative nature dealing with examinations. Such studies as exist are mainly quantitative and deal largely with topics like social class and academic performance (Bajema, 1968; Sexton, 1961, 1967, 1968). Where this literature touches on examinations, it does so more from the standpoint of examinations as functional for accreditation for social roles (manifest) and maintenance of the established stratification system (latent) (Giddens, 1973; Pascarella & Terenzini, 1991; Weber, 1968, p. 1000). It does not deal with the everyday dynamics of preparing for and writing examinations from the standpoint of the students themselves.

In this work, we attempt to spell out in five examples how sociological sense can be made of and theoretical explanations given for the everyday experiences of university student life. The first part of the chapter deals with various techniques of data gathering and then discusses the inextricable linkage of methodology and theory. Then, using previously published studies (C. Albas & D. Albas, 1988; Albas & Albas, 1984, 1988a, 1988b, 1989a, 1989b,

1993) we demonstrate how the data obtained as described in the first section of the chapter are made sense of theoretically. In carrying out these objectives, we attempt to lead readers through our thought processes as our empirical findings are submitted to examination in the light of existing theories. This is what Burgess (1984, p. 160) suggests is widely lacking in current research reporting. These theories are then used to direct the collection of further, more focused data on the basis of which existing theories are modified and occasionally new ones are suggested. A secondary function of the chapter is to elucidate theoretically the underlying motivations of students and their reactions to stress.

Getting Access to and Collection of Data

The requisite of any research project is to gain access to both a setting from which data may be obtained and to subjects who can supply these data (Shaffir, Stebbins, & Turowetz, 1981). In our case, access to the research setting could be said to come naturally in that the setting is the university classroom and we are faculty members. The university in question is located in a large midwestern Canadian city and has approximately 24,000 students. It offers a wide variety of undergraduate, graduate, and professional programs. In regard to the subjects (mostly students), though indeed we have access to them as informants, we nevertheless observe scrupulously the ethics relevant to the issue of human subjects in research (i.e., confidentiality, refraining from undue pressure or any semblance of coercion). In addition to data obtained from student subjects, we also obtained data by observation, interviews, "Garfinkling," and unobtrusive measures.

Observation

When a researcher observes social action taking place, the observation may occur while participating with the subjects being observed as they carry out the activities in which they are engaged. In this method, referred to as participant observation, subjects may or may not be aware that there is an observer-researcher in their midst. Such an approach is especially useful for getting an "inside" view of the situation. Observation, Adler and Adler (1994, p. 38) indicate, is especially "well suited to the dramaturgical perspective because it enables researchers to capture the range of facts, from the minimovements to the grand gestures, of people under study."

Observation may also be carried out by an observer who does not participate in the action (e.g., observation from behind a one-way viewing screen). In our research, we employed all these approaches to observing student life, particularly at exam time. Specifically, although we made it known to students that we were studying student life and that one method of gathering data would be by observing them, they might not always have been conscious of our roles as observer and researcher while we were at the same time engaged in the professional roles of instructor or invigilator. There were, of course, times when they did realize this, particularly when they were asked to come for interviews following particular things we had observed. This fact is dealt with at greater length in the discussion on interviewing. In regard to observations made by us as nonparticipants in the action, these were situations in which we did our own reading and grading (and of course observing) in close proximity to student carrels and tables in the library. As far as they were concerned, we were merely reading or grading. For all they knew, we could have been mature students. Of course, this closed awareness context, as Glaser and Strauss (1981) call it, could only take place when we observed students other than our own (e.g., from other faculties on the campus or from the other university in the city).

In a somewhat larger focus, we had professionally taken photographs of students writing examinations—hundreds of students in straight lines and rows in examination halls and classrooms. From these photographs, we observed arrangement of legs, use of the hands (e.g., to cover their papers), directions of the eyes, and tilt of the body with respect to neighbors. The study of these photographs often provided us with particular positions and gestures to pursue for meanings and to look out for during actual examinations. In addition to our observations, we also made use of the observations related to us by our teaching assistant invigilators. We attempted to select teaching assistants for this function who had minimal, if any, experience in the role of invigilator. In this way, we obtained the unique focus that could be called "stranger value" (Burgess, 1984, p. 23). It was interesting to note that after these tyro or novice invigilators became more blasé about their role, they also became (perhaps like ourselves) less perceptive of subtle nuances. In addition, we also solicited observations of examination behaviors from exam invigilators in other disciplines and faculties.

All these observations by ourselves and others had to be recorded, sometimes on the spot (if this could be done unobtrusively) and always after, in as much detail and exactness as possible. Prolific note taking resulted in the accumulation of a veritable mountain of recorded observations that had to be sorted through for relevance and sense making. The material suggested, by the particular relevance of its various facets, a number of different theoretical approaches to understanding it (e.g., magic, impression management, and emotion work). Accordingly, in the later phases of the data collection process we began to be less omnivorous and to focus on these specific theoretical areas. This procedure, referred to by Strauss and Corbin (1990) as theoretical sampling, is more typical of ethnographic methodology than of more formal mathematical quantitative approaches. Throughout this process of observation (participant, nonparticipant, use of photographs, and use of assistants), every attempt was made to avoid a Hawthorne effect (i.e., allowing our procedures to affect the behavior of the subjects being studied). This we did by making notes as inconspicuously as possible, and when we did have to take notes in front of people, we jotted down only the minimum necessary. Whenever possible, note taking was confined to the back of the room where we could not be observed by the students writing their exams. Even obvious close observation of students need not necessarily be interpreted by them as information gathering about them because it is the natural role of the invigilator, just as scribbling in a library is what one does naturally. There were occasions though in which it was inevitable that we "blew our cover" and thus affected the interaction under investigation. For example, on occasion we were observed taking notes, and students interpreted our behavior as gathering information to build a case against cheaters. This undoubtedly produced in our subjects a more than normally assiduous scrupulousness. We also engaged in a variety of other research techniques because, as

Adler and Adler (1994, p. 382) state, observation produces "especially great rigor when combined with other methods."

Interviewing

Over the years, a considerable amount of data was collected by interviewing students, faculty members, and members of the university administration. Most of these interviews were informal, spontaneous, on-the-spot episodes when we casually asked students to explain some strange behavior. For example, one student accidently kicked over a pile of books and notes piled on the floor under his desk. As he reached down with his hands to reorder the pile, he suddenly realized he was being observed by an invigilator. In mid reach, he froze and then proceeded to attempt to rearrange the pile, this time with his feet. When asked why he behaved in this manner, he replied, "guilt based on a smoking gun is more credible if the gun is in the hand rather than in the foot."

In asking on-the-spot questions, we tried, in the spirit of Howard Becker, to "time, shape, and minimize [our] provocations in order to induce [our respondents] to express themselves with a 'natural' sense of their familiar situations" (Becker as quoted in Katz, 1994, p. 272). However, we also carried out other interviews that were longer, more formal, and in some instances taped. Virtually all the interviewing, formal and informal, revolved around questions emerging from our observations. In this way, we were able to minimize or at least explain discrepancies between verbal claims made by subjects and their actual behavior (Becker & Greer, 1957). In some cases, interviews changed our perspective on the scenes we were observing and alerted us to look out for aspects we had previously overlooked.

Garfinkling

This term implies an ethnomethodological manipulation of a situation in which the conventional pattern of interaction is made problematic or troublesome in order "to demonstrate what societal members commonly assume or do that prevents such 'troubles' " (Cahill, Fine, & Grant, 1995, p. 612). At the very least, a researcher can elicit from the intensity of reaction to the breach the degree of importance that the subject attached to the rule that is violated (Garfinkel, 1967). For example, we were aware that in student culture there exists a norm of courtesy and face-saving for others. Accordingly, we employed a stooge, who to all appearances was one of the less able students referred to (among ourselves) as bombers, to join a group of other bombers commiserating with each other at a pity-party over their recent examination debacle. In response to cries of indignation at the stupidity of the professor, the impossibility of the exam, and the general bleakness of life, the stooge was instructed to say, "For anyone who did the least bit of studying, the exam was a piece of cake." As predicted, the response was one of scandalized horror and indignation. The stooge was also instructed (in mercy) to add immediately after, "Of course, I'm kidding." However, we clearly established the existence of the norm, which was the point of the experiment. Although we made use of a number of such contrived episodes, we always attempted to avoid lasting harm to the subjects.

Unobtrusive Measures

In all three approaches described previously, there is inevitably some possibility of observer effect on the subjects observed, interviewed, or manipulated. To compensate for this Hawthorne effect, we made use of unobtrusive measures (Webb, Schwartz, & Sechrest, 1966). The distinct advantage of this procedure over surveys (which record merely what people say) has been elaborated by Deutscher (1973) and Becker and Greer (1957). This fourth approach involves contact not with subjects themselves but with "traces" left by them. These traces are physical items left behind by people that are connected to their goals and as such tell us something about them. Because these traces are left behind without the producers' knowledge of their potential usefulness to researchers, they are clearly not affected by research influence. For example, to measure frequency of library and study space usage we used turnstyle counts in the library and items left behind in a study room. One measure of "exam fever" was the prevalence of graffiti and messages on notice boards left by students reminding each other of the approaching "Armageddon." Such physical artifacts added context and "thickness" to the descriptive report.

Student Logs

The most explicit and significant data sources employed but that we cannot claim to be completely free of observer effect are the logs or detailed accounts that students wrote for us describing their life experience with particular regard to examinations. These logs, as Cahill et al. (1995, p. 610) indicate, can "compensate for gaps in the direct experience of subjects' everyday lives." These accounts provided for us what the letters and diaries of Polish peasants provided for Thomas and Znaniecki (1918). The assignment was intentionally nondirective except for its focus on examinations. However, we did employ a number of techniques to check whether accounts were spurious and written so as to please us. For example, when a log was handed in we asked students what effect the writing of it had on them. Many expressed painful relief at facing issues for the first time and getting them off their chests. Many of the accounts were self-deprecatory and could hardly have been attempts to over-represent themselves in the best light. Students were reminded at the outset of the scientific importance of what we were asking them to do and warned that we were able to discern fraud, which would merely waste our time and theirs. We used as typical examples only those that appeared repeatedly in the logs and represented the experiences of a significant number of the students.

Data Analysis and Interpretations

In science, methodology and theory are inseparable if useful and valid understandings are to be achieved concerning any subject of inquiry. Indeed, the term inquiry implies the asking of questions. The type of questions asked about a phenomenon, usually at an abstract, general level (i.e., the paradigm or frame of reference), and the tentative, suggested answers (i.e., hypotheses) constitute the theoretical component of the enterprise to understand the what, why, and how of the phenomenon. The methodological component consists of (a) generating the empirical data validly germane to the paradigm (e.g., operationalized forms of the questions and their answers on the basis of observations, interviews, official documents, etc.) and (b) analyses of these data to determine whether the tentative answers (hypotheses) do indeed conform to the empirical find-ings. Either component without the other is virtually useless be-cause, as Blumer (1931, 1954) stated and as was later reiterated by Merton (1957), they both play back on each other to their mutual refinement, clarification, and precision. To regard theory and method as dichotomous is spurious.

As noted earlier, our data collection procedures involved a number of sources. These multisource data were brought together in the same way that photographs may be taken from a number of different angles and in different conditions of light. In this way, a given approach with inherent weaknesses (such as the subjectivity of the student logs) is, it is hoped, corrected for by the objective strength of another approach (e.g., the use of traces). Both logs and traces are further validated or corrected by the data from interviews and observations. Thus, in this chapter although the emphasis is on the methodological component of ethnographic research, the proce-dural techniques will, of necessity, be described with reference to established theoretical orientations and assumptions.

Examples From Selected Studies

The following five examples are very abbreviated versions of previously published papers and of course in this space cannot include all the details of each study. However, it is hoped that enough is offered so that the reader will have a sufficiently clear idea of what was done. In any case, the emphasis here, as was stated before, is on demonstrating Blumerian strategies of observation (perception), conceptualizations, and explanation (theory).

Student Magic for Exam Success

We observed that, particularly at exam time, students display nonrational and bizarre behavior in an astounding array of seem-ingly inexplicable and often contradictory practices that seem very much like magic (Albas & Albas, 1989a). Yet, it is the late 20th century, and the setting is one where one might expect maximum rationality, and so this can hardly be magic in the commonly ac-cepted sense. Our definition of magic in this context was "action directed toward the achievement of a particular outcome with no logical relationship between the action and the outcome or, indeed, any empirical evidence that one produces the other." The majority of these practices categorized as magic also had a mystical component. For example, if a subject reported that she studied for exams in the same classroom where she had her lectures because of the efficacy of familiar cues in stimulating memory, it was not included as an example of magic. However, if the reason given for studying in the classroom was that there remained in it all the bits of knowledge taught for the term "still swirling around to be caught again," that response was included as an example of magic. When we wrote a representative sample of such practices on a large chalkboard, we found that it was possible to classify them into two major categories: do's for good luck and dont's to avoid bad luck (i.e., taboos about what should be scrupulously avoided and what should be religiously conformed to at exam time). This procedure is a form of *coding* in which a number of various observed practices are translated and grouped into categorical concepts (e.g., "luck bringing"). This form of coding Charmaz (1995) calls "qualitative." She calls another form of coding "quantitative" because the codes are numbers rather than terms denoting qualities. For example, Question 26 in a questionnaire asks, "In what kind of community do you live?" The choices are (1) urban, (2) suburban, and (3) rural. If the answer is suburban, it would be coded as "26.2." Quantitative coding is a convenient method for survey studies. Charmaz stresses her preference for qualitative coding for grounded theory, which permits researchers to build analysis from the "ground up" rather than "taking off on theoretical flights of fancy."

Furthermore, within each of the two major categories of practices we found consistent subpatterns, such as the wearing of "oldies and oddies" (the sweatshirt of a brilliant boyfriend or the ring of a scholarly mother) and the performance of symbolic rituals (e.g., breakfasting on one slice of bacon placed vertically on the plate and two eggs, sunnyside up, beside it imaging 100%). In this way, the "what" of student magic was able to be conspicuously documented. Discerning the "why" was what brought theory to bear on the matter in order to make sociological sense of (superficially) seemingly senseless behavior. We knew that Malinowski (1954) attributed the magic practiced by Trobriand Islanders to the anxiety they experienced when they fished in the dangerous waters beyond the lagoon. We also knew that miners (Wilson, 1942), actors and athletes (Gmelch, 1971), and soldiers (Stouffer et al., 1949) used totems of one kind or another to protect them and bring themselves success. All these are high-anxiety activities. It was therefore feasible to think that the Malinowski hypothesis of magic as a stress-coping mechanism was supported in the cases of miners, actors, athletes, and pilots. We then returned to our own data for evidence of how students said that they felt after a pet dog "had waved a paw" and woofed "good luck" before an exam or after eating a specific muffin purchased from a specific vendor. In all cases, the feelings experienced were relief as well as belief that without the woof or the muffin the exam outcome would have been problematic. At this point, we accepted the hypothesis that student magic is indeed a stress-coping mechanism. *Thus, observations and perception (i.e., paw waving and muffin munching) became concepts (i.e., good luck behavior) and were theorized as magic for stress coping.*

However, our investigation did not stop there. For the sake of theoretical integration, we attempted to establish the position of student magic in the hierarchy of magic and why it might differ from the magic of preliterate people. From the literature, we constructed the ideal type polar construct of a continuum of magic with preliterate society at the left and contemporary society at the right (Table 7.1).

After examining hundreds of reports from students, we decided that student magic falls well to the right end of all four continua. This means that student magic differs considerably from primitive magic and even from some other contemporary forms midway on the continuum where, for example, the meaning of rituals is more socially shared (wishing an actor to "break a leg" or not referring to a winning streak in baseball). We suggest that societal difference over time and subcultural variations in contemporary society can explain the existence of these differing forms of magic. That is, a troop of actors and preliterate societies, unlike modern students, subscribe to homogeneous subcultures. The division of labor in preliterate society is less complex than it is in contemporary society, and both preliterate communities and troops of actors work together

TABLE 7.1 Characteristics of Magic

Characteristic	Society	
	Preliterate	Contemporary
Performance	Public (i.e., carried on ritualistically with the whole community present and with approbation of all present)	Private (i.e., carried on alone with minimal interaction with others)
Transmission/ generation	Cultural (i.e., handed down from generation to generation)	Spontaneous (i.e., invented by practitioners themselves; little or no historical precedent)
Community involvement	Shared (i.e., an act of the community)	Private (i.e., performed by individuals for themselves; meaning is often idiosyncratic)
Rubric	Fixed (i.e., details of ritual stylized and meticulously followed)	Varying (i.e., no official prescription other than whim of practitioner)

as groups rather than individually as do students preparing for exams. Therefore, the magical practices of all three might be expected to be different. Thus, existing concepts (of group homogeneity, complexity in the division of labor, and form of interaction—cooperation vs. competition) can be involved to provide the explanatory aspect of the "new" theory developed concerning student magic. We hope that, by making this explicit, somewhat of a contribution may have been made to the theoretical understanding of student life.

In sum, in the study of student magic, our procedure was to *begin with the raw data* (namely, the *what* of student magical practices) and then to classify these practices *(coding)* and look for patterns *(widespread uniformities)*. From these patterns, and guided by existing theoretical literature, we were able to establish the *why* of the practices as being consistent with those in several other areas of life where stress, uncertainty, and anxiety exist *(conceptualization)*.

Finally, we distinguished along the four continua where these student practices we call magic fall relative to and are different from other forms of magic *(theoretical refinement).*

Emotion Work at Exam Time

In the study of student magic described previously, we excluded a considerable amount of data describing student stress-coping practices because they had logical, naturalistic explanations and thus did not conform to our definition of magic. For example, wearing a soft cuddly sweater feels comfortable and homey and may thus reduce stress, but the effect is not a magical one. We now come to a more detailed examination of nonmagical stress-coping practices used by students at exam time (C. Albas & D. Albas, 1988). In this study, we began with three formal hypotheses derived from Arlie Hochschild's (1979) theories regarding "feeling rules" and "emotion work" done by people under stress to contain their feelings within the parameters defined by the rules. Our hypotheses were (a) rules exist in the student culture defining the appropriate level of emotional intensity at examination time; (b) because we think most students' level will exceed the defined norm, the direction of emotion work will be in a suppressing direction; and (c) the duration of emotion work done will coincide with the examination period.

The methodology in this study is a good example of the procedure used extensively in most of our studies of student life—namely, *triangulation,* in which data of different kinds were collected from a variety of sources. Also, under this rubric of triangulation, we used photographs of examinations in progress as a projective technique to elicit from students their empathy with "other suffering souls" and their insights into explanations of the postures and facial expressions in the photographs.

On the basis of this body of mainly qualitative data, we were able to show that during the examination period students attempt to keep their feelings within an optimum range. They seem to recognize that they have to be sufficiently "up" and yet not excessively so. Because most of them (according to self-reports) sense themselves to be on the excessive side and overstressed, they compensate by engaging in intense emotion work of a dampening kind—for example, listening to music, jogging, or avoiding talking about the exam. In addition we documented, from observations, the variety of forms of emotion work and coded them as *physical* (e.g., compulsive cleaning and tidying of rooms, leg-jiggling, or taking deep breaths), *cognitive* (e.g., establishing a hierarchy of preparation procedures or arithmetical estimation of possible minimum final grade that usually is at a safe enough level to allay anxiety), *spiritual* (e.g., praying—one respondent stated that her praying is more specifically for peace of mind and emotional fortitude than for divine intervention to achieve success), and *affiliation* (e.g., seeking the company of others who are in the "same boat"). All these forms of emotion-dampening work take the mind off the examination and, in the case of the physical, dissipate anxiety-generated energy.

Our conclusions from the study are as follows. In regard to the first hypothesis, it is clear that students have a generally understood feeling for the appropriate emotional level that best contributes to their exam success. In regard to the second hypothesis, it is also clear that students, for the most part, when working for this optimal emotional level find themselves having to dampen down rather than pump up their emotions. In the case of the third hypothesis, we observed, and students reported to us, that from the time they leave the exam room and for several days after the burden of stress dissipates, it becomes drinking and party time and for many they seem never to have had a care in the world.

Doing emotion work to pump up or repress levels of emotion to a desired optimum is widespread in all aspects of everyday life. It occurs at mine heads after explosions, at sea jetties after ferry accidents, and especially among athletes at competition time. In terms of the application of grounded theory, then, emotion work as stress management is highly generalizable.

The Examination as a Dramaturgical Stage

In this study, we introduce the concept of dramaturgy as an elaboration of impression management, which is an important facet of symbolic interaction (Goffman, 1959, 1963). Blumer (1969, pp. 16-17) stresses that symbolic interaction is a process that goes on between individuals, between individuals and organizations, and even between organizations. Thus, the concept of the actor is expanded from the individual to include also a community of individuals such as an organization. This study focuses on the university institution as an actor presenting the examination as a dramaturgical performance to the student audience.

The study (Albas & Albas, 1988b) began with a presumption on our part that the latent function of universities in our society is to transmit the values of universalism and individualism. We hypothesized also that the manifest function of the institution in its examination procedures is to assure scrupulous honesty (no cheating) and maximum achievement. Because of the highly ritualistic, formal, and solemn conduct of exams at universities, it was decided that the paradigm of dramaturgy (conceptualization) developed by Goffman would be a useful framework for understanding how the institution (i.e., the actor) conveyed its messages to the students (i.e., the audience) via the use of spaces, props, equipment, and bodies—all with specific social meanings like seriousness, high thought, individualism, honesty, ordered formality, and bureaucratic aplomb. To demonstrate this, we employed the conceptualization and terminology of dramaturgy. Specifically, we identified the spaces, props, equipment, and bodies in the exam setting and how these are used to convey the university's message. The data were largely our own observations of exam settings and their conduct over the past 15 years as well as interviews with university administrators, other professors, and invigilators.

On the basis of observations and interviews, we concluded that indeed the large halls in which final exams occur, the placement of the desks with partitions between them (or having greater than usual distances between writers) to prevent copying, the specifically printed examination booklets for answers (which have on their covers elaborate formal instructions as well as a flap to place over the candidate's name to ensure anonymity), plus the presence of vigilant invigilators all conspired to send the message intended by the university, which is regarded as the actor in this drama.

In sum, the elaborate ritual and the use of props employed by the university in staging examinations are manifestly functional in that they do convey the intended message to the audience. In turn, however, the conveying of the message should result in complete fairness to all and equality of treatment. It may well be though that, like Lady Macbeth, the university in its dramaturgy might be protesting too much. For example, exams differ in difficulty and content from section to section and from year to year. Different instructors also employ different standards of grading. Consequently, a latent function of the examination dramaturgy for the university actor is that it constitutes a "rhetoric of idealization" wherein weaknesses are ceremonially masked. This is a serendipitous finding that may be regarded as an example of the reformulation of theory that results from close reexamination of existing and accepted cultural usages.

Examination Candidates as Audience in the Drama

In this study (Albas & Albas, 1988b), which is a companion to the one concerning the exam as a dramaturgical stage, we investigated the effect on students writing examinations of the dramaturgical messages the institution endeavors to send by its staging of the examination act. The staging process is characterized as being functional if the responses elicited from students as to the effect of the staging on them corresponded to the intended messages. The staging was categorized as being dysfunctional in cases in which student responses seemed either alien from or inimical to the intended message.

The data for this study were drawn mainly from the examination logs provided by students and supplemented by probing interviews with them as well as from our own observations. The data were then arranged in the schematic table shown in Table 7.2 (coding).

From Table 7.2, it is clear that in most cases students' interpretations and reactions are congruent with the messages sent by the institution. Thus, we concluded that for the most part the dramaturgical message sending was functional and effective. However, there were cases in which students' interpretations and reactions differed from the intended messages of the university. For example, sometimes students legitimated the perceived status and police role of invigilators, whereas in other cases, even though the students' interpretations of the messages were as the institutions intended, their reactions were somewhat deviant and challenging. For example:

On occasion I have stuck my foot out across the aisle so that I can assume a more comfortable (body) position. It also serves to reduce

TABLE 7.2 Schematic Representation of Student Response to Institutional Messages in the Staging of Examinations

Media	Message		Response	
			Interpretation Through Verbal Accounts	
	Value	*Norm*		*Overt Behavior**
Space			*Functional*	
Auditoriums	Achievement	Effort	Exaltation	Circumspection
Great halls	Bureaucracy	Silence and sobriety	Exhilaration Competition	
			Dysfunctional	
			Belittlement Inhibiting	Suppression of spontaneous urges
Props			*Functional*	
Desks	Individualism	Eyes front	Discipline	Attempts to
Dividers	Asceticism	No levity	Straightness	dramatize
Rows	Order	No wandering	Constriction	conformity
			Dysfunctional	
			Overcon- formity	Challenges
Equipment			*Functional*	
Exam books and instruc- tions	Assurance and verification of fairness	Bring and show cre- dentials	Validity of red tape	Exaggerated cau- tion regarding hands, legs, and
Stickers	and justice			trunk
I.D. card				
			Dysfunctional	
			Suspicion awareness Context	Disappointment at anonymity and attempts to circumvent
Bodies			*Functional*	
Invigilators	Validity of procedure	Respect	Increased sense of profess- or's status Perception of police role	Attempts to foil oversurveil- lance
			Dysfunctional	
			Inhibition of thinking	

*Some examples of this column have not been made explicit in the summary of the study presented here.

the surveillance aspect of the exam because it prevents invigilators from walking up and down that aisle.

On one occasion I purposely started to stare at a point under the table. As I expected, an invigilator was behind me, just like a hawk. When she saw that I was not cheating she walked away and remained at the other end of the room for the duration of the exam. I often look around me; sometimes I catch a friend's eyes and we nod to each other. I refuse to cease being a human being just because I'm writing an exam. Anybody who really wants to cheat can do it, in spite of all the song and dance (of invigilators).

In sum, in this study we hypothesized that the dramaturgical message of the university would be read correctly and complied with by students. The data largely supported these hypotheses, but some aberrations did emerge. Further pursuit and closer examination of them resulted in a refinement of the theory. Specifically, we employed a modification of Thomas's definition of the situation by Perinbanayagam (1974), who views it as a "rivalry" between and eventual synthesis of the sender's message and the receiver's subjective interpretation of it.

Disclaimer Mannerisms

The previous study described the cognitive responses of the student audience to the university's dramaturgical staging of examinations. In the present study, we demonstrate that these cognitive responses of the student audience went beyond the merely cognitive and involved considerable acting out on their part. This special kind of acting out has come to be known progressively over the years as "motive talk," "accounts," "disclaimers," "disclaimer mannerisms," and "account mannerisms." A brief history of the evolution of these accounts follows.

In 1940, C. W. Mills employed the term *motive talk* to describe the rationalizations people use to explain their behavior to others and to themselves. In the 1960s, Scott and Lyman introduced the term *accounts* (including excuses and justifications) as an elaboration and refinement of motive talk. In the 1970s, Hewitt and Stokes further differentiated excuses and justifications into disclaimers (occurring before the act) and accounts (occurring after the act). In effect, the distinction was chronological. No explicit distinction was made between verbal and nonverbal as to the accounts and disclaimers, and the implication was that both were verbal.

Since behavior in the examination room does not allow for vocal proclamations, the artifices students use must of necessity be nonverbal but nevertheless dramatic enough to be noticed and effective. To meet the anomaly of identifying the behavior as a disclaimer and yet recognizing that historically the term is confined to verbal behavior, the first task was to develop an appropriate terminology that would recognize both chronology and nonverbal expression. Accordingly, we coined the term *disclaimer mannerisms* for the nonverbal before behavior and *account mannerisms* for the nonverbal after behavior (Albas & Albas, 1993). In this way, we respect the traditional boundary in the literature between verbal and nonverbal behavior (e.g., Stone's universe of discourse and universe of appearance) and, at the same time, make clear that the behavior, though nonverbal, is of disclaimer and account types.

In the fourth study describing students as audiences in the examination drama, we saw, as shown in Table 7.2, that they responded to the university's message by dramatizing conformity and exaggerated shows of caution in regard to the use of their eyes, hands, and legs. For example, one student states: "Occasionally I need to look away from my paper. When I do I'm always afraid the prof will think I'm cheating. To show I'm not I look at the ceiling or at the prof." This behavior can now be recognized as a disclaimer mannerism used prior to and during exams to demonstrate innocence before being challenged and to avoid being challenged.

We feel the principal contributions of this study are twofold. First, as an ethnography it provides numerous examples from student self-reports of efforts and successes in avoiding challenge and blame as they negotiate the trip wires in the minefield of examination dramaturgy. Second, we recognize an insufficiency in the conceptualization of aligning acts (theory) and we rectify it.

Conclusions and Implications

The point made at the outset of this chapter is that methodology and theory are inseparable components of any scientific strategy to understand and explain. We feel that we have demonstrated the reciprocal process of asking a question, suggesting a theoretical answer, generating relevant empirical data, answering the question, and perhaps modifying or extending the theoretical framework within which the question was generated. As we attempted to demonstrate, this process does not always follow the same order of procedures. Quite often, data are collected in some particular area of interest without clear-cut theoretical directions as to the appropriate questions to ask. However, by dint of classification, the observation of patterns and relationships, as well as an awareness of the literature, theoretical sense emerges from what began as seemingly inexplicable facts. We think that all five studies described in this chapter can be seen to have a thread of theory linking them that becomes cumulative and adjusted as different facets of student life, examination stress, and university ceremonials are examined.

Note

1. Adapted with permission from Albas and Albas (1996).

References

Adler, P., & Adler, P. (1994). Observational techniques. In N. Denzin & Y. Lincoln (Eds.), *Handbook of qualitative research* (pp. 377-392). Thousand Oaks, CA: Sage.

Albas, C., & Albas, D. (1988). Emotion work and emotion rules: The case of exams. *Qualitative Sociology, 11*(4), 259-274.

Albas, D., & Albas, C. (1984). *Student life and exams: Stresses and coping strategies.* Dubuque, IA: Kendall/Hunt.

Albas, D., & Albas, C. (1988a). Aces and bombers: The post-exam impression management strategies of students. *Symbolic Interaction, 11*(2), 289-302.

Albas, D., & Albas, C. (1988b). The institutional staging of an examination. *Canadian Journal of Higher Education, 18*(1), 65-74.

Albas, D., & Albas, C. (1989a). Modern magic: The case of exams. *Sociological Quarterly, 30*(4), 603-613.

Albas, D., & Albas, C. (1989b). The staging of examinations: A student response to the institutional perspective. *Canadian Journal of Higher Education, 18*(3), 69-81.

Albas, D., & Albas, C. (1993). Disclaimer mannerisms of students: How to avoid being labelled as cheaters. *Canadian Review of Sociology and Anthropology, 30*(4), 451-467.

Albas, D., & Albas, C. (1996). An invitation to the ethnographic study of university examination behaviour: Concepts, methodology, and implications. *Canadian Journal of Higher Education, 26*(3), 1-26.

Bajema, C. (1968). Interrelations among intellectual ability, educational attainment, and occupational achievement. *Sociology of Education, 41,* 317-319.

Becker, H., & Greer, B. (1957). Participant observation and interviewing: A comparison. *Human Organization, 16,* 28-32.

Blumer, H. (1931, January). Science without concepts. *American Journal of Sociology, 36,* 515-533.

Blumer, H. (1954, February). What is wrong with social theory? *American Sociological Review, 19,* 3-10.

Blumer, H. (1969). *Symbolic interactionism: Perspective and method.* Englewood Cliffs, NJ: Prentice Hall.

Burgess, R. (1984). *In the field: An introduction to field research.* London: Allen & Unwin.

Cahill, S., Fine, G. A., & Grant, L. (1995). Dimensions of qualitative research. In K. S. Cook, G. A. Fine, & J. S. House (Eds.), *Sociological perspectives on social psychology* (pp. 605-628). Toronto: Allyn & Bacon.

Charmaz, K. (1995). Grounded theory. In J. A. Smith, R. Harré, & L. Van Langehore (Eds.), *Rethinking methods in psychology* (pp. 27-49). London: Sage.

Deutscher, I. (1973). *What we say/what we do: Sentiments and acts.* Glenview, IL: Scott Foresman.

Garfinkel, H. (1967). *Studies in ethnomethodology.* Englewood Cliffs, NJ: Prentice Hall.

Giddens, A. (1973). *The class structure of advanced societies.* London: Hutchinson.

Glaser, B., & Strauss, A. (1981). Awareness contexts and social interaction. In G. Stone & H. Farberman (Eds.), *Social psychology through symbolic interaction* (2nd ed., pp. 53-63). New York: John Wiley.

Gmelch, G. (1971). Baseball magic. *Society, 8*(8), 39-41.

Goffman, E. (1959). *The presentation of self in everyday life.* Garden City, NJ: Doubleday Anchor.

Goffman, E. (1963). *Stigma.* Englewood Cliffs, NJ: Prentice Hall.

Hewitt, J., & Stokes, R. (1975). Disclaimers. *American Sociological Review, 40,* 1-11.

Hochschild, A. (1979). Emotion work, feeling rules, and social structure. *American Journal of Sociology, 35,* 551-573.

Katz, J. (1994). Jazz in social interaction: Personal creativity, collective constraint, and motivational explanation in the social thought of Howard S. Becker. *Symbolic Interaction, 17*(3), 253-279.

Malinowski, B. (1954). *Magic, science, and religion.* New York: Doubleday.

Merton, R. (1957). *Social theory and social structure.* New York: Free Press.

Mills, C. W. (1940, October). Situated actions and vocabularies of motive. *American Sociological Review, 5,* 904-913.

Pascarella, E. T., & Terenzini, P. T. (1991). *How college affects students: Findings and insights from twenty years of research.* San Francisco: Jossey-Bass.

Perinbanayagam, R. (1974). The definition of the situation and the analysis of the ethno methodological and dramaturgical view. *Sociological Quarterly, 15,* 521-542.

Scott, M., & Lyman, S. (1968, February). Accounts. *American Sociological Review, 33,* 46-62.

Sexton, P. (1961). *Education and income.* New York: Viking.

Sexton, P. (1967). *The American School: A sociological analysis.* Englewood Cliffs, NJ: Prentice Hall.

Sexton, P. (1968). *Readings on the school in society.* Englewood Cliffs, NJ: Prentice Hall.

Shaffir, W., Stebbins, R., & Turowetz, J. (Eds.). (1981). *Fieldwork experience.* New York: St. Martin's.

Stouffer, S., Lumsdaine, A., Lumsdaine, M., Williams, R., Jr., Smith, M., Janise, I., & Cottrell, L., Jr. (1949). *Studies in social psychology in World War II: The American soldier, combat and its aftermath.* Princeton, NJ: Princeton University Press.

Strauss, A., & Corbin, J. (1990). *Basics of qualitative research.* Newbury Park, CA: Sage.

Thomas, W. I., & Znaniecki, F. (1918). *The Polish peasant in Europe and America.* New York: Octagon.

Webb, E., Schwartz, R., & Sechrest, L. (1966). *Unobtrusive measures: Nonreactive research in the social sciences.* Chicago: Rand McNally.

Weber, M. (1968). *Economy and society.* New York: Bedminister.

Wilson, W. (1942). Miners' superstitions. *Life and Letters Today, 32,* 86-93.

8

Hanging Out With the Good 'Ole Boys, Gangsters, and Other Disreputable Characters

Field Research, Quantitative Research, and Exceptional Events

RICHARD A. BRYMER

Field research methods and quantitative methods both have advantages and disadvantages in social science research. Quantitative research tends to use either official statistics or survey data and is generalizable to the populations from which it is drawn. Additionally, the reliability and validity of "rate" data can be estimated statistically. For these and other reasons (e.g., quantitative data can be generated quickly and it allows for statistical hypothesis testing), social scientists generally prefer quantitative measures. Generalizing to a population, however, requires that a random sample be drawn from that population (i.e., each member of the population has one and only one chance of being selected). Although one may be able to approximate a random sample of physicians, professional athletes, or local clergy, not all groups are equally available to the more quantitatively oriented researcher. This is particularly true for deviant populations, especially deviant subcultures and other smaller subcultural groups within the larger subculture. We quite simply do not know the population from which we are to sample. In these instances, field research (ethnography) is the preferable means by which to access these populations.

We do, however, have numerical data about these groups. Official statistics are collected by various census and survey groups, such as police forces, parole and probation agencies, correctional services, and a variety of secondary aid professionals. One of the unavoidable truisms of these data is that they are based on the accounts of deviants who have been unsuccessfully deviant. Those who are successful bank robbers, con artists, and second-story thieves are not to be found in any of the official data. We should not loose sight of the fact that data derived from those incarcerated for a particular offense self-select for those who have failed at avoiding imprisonment. If we want to access successful deviants who do not show up in the official statistics, we must use fieldwork to locate them and balance our knowledge derived from official statistics.

A similar problem of self-selection occurs in survey research that requires that the sampled individuals voluntarily allow themselves to be interviewed. In my experience, many successful deviants simply do not volunteer. There is little reason for gang members to participate in such surveys or for them to be particularly forthcoming in their answers. To the extent that this is the case, surveys teach us very little about successful deviants.

Survey research is also less helpful than one might initially imagine in elaborating on the dynamics found within small groups of deviants within deviant subcultures. Most small groups are very private and have a long-term personal history that is more or less particular to that group. One-time interviews by surveys, or even multiple interviews by official agencies, are likely to present little information. Where official data are obtained with the cooperation of a particular member of the small group, we need to attend to the rather limited and narrow representation reflected in only one member's view of events and activities. Thus, the more we rely exclusively on such quantitative measures, the more we are deprived of not only the views of other members of the group but also long-term group dynamics and history. In fact, the more private the small group, the more likely it is to be successfully deviant, and the less likely it is to appear in our database derived from official or survey research.

In this chapter, I suggest that some populations can be accessed only by field research and, given the various dynamics at work, this field research must be undertaken over long periods of time. The researcher must develop long-term personal relationships with successful deviants to contrast our field knowledge with "official" knowledge and thus develop a more comprehensive view of deviants and deviant subcultures, the small groups contained within their "boundaries," and the subculture's other levels of organizational complexity.

Over the years, I think that I have managed to do this with two deviant subcultures and their accompanying small groups: (a) Mexican American conflict gangs in the Spanish Southwest of the United States and (b) hunters and poachers in North America. In this chapter, I share some of these experiences. I do so through a series of narratives or vignettes intended to give the reader the "smell" of the field. The stories are oriented toward two important problems in research that can be managed more effectively through ethnography than through quantitative work. The first theme I address is the problem posed by exceedingly elusive, rare, and exceptional phenomena. Point-in-time research risks missing exceptional events altogether or mistaking the exceptional for the routine. Likewise, events, activities, and actions that one might assume to be exceptional given the portrait painted of social life in official statistics may in fact be much more routine, common, and everyday than the data suggest. The second theme I examine is the problem of understanding small group dynamics in the face of "real exceptional events." As researchers, we need to be in the field and we need to be there a long time to be given access to the experience of "trouble" and the accompanying attempts at the "reconstruction" of the group.

The Routine, the Exceptional, and the Problem of Knowing the Difference

I grew up in the Spanish Southwest United States on an isolated ranch working with *vaqueros mojados* (cowboys who immigrated temporarily and illegally to the United States to work on ranches). I learned a dialect of Spanish that is sometimes referred to as *pachuco* or *norteno*. Although I am losing fluency in the dialect, I can still "get around with" the people, and the people that I am interested in tolerate my inadequacies. After receiving my PhD, I went back to the Spanish Southwest of the United States and spent 7 years in a major city working with Mexican American conflict youth gangs as a researcher on a gang control research project. I worked out of a religiously based community center that had locations in three different neighborhoods and had contacts with several other community centers in the city.

I also took field trips to other Southwest cities to compare information. All had rather segregated ecologies so that the Mexican American *barrios* (roughly translated as neighborhoods) were more or less independent entities with their own distinct subculture. Because of my prior childhood experience with Mexican American subculture, I was quite comfortable with the "cross-cultural" experience.

When I went to the Spanish Southwest cities to do research on Mexican American youth conflict gangs, I was confronted with a variety of images of what the gangs were supposed to be like. I imagine that when you think of the term gang, that there are likewise a series of images that you associate with these groups. I spent much time doing ethnographic interviews and "hanging out" with the various sectors of the community that were affiliated with or had something to do with gangs. In a city of almost 750,000 people, this was a real challenge. A typical day began with a trip to my office to receive messages and hear gossip about the gang subculture. Then, I headed to my car and made ethnographic visits throughout the city that often lasted well into the evening. Because I was working in a high-crime area, I bought a 15-year-old station wagon that could transport a load of gang boys or whoever needed "hauling." After 5 years, it was a wreck, but (as will be shown) it did serve a useful purpose.

The generally accepted image of gangs was as follows. They were supposed to be relatively large groups of 75 to 150 members who were identified with a given "territory" (or bounded neighborhood). These territories were defended by various gang wars and were marked by the corresponding casualties. After 2 years in the field, however, I had never seen a gang. Given what was supposed to be "out there" and my inability to find it, I had begun to doubt my abilities as a sociologist.

What I began to understand, however, was the diversity of perspectives that affected the definition of a gang. Using official statistics, the police viewed every group of young males in the ghetto as a gang or as part of a gang. The police, however, saw the gangs only in crowd control situations, and their control techniques and interrogations revealed this.

Juvenile probation and parole officers and their records revealed that very few of their clients were identified as gang members. They saw each client in a one-on-one regular interview situation, and they were not involved in street confrontations with groups. They also did not use the bathroom in the "bull pen" waiting area. I did, and the walls were covered with spray-painted gang graffiti. If one were to rely on the agencies' documentation, it would appear that their caseload did not include gang members. Even the most cursory use of unobtrusive measures, however, suggested otherwise.

Social work agencies also viewed the gangs as large fighting units identified with a particular neighborhood, whose boundaries were identified by gang graffiti and regularly updated via the ubiquitous spray can. The elders of the neighborhood also accepted this view of the gang as a defender of the neighborhood's integrity. In fact, many of these elders were themselves active members of the gang in their youth. There are also many legends of prior "wars" of the X gang with the Y gang. These legends are also commemorated in records and tapes of famous historical events, referred to as *corridos* and *tragedias*.[1]

The various images of gangs suggest a diversity of understandings of gang organization, structure, and purpose. After sifting through these diverse views, and importantly never having seen the large gang, I began to look at what was happening in the everyday lives of people coming into direct contact with what they reported as "gang activity." The first thing that became apparent was that the social workers (and myself) interacted with the "gang guys" in small groups of approximately 8 to 10 members. These groups in fact are called *palomillas* in the neighborhood culture. The term literally refers to a group of doves. This term does not translate well, but in English it could be a "small friendship clique." Most of their routine action occurs within these groups, and within them they talk a lot about gangs. Although the larger grouping that people referred to as the gang existed in people's talk within the community, I had no direct field experience with the gang proper until one evening.

I was driving around the city with a palomilla in my wagon, cruising the neighborhood and its boundaries. As we went north on a street, we passed a drive-in restaurant and hangout that had a large parking lot in which there were groups of cars surrounded by small groups of young people. The group in my car identified the various groups assembled by their palomilla names (e.g., Jose and his guys). I asked if they wanted to stop, but they said no, "it's just the guys." Thirty minutes later, we were again passing south on the street, and on approaching the drive-in, the guys said, "Pull over, there is the X gang" of which they were members. The ecological scene had shifted. Rather than a series of discrete groups, there was now a wall of young males facing the street. The cars had their trunks open, and the girls were behind the wall of young males and the cars. I was ecstatic because after 2 years in the field, I finally saw a gang! The palomilla members in my car assumed their position in the wall, and I began to run around making field notes. The open car trunks contained massive amounts of weaponry, including semiautomatic shotguns and rifles. This gang was in fact deadly, and its members' willingness to fight had, in my view, fulfilled various definitions of a gang. What produced the symbolic and actual move from palomilla member to gang member?

When I asked what happened, the guys (now gang members and not palomilla members) said that members of the Y gang had driven by and made observations about the X gang's masculinity. This affront was accompanied by the threat that they were going to come back and kill them. They did not come back, and thus no fight occurred. I still have not observed a gang fight on scene, although I have seen some of its aftermath. At the scene, I also noted that no police, probation officers, or social workers showed up for the event. Although large amounts of weapons, mostly illegal, were present, the absence of official agents meant that this event never made it into official statistics.

So what does this tell us about field research? First, certain events, such as gang fights, are rare and exceptional events, and as a researcher you may have to hang around for a long time before you can "see" them. In this sense, they are like riots. You have to wait and wait. Access to these events may depend, in part, on our ability to attend to the cultural mythology. The stories that people tell are important for a number of reasons. For the field researcher, this collective discourse helps to identify groups or groupings to which one needs to pay particular attention. My encounter with the gang also suggests that any culture may have several different levels of social organizational complexity; small groups operate almost all the time, but large groups such as gangs occur only in certain conditions. Access to these groups requires the dedication of the researcher to be present when the conditions are right (or "wrong" as the case may be). The exceptional event may be the missing piece in the puzzle. Be patient, and do not completely trust official statistics.

The Everyday Exception: The Local-Rural Poacher

At the beginning of this chapter, I argued that we need to be cautious when dealing with data derived from failed deviants. Such information may tell us more about who is likely to be caught doing a particular criminal act than it is to inform us about what is actually happening in the field. The official picture is derived from formal regulation and the activities of rule enforcers (Becker, 1963). As helpful as this may be in some respects, official data of this type are "about" formal regulation and not deviant or criminal behavior per se. Official data may tell us something about the poachers who are most likely to be apprehended, but they do not, however, tell us much about poaching more generally. Such rate data represent a "perspective on poaching"—a narrow and limited perspective but a perspective nonetheless.

The disjunction between the official image of poaching and the perspectives developed in my recent research with hunters and poachers is striking. From my long-term involvement with these "good 'ole boys," I knew that the dominant type of poacher was the "local-rural": someone whose activities are very traditional, who hunts and poaches on his or her own land, and who takes very small amounts of game for his or her own personal and familial use. Persons of this type are rarely caught. I also know that there are other identifiable "types" of poachers. There are "market hunters," who take large amounts of game for sale, often for international markets.

There are "trophy hunters," who are willing to pay a guide to take a very big trophy animal. In this case, hunters are more selective, and small amounts of game are taken. Finally, there are "tourist hunters," who have little understanding of what they are doing. These types are the ones most often caught (Brymer, 1991). These typologies were revealed from my long-term involvement in the field as both participant and researcher. I was also interested, however, in how others involved with poaching, both directly and indirectly, understood the "breakdown" of the various types of involvements in poaching.

When I decided to make my research in this area more systematic, I began to interview various persons involved in hunting and poaching (much like my approach with the Mexican American gangs). I interviewed game wardens, wildlife researchers, officials of various state and provincial wildlife departments, taxidermists, legislators, attorneys, judges, outdoor writers—everyone to whom I could gain access who had something to do with hunting and poaching. It took 2 years (all the time I had) and many miles on the road. On a continuing basis, I take field notes on all hunting trips and visits to various areas. For me, this a lifelong project.

Without exception, all my respondents agreed with my notion that local-rurals constitute the vast majority of poachers but account for the lowest level of convictions. Therefore, local-rurals simply are not reflected in the official statistics on poaching. In fact, after 54 years of hunting with local-rurals, I know of only two that have been convicted of an offense, and the fines were less than $100. The offense was the lowest-class misdemeanor, with no possible jail time and no permanent felony record.

In my various interviews and field research, it became apparent that attention to poaching, and its image, was based on the perspectives of those involved. For example, game wardens seem to be divided into two groups: careerists, who want to move up in the system, and locals, who want to remain in a local community for their entire career and are not interested in career mobility. The differing interests of these game wardens encourage a very different orientation toward poaching activities. The "local wardens" tend to focus on local-rurals, although they rarely "catch" them. They do, however, engage in a range of informal means of social control that may develop into an ongoing relationship. In interviewing a local warden, I informed him that a local poacher had retired from poaching because of ill health. The warden had been trying to catch this poacher for 30 years and in fact was friendly with him. When I told him that the poacher had retired, the warden shook his head sadly and said, "I'm really sorry that good 'ole boy is out of the game. I will really miss trying to catch him."

Careerist wardens, however, are interested in commercial poachers. Arrests of these hunters may attract considerable media attention given the relative value and potential large number of animals involved. These wardens do a great deal of undercover work and are necessarily relocated as they move up the career ladder. This "high-stakes, high-visibility" focus pleases groups on both sides of the ecological movement with whom I talked. The pro-hunting groups like the focus on commercials because they argue that it provides more game for legitimate hunters. Antihunting environmental groups like the focus because it is "saving" the environment.

It is a basic assumption of symbolic interactionism that our knowledge of the world is perspectival (Blumer, 1969; Prus, 1996). We should not lose sight of the importance of this simple statement for our research. My study of conflict gangs and poachers leads me to conclude that our knowledge of these subcultures is contextually embedded in a large number of perspectives. Poaching is not as it is depicted and represented through the actions of careerist wardens and the media. That is but a part of the picture. Likewise, the elder's portrayal of the conflict gang as the "defender of the neighborhood's integrity" captures one important, albeit narrow, aspect of gang activity. Such questions of perspective and definition strike to the very heart of the ethnographic problem: What group are we studying? They influence where we draw the boundaries of inclusion and exclusion, what we think we are looking for, and what we eventually find. An openness to the multiple perspectives of the field and a willingness to redefine what we (as sociologists) think are "gang members," "poachers," and "hunters" are essential to ethnographic work. Being open to the field means being open to the limits of our own prior constructs of the groups we study—regardless of the various claims of reliability or validity that may be associated with those representations and other perspectives.

Unanticipated Disruption and
Small Group Dynamics

In this section, I make the case for the relative value of field research in the study of unanticipated disruptions that are "real exceptional situations." Real exceptional situations are those that disrupt subcultural rules for small groups and, as such, are a problem for both the small group and the researcher. The small group must confront the "disruption problem." Although members may engage in a range of activities, managing disruption involves the recognition of the problem, identifying deviance and the deviant, responding to "offense" on the basis of the rules of the group, and engaging in some form of "reintegration" work (oriented toward the offender or the remaining group members or both) (Becker, 1963; Emerson & Messenger, 1977; Erikson, 1962; Kitsuse, 1962). If the researcher intends to engage the various joint acts that make up the disruption problem, they must be "on scene" to observe the reconstruction efforts. Being in the field during times of organizational disruption may bring with it various risks, inconveniences, and pressures to support one "camp" or another. As in the preceding section, I present two vignettes drawn from my experience with small groups: palomillas in Mexican American gang subculture and a long-term hunting and poaching small group.

Vignette 1: Disruption in the Palomilla

Palomillas form the basic organizational unit of gang subculture. One group that I was very familiar with was *Los Grifos*. Basically, this translates as "the marijuana smokers." This group was alternatively known as *Pelon y Los Vatos* (i.e., Enrique and the guys).[2] This small group made a habit of smoking marijuana regularly and making it available to other palomillas in the neighborhood. In gang culture, this was "no big deal" because marijuana is a part of Mexican American culture, and even *abuelitos* (neighborhood elders) smoke. Because heroin use draws the attention of the police (at all levels of jurisdiction) to the neighborhood, however, it is viewed as deviant and a considerably more serious offense. Heroin use also interrupts more routine recreational drug use within the local subculture (e.g., smoking marijuana and underage drinking on street corners and on front porches). If gang members become addicted to heroin, they become *tecatos*. This is a well-defined role in barrio culture that involves the member being forced out of the local gang neighborhood into the heroin use subculture that exists as a pan-city organizational locale. It is an event that I had access to within Los Grifos palomilla. The exceptional event involved violations of the barrio subculture rules and the rules of the larger culture.

I was not on scene when the initial events happened (you simply cannot be everywhere at once), but I did get various stories of the scene and was present to observe the aftermath. One evening, Los Grifos were smoking marijuana and drinking beer at the home of person X and Y's grandmother. The grandmother was also smoking and drinking beer. At some point in the evening, X and Y passed out and went into mild convulsions and became unconscious. A quick examination of the two revealed "track marks," indicating that they had been secretly injecting heroin. None of the other members were aware of this activity. The scene became chaotic and reached a level of emotional intensity marked by the grandmother's fainting. The other members finally called an ambulance, and when the ambulance arrived the attendants assumed the grandmother had suffered a heart attack and loaded her into the ambulance, leaving the two addicts lying on the floor. There was an obvious translation problem because the attendants were English speakers, and the gang members were dominantly Spanish speaking. In this chaos, the gang members managed to phone a community center's Spanish-speaking gang worker, who showed up and transported the two addicts to a local hospital that had a clinic for addicts who had overdosed.

The aftermath of this event was the breakdown of a palomilla and its reformation. Word of this exceptional event spread throughout the entire neighborhood, and community opinion turned against the two addicts. They were quite literally exiled from the neighborhood. Even their parents and other relatives would no longer tolerate them or provide them with food and refuge. Various other palomillas in the neighborhood became increasingly vigilant about heroin use among all members of the neighborhood. For a period of time, the neighborhood even began to hide the smoking of marijuana and public underage drinking. The neighborhood also began to discourage heroin use and its dealers. Police presence in the neighborhood was increased, but after a few months "normal deviance" returned (Stebbins, 1996). The affected palomilla added another two members—the younger brothers of existent members— and reestablished its usual complement, although it continued to be viewed by the community with some suspicion and was on a kind of neighborhood probation.

Vignette 2: Disruption Among Local-Rurals

As with Mexican American gang groups, local-rural hunters and poachers also have their small groups and accompanying small group dynamics. This type of culture requires ownership of land or close personal or familial relationships with the landowners over a long period of time. The size of the group varies with the nature of terrain and ecology but is generally between 6 and 12 members. This small size ensures that each member has personal knowledge of all participants. Although there is a social organization, it is informal and is based on the various qualities of all individual members. In this example, I describe how I joined the group and ultimately became a full-fledged member, the activities and organization of the original group, and the circumstances surrounding its disruption, dissolution, and the formation of a new group.

The experience began when I purchased 300 acres of Carolinian forest with dense underbrush, creeks, and swamps. There was also an abundance of deer in the area. I had hunted in this type of terrain but was a stranger in the local area. I was an important person, however, because my land was in the center of what I later discovered was the group's hunting territory. My first encounter with the group occurred when I set up a tent in a natural clearing on a trail just prior to deer season. The leading "patriarch" of the group walked by and informed me that "we hunt this land!" It was an announcement and not a request for permission. My response was "Fine, I hunt it too. Do you want a beer?" He accepted, and we began a very exploratory description in which I told him who I was and he told me who he was and that his group hunted. The next day, his group came down the trail, but I was not invited to join them. I hunted by myself, walking up and down the trail because I was not familiar with the terrain. Later that afternoon, they came out carry- ing two deer tied on poles. They were tired, and I offered beer and soft drinks. The conversation was general but guarded. I offered to load the deer on my four-wheel-drive vehicle and transport them to their barn, but they refused, saying "it's shorter through the bush."

It was only after a 2-year period of testing that I became a member of the group (of which I have been a member for 19 years now). I am a rather good hunter and brought in my share of deer. Then, and only then, did they tell me why they refused the offer of my four-wheel transport. Both of the deer had been poached, and they did not trust me. They now trust me. Entry into a small group sometimes takes time, even though you know the subcultural argot and practices.

The usual organization of a day's hunt in this terrain is as follows. In this terrain, the most efficient mode of hunting is to use dogs and a "dog puncher" who moves the dogs along well-known deer trails. The purpose is not for the dogs to run down the deer but to move them along the trails. Hunters are assigned "stands" along these various trails to wait for the deer. The stands are set out in a half circle across the trails. Thus, it is important that each member stay on his stand until the "punch" is completed. The usual line depends on the terrain and the trails but can stretch well over a mile.

The patriarch, who knows the area best, then starts the dogs through the forest, walking at a leisurely pace and, it is hoped, flushes the deer out to the hunters. If a hunter shoots a deer, he makes sure that the deer is dead and then resumes his stand. When the patriarch and the dogs finish the punch, they end up at the last stand and then begin to walk out, picking up hunters and any "kills" along the line. Values associated with the daily hunt are that hunters (a) do not drink liquor on the stand; (b) stay on the stand until they are picked up; (c) follow the patriarch, who is the leader; and (d) share any deer produced by the hunt equally.

This organization and its accompanying values will be important in the following two sections, which involve a group, its dissolution, and the reformation of a new group. Again, this is a real exceptional situation that affords insight into the small group dynamics inside a larger subculture.

The Original Group

This group had approximately 10 to 13 members. The patriarch was the acknowledged leader, and his three sons were the next in line. Other members included a nephew of the patriarch and three of his friends as well as myself. There were also three relatives who were "temporaries"—that is, they showed up as trusted members when they could get time off from their jobs. Finally, there were two grandsons who did not yet have hunting licenses but who accompanied their grandfather on his punches. They are the next generation of the group but are not yet "full hunters."

We were all bound by personal ties, acquired in long evening discussions about each other's skills that might be valuable to the group. I was the jokester and mediocre butcher, another was the automotive mechanic, and another was the "lifter" (an incredibly big and strong man). All had their skills peculiar to the group. These discussions developed the interpersonal knowledge and trust that enabled us to act as a group and team that, during the hunt, coordinated activities, including carrying loaded firearms in the forest. We also trusted each other to know where each member was, to stay in our stands, and to follow the other rules that enabled us to hunt efficiently and safely.

We also discussed game management and when to take game, and when not to, to ensure continued populations of game. If a certain species appeared to be declining on our land, we simply did not hunt that species until it replenished itself. We also shared the knowledge of our mutual deviance—occasional poaching—and how to accomplish this without revealing anything to outsiders. This often included kin and neighbors who were not members of our group.

The Explosion of the Original Group

The group began to break up when the nephew became unreliable and "troublesome" (Emerson & Messenger, 1977). He began to violate the interpersonal rules and values necessary for the group: He began to dispute the division of meat (insisting on a larger share than was traditionally and consensually agreed on); he wanted priority to assign hunters to various stands himself (usually the prerogative of the subpatriarch); he became unreliable (by drinking and smoking various substances while on his stand); he would wander off his stand so that no one knew where he was; and he lost his job and started selling substances out of his house, which attracted increased police attention to the area. The crucial event occurred when he began to brag in local community bars about how "he was going to run [the patriarch] out of the group because he was senile, and take it over himself." The result was a public confrontation between the nephew and the patriarch, ending in the nephew being "run out of" the group. No one would trust him on a hunt, and when he left, the three members that he had sponsored went with him.

As a result, the family and the hunting group split, and the hunting group was now left with only six members. This number was too small to hunt the area efficiently. In addition, 300 acres of owned or accessed land was lost.[3]

We had to form a new group that would increase our numbers. Two of the patriarch's sons began making contacts in the area. One of the contacts was another hunting group that had also lost members. This contact also owned and accessed approximately 600 to 800 acres that was contiguous with our territory. By joining together, we expanded our total territory. Our new group now had 10 to 12 members. Some of us, however, were totally unfamiliar with the others, whereas others had known each other all their lives but had never hunted together. Thus, we had to begin the process of talking, hunting, and exploring the various personalities involved and working out a new small group social structure and a division of labor. We also had to become familiar with each other's skills and weaknesses and what might be called temperamental character or personality. As a sociologist and anthropologist, this was a very nice arena in which to study the dynamics of small group formation. You never know when an opportunity strikes. If it does, however, study it.

The Process of New Group Formation

The initial stages of group formation took approximately 10 days, although adjustments will continue for years. The first few days were rather formal, and we relied on our knowledge of the general subculture of hunting and poaching. Some of us also had to acquire knowledge of new terrain and the vocabulary associated with it. Local-rurals do not rely on compass or map coordinates but rather on folk terms that "everyone" knows—for example, "walk up on top of Rocky Hill and stand in that thick grove of trees on top and look down in the valley where Tim shot that big deer the year that it snowed and sleeted." We began acquiring each other's vocabularies for "where" as well as for "who." Fortunately, the first few days were very successful, which eased the tensions of stranger relationships. On the first day, one of the members of the new group, who had never killed a deer in 30 years of hunting, killed two, and another member killed a big deer. In terms of subcultural understandings of "efficiency," even as a new group, we were doing quite well. This contributed to a camaraderie that eased the tensions of a new group of strangers.

On the second day, another member, who had never killed a deer in 25 years, got a very big buck. This was the biggest deer ever taken in the history of the area, and this member thus assumed a rather high status in the new group. We decided to butcher the deer in the afternoon. In my original group, I was the mediocre butcher; in our new group, we had a professional butcher, so I lost my place or role as butcher. As we began to cut up the deer, we were in very close confines, drinking beer, joking, and talking about our hunting experiences. In the butchering process, we began to explore each others' personalities in-depth via jokes, taunts, ribaldry, intimate revelations, and progressively closer personal contact. We also began to sort out our interpersonal roles in the new group. I, for example, displaced the butcher, who had been the jokester in his group; I was now the new jokester. We also acquired a second patriarch, and the two patriarchs sat on the side, giving advice and talking over old times and passing these old times to the new group. We also created a new "gofer." He was a young man in his early 20s who did not drink, so his job was to collect money and go into town for more beer or whatever was needed. The spirit was one of equality, and a hat was passed into which $20 bills were tossed. After butchering, wrapping, and loading into freezers, we decided that because we were having such a good time, and because we had approximately 600 pounds of fresh meat, we might as well have a cookout. The newly "nominated" chef went to an outbuilding and started building a fire and marinating the meat. He sent the gofer out for spices and grates, and we ate and talked and joked well into the night. This group celebration included only the hunters, and more personal contacts were developed. We now knew exactly how and whom we were and had our roles sorted out.

The next day, we were feeling a little guilty about our success, had lunch, and decided to do another cookout. This time, we invited wives and other relatives and a few more members of the neighborhood, including potential members of the hunting group from other neighboring hunting groups. This successful gathering of approximately 30 people helped to establish ourselves as a group in the neighborhood. On the following day, we again decided to do a third cookout. This was somewhat different in that we invited not only members of the neighborhood but also persons from the local small town, including members from "competing" hunting groups. In effect, we announced that we were a new and successful hunting group. Equally, the public event announced our new combined territory as "ours and ours alone." These conversations between our members and members of other groups were very polite and subtle. Our hunting group now had a local history and an established niche in the local community of hunting groups. They knew that we poached and we knew they poached, and the tacit agreement was that we would not turn them in and we expected that they would not turn us in.

The new group was so successful in the first year that it began to attract the attention of many possible new recruits. Many were family members or long-term friends, and it was hard for the patriarchs and subpatriarchs to turn them away. By the second year, the group now had approximately 18 to 21 members, and the hunt was a disaster, with only three small deer taken! There were too many hunters, too close together, and they were too difficult to coordinate. We had become too successful. This exceptional event required changes to ensure future success.

The patriarchs and subpatriarchs met and worked out a tentative solution. Rather than the unproductive 18- to 21-member group, we would divide into two teams of 9 or 10 members that would vary in size. Each team would hunt two different ecologies, and the team size and assignment would vary.

This itself is an exceptional solution to an exceptional situation. It has not yet been put into practice but will this year. It will require a higher division of labor and more coordination on the part of the subpatriarchs. I will be on scene to hunt and participate in whatever happens. Maybe another exceptional event will occur, and this will be part of my ongoing history with this group.

Conclusions

I illustrate small group dynamics through two vignettes, both rich with the smell of the field, possible only through extended access to the settings and dependent on the trust of the members. As I hope you recognize from these tales of the field, entry into, ongoing participation in, and access to disruption and exceptional events within small groups requires a particular commitment on the part of the researcher. What the researcher needs is time, patience, and a sensitivity to cultural organization and exceptional events.

Although the relations we establish with others and the groups we come to identify with (as members and participants) are fundamental to social life generally, we know relatively little of small group dynamics. Rather fundamental aspects of small group activity (e.g., forming allegiances, dissolution, and reconstruction) may in fact be relatively exceptional events. Knowing this, it should not surprise us that we can be in the field a very long time before we see a gang, observe the expulsion of a member, or participate in the deconstruction of a small group. There is no solution to this problem—only the recognition that it is through extended participation with a particular group that we come to understand and experience the range of dynamics present within it. For those beginning field research projects, it means remaining attentive to the reality that you are "jumping into" a group with an established social organization, history, and sense of the routine.

I began this chapter by suggesting that field research was an "antidote" and "corrective" to prior quantitative and survey studies. I now suggest a reversal of priorities. Field research can and should establish "categories of importance"—indications of the various roles and obligations that are established by the people and groups doing the behaviors. Then and only then can we begin doing valid and reliable statistical and survey research. For example, a survey of hunters should not focus on hunters as individuals but as members of various types and members of small groups. Likewise, survey research on Mexican American gang members should not focus on individuals in a gang neighborhood but rather on individuals as members of a palomilla, within a larger neighborhood, embedded in a larger pachuco subculture, embedded in an even larger Mexican American subculture. Without adequate and detailed field research to draw from, more quantitatively oriented research will lack appropriate analytical categories and will simply replicate externally derived classification schemes that reflect little of the lives of gang members, hunters, poachers, or other members of small groups.

Notes

1. A *tragedia* is the celebration of a tragic event occurring to a gang hero; a *corrido* celebrates a gang victory.
2. Pelon was a nickname for Enrique (first name). It referred to his hair line, which was very high and approaching baldness.
3. Accessed means that we do not own the land but that we have permission to hunt on it or had traditionally hunted there for years.

References

Becker, H. (1963). *Outsiders*. New York: Free Press.

Blumer, H. (1969). *Symbolic interactionism*. Englewood Cliffs, NJ: Prentice Hall.

Brymer, R. A. (1991). The emergence and maintenance of a deviant sub-culture: The case of hunting/poaching sub-culture. *Anthropologica, 33*, 177-194.

Emerson, R. M., & Messenger, S. (1977). The micro-politics of trouble. *Social Problems, 25*, 121-134.

Erikson, K. (1962). Notes on the sociology of deviance. *Social Problems, 9*, 307-314.

Kitsuse, J. (1962). Societal reaction to deviant behavior: Problems of theory and methods. *Social Problems, 9*, 247-256.

Prus, R. (1996). *Symbolic interaction and the ethnographic tradition*. Albany: State University of New York Press.

Stebbins, R. A. (1996). *Tolerable deviance: Living with deviance* (2nd ed.). Toronto: McGraw-Hill Ryerson.

PART IV

Ethics, Intervention, and Emotionality

At times, ethnography brings with it its share of disappointments, anger, frustrations, and dilemmas. Because ethnographers are the "research instruments," everything that we are gets thrown into the mix. What we cherish, our sense of justice, our perceived obligations to others, and our understanding of what it means to be a social scientist are portrayed in how we interact and form relationships with others in the field. This is not always an easy or nonproblematic process. Ethnographers may find themselves in difficult positions. At times, we confront the disjunction between our professional obligations and those obligations we owe to our intimate relations, the generalized other, and ourselves.

For example, a fundamental ethical principle of social science research is the principle of informed consent. Stated simply, we are not to "collect data" from "subjects" who have not been (a) informed of the purpose of the research, (b) given a chance to withdraw from the research, and (c) made aware of any reasonably anticipated risk or harm associated with participation. This may work reasonably well in an experimental or laboratory setting. It is a far less straightforward matter, however, when conducting research in the context of a deviant subculture, a public location, or a setting in which access is granted to a group on the condition that members are not collectively informed of the research project.

Chapter 9 takes up this general problem by examining the disjunction between the organizational ethics of the university and the ethics located situationally within the author's research site— the 12-steps group Codependents Anonymous. By asserting that "in some settings, obtaining informed consent becomes an impossibility" (Chapter 9, p. 181), Irvine illustrates the problem that ethnographers face as they move between the competing obligations of "research practice" and the obligations to and from the field.

Our diverse commitments to the field may give rise to serious questions as to how our participation within the setting will be created and sustained. In the course of obtaining an intimate familiarity with our field sites, we may also (at the same time) be dismayed, offended, angered, or otherwise disaffected by the actions and ideas of others. In such circumstances, how do we select from the various lines of action available to us? More conventional or traditional ethnographic research postures encourage the researcher to adopt a noninterventionist stance (akin to a sociological version of the "prime directive" familiar to science fiction fans). By allowing things to unfold "as they would," the ethnographer avoids aligning himself or herself with a particular position and distances himself or herself from the possible negative consequences of intervention.

Nonintervention may serve well as an ethical position, but it may prove to be situationally problematic. When intended, inaction is a decision to not act. Like other choices, such decisions may be interpreted in a variety of ways by participants. Some of these interpretations may prove disruptive to the research enterprise (e.g., a failure to intervene may be seen as indicative of disinterest, incompetence, or immorality). Likewise, nonintervention may be unpalatable to the researcher when confronted with circumstances or events defined as unacceptable.

As Chapter 10 illustrates, the pleasure and burden of ethnography is that it involves the whole person. Our relationships with those we study are not mediated by text or quantitative reconstructions. Rather, the world of the other is engaged with an intensity that involves the researcher as an emotional, ethical, and committed actor. "Engagement" provides ethnography with a resource shared by few other colleagues within the social sciences. Our ethical dilemmas, emotive responses, and inclinations toward intervention should be understood as ethnographic resources—as "data."

Although focusing on very different settings, students are encouraged to attend to the following generic themes in this part:

- The disjunction between formalized codes of conduct and the accommodations required by being "in the field"
- Self-identity within relationships and obligations that develop in the field
- The problem of intervention—problems of action, inaction, forming alliances, and altering relations
- The importance of the moral and emotional engagement with the field as sources of ethnographic information
- The utility of lived experience as an ethnographic resource

9

Organizational Ethics and Fieldwork Realities

Negotiating Ethical Boundaries in Codependents Anonymous

LESLIE IRVINE

This chapter discusses a dilemma that I faced in my fieldwork. Specifically, it addresses the disjunction between my desire to obtain the informed consent of the people I studied and the impossibility of doing so in the setting of an anonymous, 12-step group. I suspect that many fieldworkers have similar experiences. One would not know this, however, from reading ethnographies or methodological treatises on how to do fieldwork. Typically, the ethical compromises that a researcher makes in the field are glossed over in "the smooth methodological appendix" of the research report (Bell & Newby 1977, p. 63). Ethical issues are, for the most part, treated in separate volumes or sections of volumes devoted to the topic (e.g., see Emerson, 1983, Part IV; see also *Social Problems,* 27[3]). In this chapter, I argue that this segregation of ethical discussions does less experienced researchers a disservice. Moreover, "sanitized" presentations of research contradict the reflexive involvement that is part of the ethnographic tradition.

Fieldwork, as Emerson (1983, p. ix) wrote, "is learned in and through its doing." To begin "doing," however, a researcher must describe to an institutional review board (IRB) what he or she intends to "do." Since the 1970s, the Department of Health, Education, and Welfare (DHEW) has regulated social research in the

United States in keeping with the National Research Act (DHEW, 1974, 1978). These regulations emerged in response to decades of biomedical and psychological research that put participants at considerable risk without their knowledge. The Nazi abuses, the Tuskeegee syphilis study, the Jewish chronic disease hospital case, the Willowbrook State School controversy, and Milgram's research on obedience constitute the better known instances of research prior to regulation (Faden & Beauchamp, 1986, Chapter 5). From these and other cases, the United States developed a set of policies requiring the consent of those participating in research. In addition, individual disciplines developed professional codes of ethics. To enforce the new consent requirements, universities established IRBs that review proposed research. In particular, IRBs are concerned about the procedures for obtaining the consent of those involved. A researcher must document that the "human subjects" participated voluntarily and with knowledge of the possible risks and benefits of the research. All institutions and projects that receive federal funding must comply with these regulations, which also apply to research carried out by students.

Human subjects regulations no doubt protect innocent people from undue harm at the hands of unprincipled or overzealous researchers. Because much of what takes place in ethnography appears to pose little risk, fieldwork proposals may qualify for "expedited review" with little trouble. In my experience, however, the IRB requirements can constitute a force that shapes research according to a formality that does not exist in ongoing social interaction. Initially, I thought I could simply observe the people I studied; I ended up trying to pass as one of them, however. In moving from observer to participant, I learned that it is one thing to write a research proposal from the safety of a desk and quite another to try to execute it in the field. Although I understood that working within the ethnographic tradition would require sensitivity to the emergent nature of group conduct, I had anticipated expressing that sensitivity from behind the identity of a researcher. Instead, true sensitivity to the setting meant putting that identity aside. It also meant doing without the informed consent of my human subjects.

My Research

I studied Codependents Anonymous (CoDA). It is a 12-step group, and, as such, it has explicit rules about anonymity that make disclosing a research identity impossible.[1] In addition, CoDA has no leaders who can grant a researcher formal permission to study it. Moreover, anyone may attend its meetings. For a researcher seeking to obtain informed consent, this open quality means that there is no permanent entity that one can immediately recognize as "the group" and inform them of one's purposes. To be sure, certain people attend particular meetings regularly, but CoDA maintains no membership roster and no one takes attendance. Although I knew about CoDA's anonymous tradition before I began my fieldwork, I could not have foreseen what it would mean for me as a researcher. Because little empirical work on CoDA existed, I could not find out about the group without attending a significant number of meetings. I could not attend meetings—at least not as a researcher—without first explaining to the IRB what I expected to do at them.

The weight of the IRB's regulations, light though it was, influenced me to forget my sociology. I knew that fieldwork would involve sensitivity to the emergent quality of group interaction. At the same time, however, I had an inflated sense of my status as researcher, created largely through the assumption that I should—and could—seek and obtain the consent of those I wanted to study.

Regulations for the protection of human subjects are based on a model of experimentation. They assume that a researcher can openly disclose his or her identity to less powerful subjects, who, on an individual basis, consent or refuse to participate in the research. A typical application for approval for research requires a discussion of the scientific significance and goals of the study, an estimate of the number of subjects involved, an explanation of how the researcher intends to recruit them, a discussion of potential risks and benefits that they may face, and a description of how the researcher intends to obtain their consent. Fieldworkers have questioned the feasibility of answering such questions beforehand (Cassell, 1978, 1980; Emerson, 1983; Thorne, 1980; Wax, 1980, 1983). As Wax (1983, pp. 294-295) points out, "To know the exact questions to study and the precise procedures for studying is in fact to know most of the answers." Fine (1993, p. 274) adds, drawing on Glaser and Strauss's (1967) *The Discovery of Grounded Theory*, that "good ethnographers do not know what they are looking for until they have found it." Nevertheless, I wanted to respect the rules that would enable me to do my research. I filled out the necessary forms and obtained the necessary signatures.

The study that I outlined involved observation of CoDA meetings and interviews with self-identified codependents. To recruit people for interviews, I designed a small advertisement to place in pennysaver-type newspapers and a flyer to post on community bulletin boards and distribute at meetings. The ad and the flyer explained the research in a sentence or two and asked for self-identified codependents to volunteer for interviews. I submitted samples to the IRB with my application. Because this exerted no coercion over potential subjects, the IRB gave their approval. I placed the ad, posted the flyers, and waited for the phone to ring. I received one phone call during the course of several months, and even this was from someone who knew me in another setting and recognized my name on the flyer. I gradually learned just how ridiculous it was to assume that members of anonymous group would step forward and identify themselves to a stranger, even if that stranger had an affiliation with a local university.

The IRB had also given me approval to observe CoDA meetings. I planned to announce my research there, make my flyers available, and ask for volunteers for interviews. At this time, I had not yet attended any meetings. Because I knew that I would eventually do research there, I did not want to go to a meeting only to turn up later as a researcher. My lack of exposure to the setting, however, led me to presume a structure that did not exist within it. When I began the fieldwork, I thought it made sense to seek permission by starting at what I imagined would be CoDA's gatekeeper. I called the telephone listing for CoDA and got a recorded message that included the number for Intergroup, their local decision-making committee. I called it, imagining that I might even get a letter that I could then take around to meetings to show that I had permission to be there. I quickly learned that, in an anonymous group, my assumptions about gatekeepers would not hold.

CoDA, like all 12-step groups, simply has no gatekeepers to ask for permission. Intergroup has nothing to do with leadership; it consists of a committee that makes decisions on a local level. The chair said that only individual groups could decide whether I could research them. He added, however, that researchers had attended meetings openly before, and it "had not gone well." Some people feel like guinea pigs, he said, and others "grandstand," thinking they will get into somebody's book or article. Both behaviors violate the anonymous principles of the group. The chair encouraged me to go to the meetings "for my heart." He asked me if I thought I was codependent. I knew better than to say that I did not; he would take any denial on my part as a sign of the depth of my codependency. He pressed me: "But you do think you're codependent, don't you?" I danced around the question by saying that I was sure that I had my share of issues to work through, but my real interest was in studying the group. He said that Intergroup had no authority to give me blanket permission to study CoDA. Only the individual groups could make that decision.

I went to my first meeting. I thought I would arrive at the site and find a distinct entity called "the group," not to mention that I still hoped to find someone more or less in charge. I would explain who I was, and I would sit and watch the meeting without disturbing the interaction. I would leave my stack of flyers and ask for volunteers for interviews. I believed that the credibility attributed to the words sociology, dissertation, and research would open doors for me. I assumed that the members of CoDA would welcome a curious scholar into their midst.

Instead, I found no one in charge. "Leading" a CoDA meeting consists of reading a printed text; the position has no power attached to it. I watched the interaction and waited, looking for cues from the setting. Lacking an official gatekeeper, I thought that, alternatively, I could introduce myself to those in attendance. I would just have to find the right moment in the meeting and make my introduction.

Next, I discovered that CoDA meetings have no moment at which to introduce oneself. Twelve-step culture takes the concept of anonymity very seriously. I had understood that everyone would use first names only. I had also understood that one's identity outside the meeting, one's occupation, and social location become secondary in what are referred to as "the rooms," the places where meetings take place. I knew that, in the rooms, the focus would be on the common problem. It would make no difference whether one is a lawyer, a waitress, or a student. Although I had understood that anonymity meant that no one could call attention to his or her identity, I had thought that my legitimate research agenda would allow for an exception to the rule. It took me only minutes to understand that I would have disrupted the meeting if I did what I planned to do.

Even if I had been able to make an introduction, I had no idea of who my audience was. I had not even found anything that I could confidently call the group. As a newcomer, I did not know the other newcomers from the regular members. I could not tell those who had made a commitment to the group from those who were only marginally involved or just visiting. For all I knew, most of the others were doing research too.

I sat through that first meeting in stunned silence, seeing my best laid plans fail at every turn. Without a gatekeeper at the organizational level or at the meeting itself, and with an introduction out of the question, I knew I had to improvise something else. I also knew that I had to keep coming to meetings to figure out what form that "something else" might take.

Next, I considered using the meeting's time for announcements to let the others know that I planned to leave a stack of flyers and that I wanted to do interviews. I soon discovered problems with this strategy as well. First, CoDA, like other 12-step groups, does not promote or endorse any outside concerns. All the announcements at meetings have to do with 12-step activities. I knew mine would count as "outside" and would violate the norms of the group. Second, CoDA, like other 12-step groups, controls the type of literature it makes available. The group distributes only "conference-approved" literature, meaning that which comes directly from CoDA's service office. Because CoDA does not promote any causes or accept any outside sponsorship, the rule about only conference-approved literature helps avoid conflict in that area. Some groups make other kinds of inspirational literature available but only with the approval of the members. A person cannot simply walk into a meeting and leave a stack of flyers on a table. Although the announcement and the flyers seemed like perfectly neutral tactics to me—moreover, they had the IRB's approval—they lost that neutrality in the 12-step setting.

Crossing the Line

Over time, as I struggled to figure out how to do the research, the research had already begun to take place. It was, however, taking a course very different from the one that had met with the approval of the IRB. During the first few meetings that I attended, I only observed. I listened and watched carefully for an opportunity to disclose my identity to the group and begin my research in earnest. Soon, however, my silent observation had to end. Most of the meetings have a format designed to encourage everyone to "share" their experience, so consistently not speaking would have violated group norms. Few members—even first-timers—pass up their turn to share. Codependents believe that they have put the wants and needs of others before their own. It would be "acting out one's codependency" to go to a meeting, look around, and think, "Oh, we won't have enough time for everyone to talk, so I'll just listen." To discourage that behavior, the meetings give everyone an opportunity to speak. Not speaking would be so unusual as to arouse the suspicions of those at the meeting. Only by "sharing" could I attend any one particular group for an extended period of time. Thus, without intending to, I stepped into participant observation. As I did, however, I lost the ability to claim an identity as a researcher. My sharing enabled me to stay at the meetings, but it also ruled out revealing myself later as a researcher who had been there all along.

Given the ambiguity of the concept of codependency, I had no trouble finding things to share. I suspect most adults would agree with this as well. Concurrent with my research, my 5-year, live-in relationship ended. Before that, I had experienced a divorce. I came to CoDA fully qualified to talk about failed relationships. I met other requirements as well. As the elder daughter of two hardworking professionals, responsibility and competence were expected of me from an early age. My sister and I were latchkey kids. My parents divorced when I was a teenager. In CoDA, that combination indicates a wounded "inner child." I do not like to disappoint people and will often do things for the sake of getting along. In CoDA, that makes me a "people pleaser." In many areas, I would describe myself as an overachiever. When I know how to do something, I tend to take over. In the language of CoDA, I have "control issues." In short, I did not have to lie about or embellish any of the events in my life. The discourse of codependency has sufficient leeway to accommodate almost anyone's life history; therein lies much of its appeal. I listened carefully to what the others said, and I put my own experiences into the language they used. I hoped that the words of Herbert Gans (1982, p. 405) would ring true for me: "Most people are too busy living to take much notice of a participant-observer once he [or she] has proven to them that he [or she] means no harm."

Although I did not find it hard to think of things to say at meetings, I did find it difficult to actually speak. I did not like confiding in strangers. As one woman explained to me, in CoDA, talk comes "from the gut." Typically, I spill my guts only to my closest of friends. Other researchers have found attending CoDA equally unsettling. For example, Carol Warren (as quoted in Mitchell-Norberg, Warren, & Zale, 1995, p. 129), "attended one meeting and found the experience too intense to return." The one-dimensionality of the interaction grated on me. I knew the people in CoDA—and they knew me—only as a series of problems. I also found it difficult to interact with the members knowing that I had deceived them about my reason for attending. I cringed when others thanked me for something I had shared in a meeting or when a member told me that I had said something that he or she "really needed to hear." I could not have foreseen that I would contribute to anyone's recovery program. I wanted to say, "Don't mind me. I'm just a sociologist." I wanted to tell them that I did not really believe I had a problem. I knew, however, that within the context of the group, my resistance would only have signaled to them the depth of my need to be there.

All told, I attended CoDA for 1 year and 5 months. I attended only what 12-step groups refer to as "open" meetings, meaning those that interested members of the public may attend. CoDA has "closed" meetings for gay men and lesbians and for in-depth study of the Twelve Steps in sequence. I did not attempt to attend any of these. I went to at least two open meetings a week—sometimes as many as four. I attended one particular meeting consistently over the course of the research, tapering off my attendance once I felt that I did not stand to learn much more by continuing. I attended a second weekly meeting at that same location for approximately 6 months. The rest of the time, I drove to other locations to visit a total of 18 groups. I also attended a CoDA picnic and an all-day event called a CoDA-thon, a combination of meetings, meals, and entertainment held once a year. After I had attended a group long enough to become acquainted with the members, I approached some of them individually for interviews. I explained the research to them in more detail and said that I wanted to ask them some more in-depth questions. We then arranged to meet privately. At the interview, I explained that I would protect their anonymity, and I had each person sign a standard consent form. This one-on-one approach worked where the distance of ads and flyers had failed.

Even if I had been able to disclose my identity, I would have had no control over what the members of CoDA made of the information I gave them about myself. As Shaffir (1991, p. 79) explains, "the researcher does not simply appropriate a particular status, but discovers that he or she is accorded a status by the hosts that reflects their understanding of his or her presence." In my case, the power of codependency as something approximating a "master status" for those at the meetings would have overridden any other information I could have given them. For example, some of the members knew about my research. Some found out because I had approached them for interviews. Others learned through my sharing that I was writing a dissertation. Regardless of how they heard it, they fit their new knowledge of my research interests into their prior understanding of me as a codependent. They believed that my desire to help people (a "symptom" of codependency) had brought me to the group and to my chosen profession. They generally thought that my research would, in turn, help people who "had" codependency. When I explained that I planned to become a university professor and not a therapist, some would say, "Well, that's helping people, too." They saw what they were prepared to see. They filtered the information I gave them through their own presuppositions. I had little power to shape their understanding of my presence.

The Limits of Consent

The same dynamics apply to the process of obtaining consent. As Roth (1962) stated,

> [E]ven if the subjects of a study are given as precise and detailed an explanation of the purpose and procedure of the study as the investigator is able to give them, the subjects will not understand all the terms of the research in the same way that the investigator does. (p. 284)

My stock explanation—and the one that appeared on the consent forms I used in my interviews—was that I was studying codependency and emotion management. Most of the time, however, even I would have been hard pressed to explain exactly what this meant. To complicate matters further, sometimes I was more interested in things far removed from emotion management.

Informed consent, in principle, suggests that a researcher knows what he or she is looking for. Moreover, it assumes that he or she is looking for the same information from each person. In the context of fieldwork, this kind of prescience seems absurd. The assumptions underlying informed consent, however, have shortcomings even in the arena in which it originated.

Informed consent as a legal doctrine comes from a 1957 California court decision (*Salgo*) that held physicians liable for withholding information necessary for consent to proposed treatment (Faden & Beauchamp, 1986; Lidz & Meisel, 1982; Lidz et al., 1984).[2] Zussman (1992) stated that informed consent is

> intended to enable patients to make decisions about their own medical care by requiring physicians to provide them with sufficient information about the risks and benefits of treatments and procedures as well as about alternatives to any proposed treatment or procedure. (p. 82)

Even in medicine, however, the notion of consent seldom corresponds with actual practice. For example, consent assumes "that medical practice is discrete—that is, broken into distinct parts, or decision units—and that there can be consent by the patient to each of these individual parts" (Lidz & Meisel, 1982, p. 401). In practice, medical treatment takes place on a continuous, not a discrete, basis. Prior treatments change the degree and kind of risk incurred by subsequent treatments, making the possibility of providing truly accurate information about each unlikely. In addition, many patients have no desire to become as involved in the process of consent as the doctrine allows. Others, due to the severity of their illness, simply cannot participate in the decisions that affect them (Zussman, 1992). In short, the concept of informed consent, although intended for use within the practice of medicine, does not articulate with the realities of medicine as practiced.

If informed consent presupposes a formality that does not exist even in the setting for which it was designed, its pitfalls become even more glaring in ethnographic realms. Consent assumes that the researcher "confronts a series of individual subjects" (Emerson, 1983, p. 264) over whom he or she has power. In fieldwork, however, researchers confront ongoing group interaction. As Thorne (1980, p. 264) has explained, "the contours of the natural groups and settings of field research run against the individual model of informed consent." In fieldwork, "consent is a continual process, dependent upon mutual learning and development" (Wax, 1980, p. 275). It is "a negotiated and lengthy process—of mutual learning and reciprocal exchanges—rather than a once-and-for-all event" (p. 275).

This continual quality became clear to me when I started visiting CoDA and saw no way to stop the course of events and explain my presence. The experience of another sociologist shows what happens when this is done. Rice (1996) identified himself as a researcher at one of the many CoDA meetings he visited. He found disguised or covert research unethical but, in my view, chose an option that also produced troublesome consequences. Rice explained his research to the group, and the members asked him to leave the room while they voted on whether to let him stay. They decided to let him stay, but they had to repeat the vote each time a member arrived late, and they would have to repeat the entire procedure each time he attended. Rice and the members agreed that this interfered with the meeting. He realized that, in a setting such as CoDA, asking for consent created far more disruption within the group. From then on, he just observed the meetings of other groups, saying that he was only there to learn more about CoDA.

Although I would have felt more comfortable doing what Rice did, the kind of information that I sought required sustained attendance, which in turn required participation. I wanted to understand how CoDA functions as an institution. I wanted to know what opportunities for involvement it offers its members. I wanted to understand the group perspectives on the process of sharing. Silent observation would have defeated these research goals. In addition, even silence would have ultimately felt and been deceptive. I could not have, in good conscience, kept quiet, saying that I just wanted to learn more about CoDA over the entire course of my research. Rapping (1996) used this strategy to study several 12-step groups. Although keeping silent made her feel less "sleazy" than deception, which she initially tried, she found maintaining it over time both "awkward" and "anxiety provoking" (p. 95). I used the silent strategy at the groups I visited only once or twice and where the format did not require each person to share.[3]

During one interview, I asked a longtime member of CoDA how she felt about my being at the meetings. She explained that CoDA meetings are open to the range of needs and interests that people bring to them—mine included. She stated,

> People come to CoDA for all sorts of reasons. Not everybody in these rooms is working a program. Some people just need contact. They're lonely. Some people have nothing to do on a Friday or a Monday night. Some people come here looking for a date, or a mate. Some people are just checking it out, and it might take some time for them to figure out if they belong here or not. CoDA welcomes anyone. We don't ask what your reasons are for coming.

According to IRB regulations, I deceived the people in CoDA in that I did not inform them that they were part of my study. According to the standards of the group, however, I did not do anything that does not take place there already—when someone goes to a meeting for some reason other than "working a program." The woman quoted previously shows a more sociological understanding of the range of interaction that could take place within the group—and of the inappropriateness of requiring that people reveal their motives—than do the regulations for research.

The Invisibility of Ethical Dilemmas

I do not want to convey the impression that I see my fieldwork experience as particularly perilous. I know that field-workers have entered settings far more menacing and ethically complex than CoDA meetings. They have struggled with ethical compromises of this magnitude and greater. Why, then, have I not read about these compromises in the methodological appendixes to their studies? Why do researchers typically gloss over the perils of their research? Why do they so often portray it as smooth and unproblematic? Why does a student have to go looking for accounts of the ethical dilemmas that others have faced in fieldwork?

Two reasons come to mind immediately. First, the smooth methodological appendix satisfies the expectations of publishers "who find such accounts superfluous" (Punch, 1983, p. 14). Although publishers may indeed shape the final product, it is worth keeping in mind that some reports of field research are sought out for their methodological insights over and above the conclusions of the study. For example, much of the fame of a fieldwork classic such as *Street Corner Society* comes from Whyte's openness about the "serious mistakes" he made in Cornerville (1981, p. 359; see also Punch, 1983). One wonders, however, what "mistakes" Whyte would have reported if he had done the research in the era of IRBs.

Second, I may have read mostly "smooth" reports of field research because the validity of fieldwork rides largely on the integrity of the fieldworker. In quantitative research, the collection, interpretation, and presentation of data are less subjective (or are at least assumed to be so). In contrast, only the field-worker sees his or her field notes. Interviews take place in private, tapes are often erased after transcription, and others seldom read the transcripts. Moreover, the researcher has his or her own motives for selecting particular quotes or illustrative cases (Punch, 1983). This degree of subjective judgment places the burden of proof on the integrity of the field-worker. If a compromise appears or a breach of regulations occurs, what might it mean for the whole of the research, not to mention the reputation of the researcher?

I argue that the integrity of the researcher makes it especially important to "come clean," as Punch (1983) states, about the course of the relationship that he or she has had with those in the study.

Readers should have a sense of the constraints and compromises that shaped a given interpretation and not be treated to a sanitized explanation of coding schemes and categorizations. An account of the researcher's ethical dilemmas could enrich the work in the way that Kleinman's (Kleinman & Copp, 1993) account of her emotional reaction to her research enriches her findings. Her frankness about the disillusionment she experienced in the field does not diminish her integrity; on the contrary, it strengthens it. Moreover, "sanitized explanations" contradict the reflexive involvement that ostensibly drew the researcher to the ethnographic tradition. If one's ideal is detached objectivity, then other methods lead to it more directly.

The demands of publishers and the reputations of fieldworkers strike me as weak reasons for glossing over research problems. I believe that the practice of publishing sanitized research reports in one place and ethical discussions in another does new researchers a disservice. If, "in our teaching and publications we tend to sell students a smooth, almost idealized, model of the research process as neat, tidy, and unproblematic" (Punch, 1983, p. 14), we do little to prepare them for what may lie ahead. Openness about the ethical perils of research can do more to prepare new researchers than can abstract talk about sensitivity. It can train fieldworkers to think about ethical decisions before they have to make them. It can "sensitize [fieldworkers] to situations in which ethical concerns become particularly salient" (Rubin & Rubin, 1995, p. 96).

I do not advocate an outpouring of "sentimental, emotional, pseudo-honest accounts detailing every nervous tremor and moment of depression or elation" (Punch, 1983, p. 14) experienced in the field. Rather, I advocate a reconciliation between two literatures. Currently, research reports and methodological manuals mirror little of what appears in the separate treatments of ethics and vice versa. Van Maanen (1988, p. 75) explains that although addressing "confessional tales" of fieldwork and not ethics in particular, accounts of the research experience "are distinct . . . from the ethnography itself." This conveys the illusion of "a clean break between the representation of the research work itself and the resulting ethnography" (Van Maanen, 1988, p. 75). Mending this break can demonstrate to students and other readers "that fieldwork is a craft, requiring both tenacity of purpose and competence in a number of social skills" (Punch, 1983, p. 16). From my own experience, I know

that, without exposure to a variety of dilemmas of the field, fledg-
ling researchers will have little preparation for what may lay before
them. To be sure, fieldwork cannot be learned in advance; it "is
learned in and through its doing" (Emerson, 1983, p. ix). Precious
little can be taken from one setting and applied to another. Nevertheless, making ethical considerations a part of research reports can
steer fieldworkers away from the flawed assumptions that I
adopted.

Conclusion

There are strong reasons why it is preferable to give people the
information they need to consent to participate in a study (Erikson,
1967). Although insisting on full disclosure and informed consent
makes good ethical sense, it makes little sociological sense. It reveals
an unsociological approach to the world of lived experience. As
Roth (1962) points out, most social settings lack a clear point at
which consent becomes an issue. He asks,

> Is it moral if one gets a job in a factory to earn tuition and then takes
> advantage of the opportunity to carry out a sociological study, but
> immoral to deliberately plant oneself in the factory for the express
> purpose of observing one's fellow workers? (p. 284)

If we push the idea of consent to its logical limits, sociologists could
produce few ethnographic studies at all.

My experience indicates that, in some settings, obtaining informed consent becomes an impossibility. Twelve-step groups do
not allow a researcher to distinguish himself or herself within the
group setting. In addition, the tradition of anonymity does not allow
for the open recruitment of human subjects. I could only learn these
things in the field, however, when I would have to make on-the-spot
decisions and hope for the best. Although I understand that this kind
of decision making is an ethnographic commonplace, its ethical
dimensions remain obscure—almost taboo. Their absence from ethnographic reports can lead new researchers to misread the degree
of formality that exists in the field. Moreover, their absence does a
disservice to the fundamental ethnographic belief that fieldwork

requires sensitivity to the setting. Real sensitivity may require ethical compromises. Although sensitivity cannot be taught, it can be enhanced. The best way to do so, I suggest, is by adding an ethical dimension to the discussion of fieldwork realities.

Notes

1. Twelve-step groups are psychospiritual programs based on Alcoholics Anonymous (AA). They exist to help people give up or manage more effectively their dependencies on substances and behaviors. The Twelve Steps are a set of principles for acknowledging one's lack of control, for surrendering it to a higher power, and for making a regular self-assessment in a serious effort to change one's life. In addition to AA, approximately 150 other programs have permission from AA to use its copyrighted steps.

2. With *Salgo*, " 'informed' was tacked onto 'consent,' creating the expression 'informed consent' " (Faden & Beauchamp, 1986, p. 125).

3. Some groups use a show-of-hands method in which each person calls on the next person to share. Those not wishing to share do not raise their hands.

References

Bell, C., & Newby, H. (1977). *Doing social research* (1st American ed.). New York: Free Press.

Cassell, J. (1978). Risk and benefit to subjects of fieldwork. *American Sociologist, 13,* 134-143.

Cassell, J. (1980). Ethical principles for conducting fieldwork. *American Anthropologist, 82,* 28-41.

Department of Health, Education, and Welfare. (1974, May 30). Protection of human subjects. *Federal Register, 39* FR 18914.

Department of Health, Education, and Welfare. (1978, November 30). Protection of human subjects: Institutional review boards. *Federal Register, 43* FR 56174.

Emerson, R. M. (1983). *Contemporary field research: A collection of readings.* Boston: Little, Brown.

Erikson, K. (1967). A comment on disguised observation in sociology. *Social Problems, 14,* 366-373.

Faden, R. R., & Beauchamp, T. L. (1986). *A history and theory of informed consent.* New York: Oxford University Press.

Fine, G. A. (1993). Ten lies of ethnography: Moral dilemmas of field research. *Journal of Contemporary Ethnography, 22,* 267-294.

Gans, H. (1982). *The urban villagers* (Updated and expanded ed.). New York: Free Press.

Glaser, B. G., & Strauss, A. L. (1967). *The discovery of grounded theory.* Chicago: Aldine.

Kleinman, S., & Copp, M. A. (1993). *Emotions and fieldwork.* Newbury Park, CA: Sage.

Lidz, C. W., & Meisel, A. (with Holden, J. L., Marx, J. H., & Munetz, M.). (1982). Informed consent and the structure of medical care. In *Making Health Care Deci-*

sions. Vol. 2: Appendices, Empirical Studies of Informed Consent (President's Commission for the Study of Ethical Problems in Medicine and Biomedical and Behavioral Research). Washington, DC: U.S. Government Printing Office.

Lidz, C. W., Meisel, A., Zerubavel, E., Carter, M., Sestak, R., & Roth, L. (1984). *Informed consent.* New York: Guilford.

Mitchell-Norberg, J., Warren, C. A. B., & Zale, S. L. (1995). Gender and codependents anonymous. In M. Flaherty & C. Ellis (Eds.), *Social perspectives on emotion* (pp. 121-147). Greenwich, CT: JAI.

Punch, M. (1983). *The politics and ethics of fieldwork* (Sage University Paper Series on Qualitative Research Methods, Vol. 3). Beverly Hills, CA: Sage.

Rapping, E. (1996). *The culture of recovery: Making sense of the self-help movement in women's lives.* Boston: Beacon.

Rice, J. S. (1996). *A disease of one's own: Psychotherapy, addiction, and the emergence of co-dependency.* New Brunswick, NJ: Transaction.

Roth, J. (1962). Comments on "secret observation." *Social Problems, 9,* 283-284.

Rubin, H. J., & Rubin, I. S. (1995). *Qualitative interviewing: The art of hearing data.* Thousand Oaks, CA: Sage.

Shaffir, W. B. (1991). Managing a convincing self-presentation: Some personal reflections on entering the field. In W. B. Shaffir & R. A. Stebbins (Eds.), *Experiencing fieldwork: An inside view of qualitative research* (pp. 72-81). Newbury Park, CA: Sage.

Thorne, B. (1980). "You still takin' notes?" Fieldwork and problems of informed consent. *Social Problems, 27,* 284-297.

Van Maanen, J. (1988). *Tales of the field: On writing ethnography.* Chicago: University of Chicago Press.

Wax, M. (1980). Paradoxes of "consent" to the practices of fieldwork. *Social Problems, 27,* 272-283.

Wax, M. (1983). On fieldworkers and those exposed to fieldwork: Federal regulations and moral issues. In R. M. Emerson (Ed.), *Contemporary field research: A collection of readings* (pp. 288-299). Boston: Little, Brown.

Whyte, W. F. (1981). *Street corner society* (3rd ed.). Chicago: University of Chicago Press.

Zussman, R. (1992). *Intensive care: Medical ethics and the medical profession.* Chicago: University of Chicago Press.

10

Animal Passions

The Emotional Experience of Doing Ethnography in Animal-Human Interaction Settings

CLINTON R. SANDERS

Above and beyond the world of facts and law, with which alone Science concerns itself, is an immense and almost unknown world of suggestion and freedom and inspiration, in which the individual . . . must struggle against fact and law to develop or keep his own individuality. . . . Though less exact, it is not less but rather more true and real than Science, as emotions are more real than facts, and love is more true than Economics.

—*Long (1903, p. 688)*

The scientistic ideology that governs conventional sociological re-search holds that the investigator's emotions should have no place in his or her work because emotions simply contaminate the data and impede the "objective" process of acquiring valid information. For quantitative researchers, avoiding such "emotional contamina-tion" while collecting data is rather easy because, unlike ethnogra-phers, they are not required to build relationships or engage in intimate interactions with those they study. Furthermore, the very act of quantification—transforming the words people speak in structured interviews or the preordained responses they check off on questionnaires into categories represented by numbers—effec-tively washes the emotional elements out of "subjects'" experiences (Young, 1981).

Traditional instructions about doing ethnography have tended to repeat the positivist caution about the possible contamination of data due to the fieldworker's intimate involvement in the lives of those with whom he or she works and his or her emotional response to happenings in the research setting. This condemnation of emotion has, in the past few years, been tempered considerably. This change has largely come about because of the emphasis by feminist scholars (e.g., DeVault, 1993; Kleinman & Copp, 1993; Krieger, 1991; Mies, 1983), some postmodernist ethnographers (e.g., Denzin, 1989, 1990; Ellis, 1991), and others (e.g., Lofland & Lofland, 1995) on the inevitability and methodological utility of emotion in the field.

Emotional experience is, in fact, central to doing ethnography. The fieldworker is routinely confronted with the uncertainties of being a stranger in other people's home territories and having to navigate through the field without the comforting compass of a testable hypothesis. Ethnography also offers considerable emotional rewards, however—the joy of discovery, the pleasure of eventual acceptance, and empathetic connections to the lives of participants. Because experiencing emotion is an unavoidable feature of doing fieldwork, it is most sensible to pay close attention to the emotions displayed by participants and those that are inevitably called forth in the ethnographer as he or she shares in the activities of interest. Emotional experiences, when reflectively examined, can prove to be valuable sources of ethnographic information.

One type of social setting in which emotional issues are most vividly apparent is that in which people routinely interact with nonhuman animals. Our cultural definition of animals is fraught with ambivalence (Arluke & Sanders, 1996; Sanders & Hirschman, 1996). On the one hand, we callously use animals for food and objects of entertainment, treat them as functional servants, and subject them to often painful and cruel scientific experiments. On the other hand, we bring animals into our homes and come to regard them as members of our families (Beck & Katcher, 1983, pp. 39-59; Cain, 1985; Veevers, 1985). As intimate participants in our daily lives, we regard companion animals as thoughtful, emotional, empathetic, and uniquely individual. As such, they typically are loved and seen as freely returning the love they receive from us. Companion animals are, in short, assigned a "person-like" status, and our interactions with and feelings for them are parallel to those that are bound up in our relationships with other intimates (Sanders, 1993).

The intimacy of human relationships with animals means that emotions are routinely encountered when one does ethnographic work in settings that revolve around human-animal interaction. Fieldworkers who investigate, for example, the culture of scientific laboratories (Arluke, 1988; Phillips, 1993), the activities of dog trainers (Gillespie, Leffler, & Lerner, 1996), workers in animal shelters (Arluke, 1991), interactions in veterinary clinics (Keto & Gregory, 1991; Sanders, 1995), and both public and private settings in which people are in the company of animals (Belk, 1996; Holbrook, 1996; Sanders, 1990) are thrust into a world of emotion. Prior commitments held by researchers, who themselves tend to be animal people, may serve to amplify or otherwise draw out emotional aspects of being "in the field." How the ethnographer experiences, works to manage, and draws analytic lessons from the emotions he or she feels and encounters in these settings potentially reveals much about the intimate work of doing ethnography.

The Research

For almost a decade, I have been exploring the development of relationships between people and animals. This exploration first took me into a puppy kindergarten in which owners were introduced to the most basic elements of dog rearing and their young dogs were introduced to other people and canines. I next asked a veterinarian who was a partner in a large mixed-practice veterinary hospital if he would help me gain access to do fieldwork in the clinic. He agreed, and I soon found myself in a major setting in which I could observe owners interacting with their dogs and other companion animals. Although my initial concern was with the interaction between owners and their pets, I soon realized that the occupation of being a veterinarian was of considerable sociological interest. During more than a year of fieldwork in the clinic, I collected a rich body of data focusing on veterinary exchanges with both animal patients (Sanders, 1994a) and human clients (Sanders, 1994b). Having laid the groundwork for understanding human-companion animal relationships generally, I then moved to a related, but more specialized, interaction setting. Using contacts I had made in the clinic, I approached the administrators of a guide dog training program and asked permission to "hang out" in the training facility, accompany the trainers as they worked with their dogs, and interview guide dog owners. Having gained permission, for approximately 9 months I collected field notes and interviews related to the training of guide dogs and the daily experience of living with them.

During most of the time I was doing ethnographic work in these settings, I was also recording notes about my experiences as I lived with my own dogs. These "autoethnographic" data (Denzin, 1989; Hayano, 1979) proved to be especially instructive. As I watched my Newfoundlands interact with each other, accompanied them on our daily walks, systematically recorded my own emotions and thoughts as we lived together, and eventually had the experience of attending the euthanasia of one of them, I acquired the most intimate and instructive information about one's relationship with animal companions. Personal experience may teach the most vivid of lessons.

Because I address the emotions that the ethnographer experiences and encounters while doing research in human-animal interaction settings, I will concentrate on the my work in the veterinary clinic and my autoethnography. These two elements of my research project provided the richest and most instructive information about the issue at hand. It was in my research encounters in the hospital and my life with my own canine companions that I confronted the sorrowful emotions surrounding animal pain and death as well as human ignorance and mistreatment. I also experienced the joy regarding the healing of and intimate interaction with companion animals. In what follows, I describe some of these emotion-laden research experiences and use them to ground a more general discussion of the key role emotion plays in the process of doing ethnography.

Emotional Encounters

Encountering the Unpleasant

Ethnographers who explore human-animal interaction settings, especially those that revolve around medical or scientific activities, frequently find themselves exposed to rather distasteful sights and experiences. Regular participants in the settings are usually accustomed to these situations and may purposefully thrust the investigator into them—especially when he or she is new to the field—as a way of testing his or her commitment. The following is a segment from field notes I recorded early in my experience in the veterinary clinic in which I describe such an incident. This came at the end of an emotionally draining day in which I had observed two euthanasias of old and dearly loved dogs ("death encounters" are discussed later):

> As I prepare to leave and am going through the surgery area I see Martha (a veterinary technician) talking with Bob (a vet). I chat with them for a while. . . . Bob asks Martha if the old collie he euthanized earlier has been cremated yet. She says the body is still in the back and Bob asks her to help him bring it into the surgery preparation area. They leave and return with the dog in a black plastic trash bag on the blue stretcher used to move it out of the exam room. They split the body bag and put it on sink-like affair with a grill over it. The poor animal's eyes are open and it is now stiff with rigor mortis. Bob looks in a cabinet for scalpel preparing to open the dog up. I say, "I'm not sure I want to stay around for what's coming." Martha replies, "I know what you mean. I don't usually like to see autopsies on animals I know. But this is really interesting and it is a good way to learn." Bob turns to me. "In cases like this I like to do an autopsy—if the owner says it is OK. If they tell me not to touch their dog, I won't. But this is useful. If I find that the dog is filled with cancer I can call the owner and tell him. They often seem grateful to know. If I don't find anything I won't call." He turns the dog so that its stiff legs are pointed up and asks me to hold the front legs. I say, "OK, but I don't think I will watch this process too closely if you don't mind." Bob makes an incision in the dog's belly and large quantities of black fluid gush out. Bob nods and remarks, "Ah, it was bleeding into the abdominal cavity. That's why she was so anemic." He continues to squish his hands around in the dog's exposed entrails. "Hey, this liver is kind of funky. Take a look at this." Martha comes over and asks if I would like her to take over holding the legs and I agree. I feel slightly nauseated and continue to be rather upset by having seen the euthanasia. Martha and Bob engage in light, friendly banter during the operation. I leave after saying that I want to ease into less savory situations like this somewhat slowly.

Some time later during my research, I described this incident to one of the other doctors, who observed, "Yeah, that's just like Bob.

He will do that sort of thing just as a joke. He was trying to see what you were made of." I felt some pleasure in the fact that I had handled the situation fairly well and realized that I should pay closer attention to the joking that went on behind the scenes in the clinic. It became clear that humor was one of the ways that hospital staff, like other workers in "death settings" (e.g., Coombs & Powers, 1975; Lesy, 1989; Smith & Kleinman, 1989), dealt with having to work daily with pain and death.

Doing surgery was the work activity the veterinarians usually found to be most interesting and potentially rewarding. Although much of the surgery they performed, such as spaying and castrating companion animal patients, was entirely routine, some operations provided the satisfying experience of, as the doctors stated, "going in there and fixing it." The veterinarians who were seen as having the highest levels of surgical skill were admired, whereas those that had only rudimentary abilities were often the focus of joking derision (usually behind their backs). Because surgery was an important occupational activity in the clinic, it was something I had to observe. I felt some initial anxiety as I anticipated watching operations because I have always tended to be rather squeamish about real-life gore and had heard staff relating stories about the occasional regular client who requested being allowed to observe surgery on their animal and passed out during the process. In general, I found my anxiety to be unfounded. Anesthetized surgical patients were covered with cloths that shrouded their individual identities and the surgery itself was far less bloody than I had anticipated. Occasionally, however, I did find operations to be a bit more than I bargained for. Surgery on animals' eyes and the grinding and drilling that accompanied orthopedic surgery were especially distasteful. After I had been in the field for a few months, however, I had little trouble observing and assisting in minor ways with surgeries. As was the case with the other regular participants in the setting, my normal emotional response to unpleasant medical routines was dulled by regular exposure.

Encountering Death

Euthanizing old, sick, or unwanted companion animals is another routine feature of veterinary work. Just before I gained access to the clinic, one of my own dogs was diagnosed as having a brain tumor. Emma's physical condition declined rapidly, and a few months into the research I had the painful experience of attending her euthanasia. This personal encounter colored my subsequent experience with observing, and sometimes assisting in, other "mercy killings." Mental health professionals who work with the families of homicide victims, clients who have been subjected to domestic violence, and others who are exposed to severely damaging ordeals refer to the emotions generated by their empathy with these clients as "vicarious traumatization." Because many of the euthanasias I observed reopened the old wounds caused by the passing of my own dog, I found these situations to be the most emotionally wearing. Although I realized that I had to put myself into the position of observing euthanasia encounters, I found it impossible to distance myself from the intense pain felt by clients during these situations. My emotional discomfort was compounded by the fact that, for the first time in more than two decades of doing ethnography, I felt like a voyeur who was looking in on a terribly painful human experience and turning it into "data" to be objectified and used to make analytic points that were far removed from the actual aching sorrow felt by those I was observing and which I shared (I discuss how intervention by the researcher may serve to limit some of these concerns in the following section). The following is a lengthy example of just such an incident drawn from my field notes:

> What a day! This one starts off with an awful euthanasia case that pushes me to the limit. I follow Mark into an exam room in which an old German shepherd cross is lying on a stretcher on the exam table. The owners are a late middle-aged couple. The dog (Heather) has recently been operated on for a cancerous spleen and is not doing well. The woman has a stack of notes about animal's mobility, eating, eliminating, etc. and proceeds to read them. Mark stops her and says he doesn't really need to hear it because he can see the dog is doing badly. He opens the dog's mouth. Even I see that the gums are dead white, an indication of severe anemia. Mark tells them that the great likelihood is that the cancer has metastasized and the dog is bleeding internally. He says that the best case scenario is that there is bleeding from a vein unnoticed in the operation but that there is only around a 2 to 5 percent chance of this. Mark outlines the options—open her up again, do an ultrasound or x ray to find if more cancer, or put her to sleep without any further trauma. He says, "I have an old shepherd cross myself. All these other things

would put a lot of stress on her and you would incur more expense." The man quickly responds that the expense is not important. Mark continues, "If it were my dog I would put her to sleep."
He says this in a very quiet voice, looking down at the floor. I also
notice he calls the dog "sweetheart" as he gently examines her.
Obviously shaken, the woman says, "You weren't sure when I
talked to you before. Would the cancer cause these sorts of ups and
downs? Some days she has been real good—she even played with
her ball." All this time I am crouched with my back against the wall
watching the scene. The dog's head is toward me and I look into
her eyes and, remembering the book I just read [on telepathic communication with animals], try to mentally communicate to her that
everything is going to be OK. At some level I realize that this is
perhaps a very silly thing to do but I am feeling terribly sad. The
talk turns to putting the dog down. The woman says, "We had a
little poodle we put to sleep. I don't think I can stay here. She let
out a yelp and I swore I would never do that again." She goes over
to the table, strokes the dog's head, and whispers in her ear. "The
way they look at you with their eyes. She's saying, 'Are you really
going to leave me?' Can you do it peacefully?" Mark replies, "It's
hard to predict how they are going to react. Usually it is peaceful,
but sometimes they let out an involuntary cry. With people (in her
situation) you do anything to keep the person alive. But . . ." The
woman says, "I don't think I can stand to stay." Mark tries to con-
sole her, "I'm sure she understands." The woman draws a deep
breath, "We have to stay for her sake. Can you give us a few minutes?" As we leave I hear her ask her husband, "What are we going
to tell Sharon?" The man says, "She'll understand." They are both
crying. I stand outside the door for a minute fighting back tears and
then go into the library-lunch room to write notes. I feel very sad
remembering my own experience with Emma. I am crying as I take
notes. I feel as if I have violated the couple in this terrible time for
them, that I am exploiting their pain. Martha comes in and, seeing me crying, touches my shoulder in sympathy and tells me
that she knows how I feel since she is not yet over the recent
euthanizing of two of her own dogs. "You just have to go through
what it takes to help people. It's really hard—especially with animals you know. You just have to learn how to distance yourself from
it some way."

Even now, it is difficult for me to extract an analytic point from
this description other than that personal emotions are part of the

burden of doing ethnography. Empathetic involvement in emotional encounters hurts and, in some extreme cases, may drive the researcher from the field—at least for a time. If our ultimate goal is to truly comprehend the rich variety of perspectives and experiences that shape interaction processes, however, we must not avoid involving ourselves in, and empathetically sharing, the sorrow and joy, pain and conflict, that are integral features of social life. Intimate confrontations with emotion will both enrich our knowledge of social interaction and expand our understanding of ourselves. Susan Krieger (1985) emphasizes this connection between self-knowledge and sociological insight:

> I think that often in social research, this is what we really do. We see others as we know ourselves. If the understanding of self is limited and unyielding to change, the understanding of the other is as well. If the understanding of the self is harsh, uncaring, and not generous to all the possibilities for being a person, the understanding of the other will show this. The great danger of doing injustice to the reality of the "other" does not come about through use of the self, but through lack of use of a full enough sense of self which, concomitantly, produces a stifled, artificial, limited, and unreal knowledge of others. (p. 320)

Intervention

It is conventional in fieldwork to expect the ethnographer to be a "silent witness" to happenings in the field. The researcher's primary goal, in this view, is to build an adequate understanding of the perspectives of those with whom he or she is working and not make judgments about whether these perspectives are true or false and the actions grounded on them are right or wrong. This hands-off stance is typically justified by claiming that the ethnographer's display of skepticism, distaste for certain points of view, or overt intervention in what happens in the setting can potentially harm his or her relationships with those in the field and limit access to important situations. Criticism or intervention can be seen by participants as a betrayal of trust.

Although this conventional concern might well be warranted and I do not intend to imply that the traditional ethnographic stance is immoral, there are other interests that I believe must be considered. At times, the fieldworker might find that directly expressing skepticism can lead to exchanges that open up new and interesting data (Douglas, 1976). Furthermore, by expressing doubt or concern and overtly acting on these feelings, the ethnographer can potentially ease some of the ethical discomforts he or she may experience, such as the feelings of being a voyeur mentioned previously. One of the ways in which the ethnographer can ease the discomfort of being merely a voyeur or exploiting the people with whom he or she is working is to use the information collected to give back something of value to those in the field. I do not believe, however, that one's ethical responsibilities are equally distributed among all actors in the research setting. As Galliher (1980) has persuasively maintained, all social settings are characterized by the unequal distribution of power and control. Those in charge typically have the resources at hand to support their own interests. It is those further down the ladder of power that can best use the information collected by the fieldworker to make their daily lives more easy to bear. In turn, should the ethnographer choose to intervene in situations that arise in the field, I maintain that these efforts are best focused on improving the lot of those with the least power.

As my own experience with studying animal-human interaction settings proceeded and I acquired more knowledge of relationships with companion animals, I was often appalled by the cruelty, thoughtless disregard, and misguided kindness people displayed in the treatment of their pets. Dogs, for example, were harshly punished when they simply did not understand what owners were demanding. They were allowed to engage in dangerous behaviors, isolated and ignored until they literally were driven insane by boredom and loneliness, and overfed until they were seriously overweight. Initially, when encountering these types of situations in the field I simply watched and recorded. As time went on, however, my discomfort grew, and I was increasingly inclined to exercise what Maria Mies (1983) calls "conscious partiality." My commitment to the welfare of animals prompted me to begin giving advice to owners about their pet's nutrition and grooming, advocate effective training techniques, explain how the animal might interpret his or her owner's commands, and, in a variety of other ways, intervene in the animal-human relationships so as to promote what I determined to be the interests of the nonhuman "subordinate." The following is an example from my field notes of such a situation in which I decided to intervene:

> I go with Martin into an exam room to see a nice young male brown Doberman in there with a middle-aged woman and her young son. She says that they just got the dog a couple of days before. The dog's ears are not cropped. She asks me if the dog is too old to have ears done. I don't answer directly but I say I like them that way. When she asks Martin he says that he also likes them that way and that were they clipped they would probably not stay upright (I realize this is not exactly true but I am happy that we have probably saved the dog some pain). As we are talking the son is showing off by whapping the dog on the muzzle. The woman half-heartedly tells the kid to stop. He doesn't. I say, "Zack, its not a good idea to hit him on the nose like that." "Why not?" "They just don't like it. How would you like it if someone did that to you?" The kid raises his hand again and I shout, "HEY!" He goes and pouts in the corner. The mother just shrugs.

Although this is, admittedly, a rather minor instance of intervention, it does illustrate the point that I am trying to make. This situation and many others like it required me to confront my own concern for the welfare of companion animals and make decisions about whether I had legitimate license to intervene. I could simply have exercised "emotional management" (Hochschild, 1983) and pushed down my empathic feelings for the animals. Early in my time in the clinic, I did this because I was worried about being seen by the veterinarians as forgetting my place and impinging on their territorial authority. As time went on, however, my relevant knowledge increased, and my relationships with the major participants in the setting became more secure. I came to realize that I possessed, and was seen by the vets as possessing, some measure of expertise. Consequently, I felt more comfortable "listening to my heart" and intervening when I believed I could have some small, but positive, impact on the lives of the people and animals I encountered.

In short, I see ethnography as less about what social scientists do and more about what people do. The quasi-positivist orientation toward fieldwork would have us assume what I have come to think of as the "zoo visitor" stance in which we are expected to simply stand back and watch the interesting things going on. Circumstances vary considerably from field setting to field setting, but I have usually found that I feel better about myself if I push aside my hesitation about speaking out of turn or possibly damaging the relationships I have fostered with some participants. There will be times when the ethnographer will encounter situations in which he or she will feel a moral responsibility to intervene (Palmer, 1991). In the final accounting, the goal of doing what one can to help is far superior to collecting data.

Conclusion

After I had had some experience doing fieldwork in a couple of different animal-human interaction settings, I recorded the following observation in my autoethnographic notes:

> It really strikes me that [what I am doing now] is very different from any of the other research projects I have been involved in. I was sitting reading in preparation for writing a paper and found myself crying while reading the section on the death of a dog and the impact of this experience on owners in Fogle's (1987) book *Games Pets Play*. He quotes from an editorial in a turn-of-the-century newspaper responding to someone who wrote asking where he should bury his dog.
>
>> There is one place to bury a dog. If you bury him in this spot, he will come to you when you call—come to you over the grim, dim frontiers of death and down the well-remembered path and to your side again. And though you call a dozen living dogs to heel they shall not growl at him, nor resent his coming, for he belongs there. People may scoff at you who see no slightest blade of grass bent by his footfall, who hear no whimper, people who never really had a dog. Smile at them, for you shall know something that is hidden from them, and which is well worth know-

ing. The one best place to bury a good dog is in the heart of his master. (pp. 208-209)

> I went out and stood by [where we had buried one of our dogs] and talked to him for a while. I also find myself touched and grinning with pleasure at the antics of the puppies [in the puppy kindergarten] or upset at the ineptitude or thoughtless cruelty of the owners. I have never had such emotional experience with research. . . . There certainly is a difference between being "interested" in a phenomenon or subculture . . . and being engaged by positive emotions like love, attachment, respect. This [research] is truly unique in that it is filled with the most "heart touching" emotional experiences.

Ethnographic work revolves around what anthropologist Mary Louise Pratt (1986, p. 32) refers to as "sensuous experience." In addition to partaking of the sights, sound, smells, and tastes of the field, the sensitive ethnographer encounters and shares in the emotions of those in whose daily lives he or she is interested. In part, the "truth value" of ethnographic accounts depends on whether the investigator can convince the reader of these accounts that he or she was intimately involved in the social setting being presented (Hammersley, 1990; Kleinman & Copp, 1993). In addition to offering richly detailed descriptions of behavior and telling quotes from interviews and field conversations, descriptions of one's own emotional experiences help serve to support the ethnographer's right to speak knowledgeably about the setting and the lives of the people within it. Emotional involvement is integral to "being there."

Furthermore, because the central (but, I would maintain, not the exclusive) goal of fieldwork is to intimately grasp the definitions and interpretations that shape people's behavior, it is necessary to pay close attention to the emotional elements of the field. Feelings are built into the experiences and cultural definitions that constrain social action. Intimate familiarity with a setting and the people within it requires more than simply observing and participating in their activities. Real understanding comes when the ethnographer attends to and shares the emotions that are felt by those in the field.

This empathetic connection to participants and their experiences promises, in turn, to provide the investigator with valuable insight into his or her self and may, at times, prompt the ethnographer to go beyond simply collecting data and initiate interventions that improve, at least in small ways, the lives of those in whom the researcher has developed an emotional stake. By ignoring or suppressing emotion, the ethnographer does a disservice to his or her self and to this most intimate means of constructing a grounded understanding of social life.

References

Arluke, A. (1988). Sacrificial symbolism in animal experimentation: Object or pet? *Anthrozoos, 2*(2), 98-117.

Arluke, A. (1991). Coping with euthanasia: A case study of shelter culture. *Journal of the American Veterinary Medical Association, 198*(7), 1176-1180.

Arluke, A., & Sanders, C. R. (1996). *Regarding animals.* Philadelphia: Temple University Press.

Beck, A., & Katcher, A. (1983). *Between pets and people.* New York: G. P. Putnam.

Belk, R. (1996). Metaphoric relationships with pets. *Society and Animals, 4*(2), 121-146.

Cain, A. (1985). Pets as family members. In M. Sussman (Ed.), *Pets and the family* (pp. 5-10). New York: Haworth.

Coombs, R., & Powers, P. (1975). Socialization for death: The physician's role. *Urban Life, 4*(3), 250-271.

Denzin, N. (1989). *Interpretive interactionism.* Newbury Park, CA: Sage.

Denzin, N. (1990). On understanding emotion: The interpretive-cultural agenda. In T. Kemper (Ed.), *Research agendas in the sociology of emotions* (pp. 85-116). New York: State University of New York Press.

DeVault, M. (1993). Different voices: Feminist methods of social research. *Qualitative Sociology, 16*(1), 77-83.

Douglas, J. (1976). *Investigative social research.* Beverly Hills, CA: Sage.

Ellis, C. (1991). Sociological introspection and emotional experience. *Symbolic Interaction, 14*(1), 23-50.

Fogle, B. (1987). *Games pets play.* New York: Viking.

Galliher, J. (1980). Social scientists' ethical responsibilities to superordinates: Looking upward meekly. *Social Problems, 27*(3), 298-308.

Gillespie, D., Leffler, A., & Lerner, E. (1996). Safe in unsafe places: Leisure, passionate avocations, and the problematizing of everyday public life. *Society and Animals, 4*(2), 169-188.

Hammersley, M. (1990). *Reading ethnographic research.* New York: Longman.

Hayano, D. (1979). Auto-ethnography: Paradigms, problems, and prospects. *Human Organization, 38*(1), 99-104.

Hochschild, A. (1983). *The managed heart.* Berkeley: University of California Press.

Holbrook, M. (1996). Reflections on rocky. *Society and Animals, 4*(2), 147-168.

Keto, S., & Gregory, S. (1991, May). *Negotiating definitions of reality in a veterinary clinic: Human mediation in construction of diagnoses for sick pets.* Paper presented at the Qualitative Analysis Conference, Carlton University, Ottawa, Ontario, Canada.

Kleinman, S., & Copp, M. (1993). *Emotions and fieldwork.* Newbury Park, CA: Sage.

Krieger, S. (1985). Beyond subjectivity: The use of the self in social science. *Qualitative Sociology, 8*(4), 309-324.

Krieger, S. (1991). *Social science and the self.* New Brunswick, NJ: Rutgers University Press.

Lesy, M. (1989). *The forbidden zone.* New York: Anchor.

Lofland, J., & Lofland, L. (1995). *Analyzing social settings* (3rd ed.). Belmont, CA: Wadsworth.

Long, W. J. (1903, May). The modern school of nature-study and its critics. *Northamerican Review, 176,* 688-696.

Mies, M. (1983). Towards a methodology for feminist research. In G. Bowles & R. D. Klein (Eds.), *Theories in women's studies* (pp. 117-139). Boston: Routledge Kegan Paul.

Palmer, C. E. (1991). Human emotions: An expanding sociological frontier. *Sociological Spectrum, 11,* 213-239.

Phillips, M. (1993). Savages, drunks, and lab animals: The researcher's perception of pain. *Society and Animals, 1*(1), 61-82.

Pratt, M. L. (1986). Fieldwork in common places. In J. Clifford & G. Marcus (Eds.), *Writing culture* (pp. 27-50). Berkeley: University of California Press.

Sanders, C. (1990). Excusing tactics: Social responses to the public misbehavior of companion animals. *Anthrozoos, 4*(2), 82-90.

Sanders, C. (1993). Understanding dogs: Caretakers' attributions of mindedness in canine-human relationships. *Journal of Contemporary Ethnography, 22*(2), 205-226.

Sanders, C. (1994a). Biting the hand that heals you: Encounters with problematic patients in a general veterinary practice. *Society and Animals, 2*(1), 47-66.

Sanders, C. (1994b). Annoying owners: Routine interactions with problematic clients in a general veterinary practice. *Qualitative Sociology, 17*(1), 159-170.

Sanders, C. (1995). Killing with kindness: Veterinary euthanasia and the social construction of personhood. *Sociological Forum, 10*(2), 195-214.

Sanders, C., & Hirschman, E. (1996). Involvement with animals as consumer experience. *Society and Animals, 4*(2), 111-119.

Smith, A. C., & Kleinman, S. (1989). Managing emotions in medical school: Students' contacts with the living and the dead. *Social Psychology Quarterly, 52*(1), 56-69.

Veevers, J. (1985). The social meaning of pets: Alternative roles for companion animals. In M. Sussman (Ed.), *Pets and the family* (pp. 11-30). New York: Haworth.

Young, T. R. (1981). Sociology and human knowledge: Scientific vs. folk methods. *American Sociologist, 16,* 119-124.

PART V

Ethnographic Text and Ethnographic Voice

The term *ethnographer* quite literally translates from its root words as "one who writes about a people." In the writing, we make decisions about the story we will tell—how the tale will be made theoretically interesting, what questions we will engage with our work, and what aspects of our research will be presented and what will be set aside. Through this process, lived research and the experiences that accompany it are represented and mediated by text. In a very real sense, the ethnographer may be profitably understood as a storyteller.

The position of storyteller, however, is a privileged one. The "voice" the teller adopts influences what is emphasized within a setting, who is heard from a community, and correspondingly what themes are silenced or neglected. As we go about the work of moving from our field settings to our textual representations of our "data," we are engaged in a process of re-presentation. Writing is social. It is reflexive, audience attentive, and negotiated. As an author, the ethnographer is somewhat uniquely positioned. The ethnographer often seeks to represent the worldview of his or her informants while writing for an audience that is, for the most part, composed of those outside the community studied. How then do we move from the socially constructed realities of field settings (in which, as has been shown earlier in this volume, our respondents may view a religious leader as the Messiah, attribute efficacy to magic in examination settings, and construct an identity in light of the rhetoric of codependency) to our sociological constructs of everyday life?

Chapter 11 takes up this general problem by examining the problematics of presenting the nonrationalist discourse of practitioners of earth-centered religions in the context of a rationalized, sociological discourse. Much like the social world that it seeks to portray, ethnographic writing is "home" to multiple realities—the truths of our informants, the truths of the ethnographer's experience, and the disciplinary truths of concept and theory. Although the disjunctions between these realities may be pronounced (e.g., these may be competing discourses), the ethnographer should feel no obligation to serve as an arbiter of truth claims—relegating one set of claims to the category of the wrong-headed, confused, or misguided while championing alternate positions. Our understanding of the social world as a socially constructed, intersubjective reality can be articulated without doing violence to the worldviews of our respondents.

As Charmaz (Chapter 12, p. 239) writes, "I contend the writer's presented images must resemble the experience. . . . [E]thnographers must strive to represent their subjects' understandings as well as their own." The point of departure and the point of return for ethnographic writing is the world of experience that we seek to represent. Our reflections of the social world rest on our ability to convey our experiences textually. Chapter 12 addresses this problem by examining strategies and practices for "turning research tales into written stories." This is accomplished by examining one such story as writing and reflecting on the provisional and tentative quality of all the stories we choose to tell.

As the reader moves between these two chapters, I encourage an attentiveness to the following generic themes:

■ The multiplicity of perspectives found within ethnographic writing

■ Managing the disjunction between competing discourses

■ The relationship between what is written and the willingness of various audiences, including informants, to accept the ethnographer's claims

▨ Issues regarding the move from experience to text

▨ The various commitments that distinguish the ethnographic story-teller from other authors

▨ The problem of attending to multiple audiences

▨ The qualities of ethnographic writing as "good writing"

11

Presenting Constructions of Identity and Divinity

Ásatrú and Oracular Seidhr

JENNY BLAIN

This chapter is an exploration of (a) how practitioners of an earth-centered religion (Ásatrú) make sense of their social and physical worlds; (b) the narratives they draw on; and (c) how they construct identity for themselves, their groups, and communities. Describing and exploring this material is, as I intend to show, neither straightforward nor simple. Practitioners' discourse sometimes draws on concepts that, to a Western rationalist audience, may seem strange, weird, amusing, irritating, frightening, distracting, or confusing. Conventionally, anthropologists and sociologists have tended to overlook such material, looking instead for explanations of what particular kinds of belief do for social groups—couched as social cohesion, fragmentation, domination, or resistance, depending on the sociologist's point of view. Some social scientists, however, are now reconsidering how we can present, and understand, experiential accounts of events that appear to lie outside the everyday reality of the Western world.

An increasing number of people in Europe and North America are drawn toward earth-centered ("alternative" or "pagan") religions. Many practitioners, particularly within the Women's Spirituality Movement, state that they look primarily to "ancient" religions and practices as suggested by archeological findings from the Bronze Age, neolithic, or even palaeolithic. Another group relates its beliefs and practices specifically to mythologies and mythological texts[1] and archeological findings from Western Europe in a period of approximately 1,000 years, from the 4th to the 14th centuries of the Common Era (CE). Others may gather information on particular deities without being historically, geographically, or temporally specific about practices. A publishing industry has appeared to cater to these markets, and a wealth of books on gods, myths, runes, magic, and practices (documented, speculative, or imaginary) are readily available.

I have been interviewing practitioners, both directly and via the Internet, for the past 2 years, and this work continues. In my work, I draw on informants' accounts to examine how members of these groups locate their practice and their "selves" with respect to present-day narrative constructions of the past, mythologies, and cosmologies. Linked with this, and woven through their talk, are concepts and discourses of power, magic, feminism, and earth or environment. Although some of these concepts increasingly form part of today's sociological and anthropological analyses, others do not: Therein lies a problem. "Magic" and "communication with the gods" are counter to the rational and liberal discourses currently dominant in North America and Western Europe.[2] How can we understand informants' constructions unless we grant validity to the premises on which these constructions are built?

This is part of the methodological question of whose "truth" we express in our work and how we present and analyze it. In traditional "objective" social research, the observer is deemed to stand at an "Archimedean point" outside the reality that is observed and, from there, see or attempt to see what is really happening. Many researchers and theorists, however, have theorized the impossibility of finding or expressing absolute truth. Each of us, as a social scientist, is located by his or her circumstances of culture, gender, ethnicity, "race," and class, by belief, and by training and affiliation within the situation that we observe and the relations that exist between ourselves and those we observe. What we see and how we see it is, necessarily, subjectively constructed. For the academic researcher, that training necessarily includes immersion within rational and liberal discourse, with its attendant concept of a "scientific" explanation for all occurrences. To understand what is happening from the point of view of my informants, however, I must both see as they do and then examine how their account emerges, discursively, from their social relations of practice and the circumstances of their lives.

Knowing the Other

This problem is not, of course, unique to "exotic" rituals or belief-linked practices or even to religions. Rather, the situation I examine can be seen as a specific case of the old problem of understanding the experiences of the "other," which faces every ethnographer. Even if the other is our best friend, that other has an emotional and cognitive life to which we can have access only through interpreting their practices, including signitive or symbolic practices, in terms of the socially constructed intersubjective reality we consider we share with them. Stated simply, we seek in our everyday lives, as well as in our research, to understand the meanings and locations of those around us by watching what they do and listening to what they say and assuming that the meanings of their practices and talk are similar to our own.

The anthropologist or sociologist, however, works in the knowledge that these meanings may not be our own. How, then, does one proceed? Anthropological literature is rife with instances in which the informants treat the anthropologist as one who does not, or cannot, know "what's what." Anthropologists have written humorous tales of their own initial failure to comprehend that there was a difference in perception. Schutz (1967) long since conceptualized the dilemma as a problem of lining up the researcher's stream of consciousness with that of the people observed: easier to state than to do. Dorothy Smith (1987) has discussed the possible distance between perceptions and meanings of social researchers and those of informants. In examining her own experiences, she found a gulf between the conventional sociological descriptions of women's lives and the experiences and perceptions—voiced, unvoiced, or possibly unvoicable—of the women living those lives. She speaks of viewing her own experiences through both a participant's and a sociologist's eyes, describing this as "bifurcation of consciousness." From this dual positioning, she commenced her project of laying the foundations of a sociology for women. The project was not only to describe and analyze women's everyday perceptions of the processes surrounding and constituting the physical, structural, economic, and political "realities" of women's lives but to validate these perceptions.

Others have discussed how orthodox social psychology relies on the concept of a unitary, "male, European, rational individual" whose behavior is studied and analyzed (Venn, 1984, p. 130). "Rationality" here speaks to a particular type of thinking, in which cause and effect are ordered temporarily, causation is subject to proof, and decisions follow careful weighing of choices in terms of costs and benefits (each of these being subject to proof). Tambiah (1990) has pointed to the cultural specificity and historical construction of such rationality, today used in conjunction with the concept of "individual." In other words, many human cultural pursuits occur within frameworks of analysis that employ different concepts, and Western concepts of people (or of their deities and religions) do not always permit interpretation or understanding of others' systems of behavior or belief. I return to the question of studying religion—any religion, but especially one that is nonmainstream and hence seen as exotic—and having difficulty expressing what it is that participants find meaningful because their discourse is not that of conventional rationalist thought.

Research on Earth-Centered Belief and Meaning

Relatively few researchers within anthropology or sociology have turned their attention to the phenomenon of present-day paganism and its construction. Earth-centered spirituality has been treated cursorily by most mainstream sociologists of religion.

Some interesting studies do exist, such as Jon Bloch's (1994) work on narrative strategies of members of "countercultural" religious groups in the United States or Luhrmann's (1989) *Persuasions of the Witch's Craft*, an exploratory ethnography of several neopagan groups in Britain. Neitz (1994) examines similarities and differences in meanings of Dianic and neopagan wiccans. Some research has focused specifically on wicce, or Dianic witchcraft. Thus, in a literature review, Luff (1990) pursues connections between wicce and feminism, whereas Finley (1991) explores links between spirituality and feminist politics in her study of participants in an annual conference of Dianic witches. Lozano and Foltz (1990) explore how feminist Dianic wicca constitutes a framework for the construction of meaning during the occasion of the funeral of a group member's father. Luhrmann (1993) implies that beliefs and practices of feminist spirituality may often have the effect of structuring gender processes in ways that empower, rather than disempower, women. Here, a strong link with earth and environmental concerns becomes apparent. Luhrmann describes images and symbolic constructions of the pagan goddess not only as mother but also as a young woman independent of males and as a destructive "crone" figure. Within feminist pagan discourse, the words "hag" and "crone" convey power. Griffin (1995) focuses on how Dianic witches use symbols, images, and consciously created myths to redefine women and power and to construct a feminist understanding of the relations of people to their world.

The pagan communities within North America and Europe, however, include many people, both women and men, who are neither Dianic nor wiccan. Other constituent groups found in Canada include Ásatrú, various groups that attempt to reconstruct beliefs and practices of Celtic or Eastern European religious origins, and goddess worshippers and women's spirituality groups. Within the United Kingdom, some of these groups have been described by Harvey (1996). It would appear that little scholarly work has been carried out on narrative and the construction of meaning, self, and identity within non-wiccan groups. Furthermore, those studies that do have a bearing on the discourse of wiccan groups have, for the most part, been specific to particular small groups observed by researchers. There is a lack of studies of how people insert themselves into the public narratives of earth-centered religions, how these discourses are spread and modified, to what extent they are shared generally across neopagan groups, or how practitioners use them in constructing their identities as members of earth-centered religions. In my own work, I have attempted to consider narratives of empowerment and earth. This chapter focuses on narratives of belief, and of deities, as presented by members of one particular reconstructionist religion.

Pagan Spiritual Reconstruction

I intend to demonstrate that to achieve an understanding of practice that is more than merely superficial, researchers need to treat what their informants say seriously. A focus for this chapter, therefore, is on my informants' use of narratives of history, prehistory, and mythology in constructing accounts of their spiritual practices and their everyday religious or spiritual life.

Narratives of paganism in the Middle Ages or ancient goddess worship not only establish authenticity, precedents for practices, and status for group members but also provide individuals and groups with ways in which they relate discursively to goddesses, gods, or earth. Perceptions of pagan religions going back even to the paleolithic provide reference points for identification and credentialing of not only group and individual practices and organization but also cosmologies and mythologies.

I differentiate three major sets of narratives. First, accounts of an unbroken chain of practice disrupted and driven underground by the period of witch burnings. These accounts are now possibly less favored then they were during the 1980s. Second, accounts of practices as modern and created deliberately and eclectically but derived from, influenced by, and possibly including survivals of early practices. This group of narratives includes accounts constructed from interpretations of (now somewhat rethought and modified) archeological findings, such as Gimbutas's concept of "Old Europe." Third, deliberate reconstructions, although within a modern context, of such practices in surviving documents, generally written during the Middle Ages, in which Celtic or Norse mythologies are detailed.

For the purposes of this chapter, I concentrate my attention on the third category. This chapter, although constituting an elaboration and expansion of earlier work describing reconstructionist groups (Blain, 1996), also gives the opportunity for a detailed investigation of how one reconstructionist uses narratives of "the gods" in her self-definitions within the context of an interview.

The expressed aim of reconstructionist groups is not usually to re-create pagan society or ritual exactly as it was but to use sources from the past to aid in the creation of religious, spiritual, and ritual structures that suit the present day. Although there are reconstructionist groups that trace cultural links to religions of many parts of the world, the groups to which I have most access look to northern Europe, to previous Celtic or Germanic peoples, for their sources of information. They draw on evidence from both archeology and literature and engage in lengthy debates over the interpretation of particular passages of ancient material and how these shed light on their spiritual ancestors' concept of soul and spirit, religious practice, or indeed attitudes to questions that concern present-day people (such as child rearing, education, individualism, gun control, or the welfare state). All the reconstructionists I have met or spoken with are relatively well-read, regardless of their level of formal education.

Reconstructionists, then, are attempting to uncover previous rituals, philosophies, and theologies and to adapt these to a present-day setting, creating religious philosophy and practice that they consider appropriate. They generally define themselves as belonging to specific faiths relating to culturally specific gods.[3] Several organizations exist, in North America, Europe, and elsewhere, whose objectives are not only to bring together like-minded people to practice religion but also to conduct the necessary background research to expand such practice. Not all reconstructionists are members of these organizations—indeed, the majority are probably not members—although many may belong to local groups affiliated with national or international organizations.[4]

One problem shared by reconstructionists is that there are few accounts of how their spiritual ancestors actually did worship, what they believed, or how their religious practices fitted in with their daily lives.[5] Most accounts of Celtic mythology, moreover, come from the pens of Christianized scribes, and available accounts may have gone through repeated copying and recopying by people who had little understanding of their contents and who perhaps engaged in substitutions that appeared to make more sense to the scribes, as Ford (1977) suggests may have occurred in the third branch of the Mabinogi. In the case of Germanic reconstructionists, the same problem arises, but because the Scandinavian countries and Iceland were Christianized relatively late in the Middle Ages, there is less distance between the writers and the events they describe. Many of the practitioners of Ásatrú acknowledge a debt in particular to the Icelandic scholar and poet Snorri Sturlusson (1179-1241), who preserved much of the material, both mythological and historical, although in a somewhat Christianized form.

A Reconstructionist Religion: Ásatrú

> Very generally, Ásatrú is "faith in the Aesir" . . . the pre-Christian deities of the northern European peoples. The beliefs and ceremonies of Ásatrú are found in Icelandic and Germanic sagas, and Eddic poetry. (L. Eirarson, personal communication, February 6, 1996)[6]

Laeknir Eirarson is an *Ásatrúarmadhr* (a practitioner of Ásatrú) of several years standing. He now works with a local group, known as a kindred. He explains (personal communication, February 6, 1996),

> I hunted for this religion since youth. Some have labeled my path "Icelandic Ásatrú," which in a sense indicates a "purity" or exclusiveness to Ásatrú. There are many different forms of Norse paganism, and "Icelandic Ásatrú" generally means that the ceremonies are based specifically on what has been found in the Icelandic sagas. This can seem a little restrictive to some. The ceremonies involved with Norse wicca, for instance, are somewhat different than those in traditional or Icelandic Ásatrú.

Laeknir Eirarson traces the roots of his practices to the Icelandic sagas and Eddas. Some others make use of Old English sources or use forms of words (e.g., the names of gods) from continental Europe. One writer for this community, Freya Aswynn, draws on forms and folk practices from The Netherlands, her country of origin. Laeknir Eirarson (personal communication, February 6, 1996) elaborates:

> The Eddas, especially, and many of the Icelandic sagas . . . tell us not only about the mythology, but also about the mind-set and feelings of the ancients. They differed in many ways from modern folk, and learning to understand how they felt gives us a good insight into how they felt about and approached the gods in daily life. Eyrbyggja saga,[7] for instance, is one of the key sagas for understanding Ásatrú faith. It holds one of the very few references to

what religious ceremonies were like. In reconstruction of these for the modern day, we do have to be careful about Christian influence (or any other influence), however. Eyrbyggja saga is one that may be tainted with non-Ásatrú beliefs, but it provides insight into the religion of our ancestors.

Many Ásatrúar folk speak of finding a religion that seemed to them to have some historical basis. They could point to historical figures, or scholars' accounts of the daily lives of ordinary people, and feel kinship. One book often mentioned by my informants is *Our Troth* (Gundarsson, 1993), published privately by the Ring of Troth, an international Ásatrú organization. This includes work on the history, religion, and philosophies of Germanic peoples in addition to accounts of present-day practices. The book includes work by academics, notably Stephan Grundy, incorporating extracts from his PhD thesis, titled *The Cult of Óðhinn, God of Death* (1995), and many of its authors draw on sources such as Ellis's (1968) *The Road to Hel* and Turville-Petre's (1975) *Myth and Religion of the North*.[8]

Most of the Ásatrú practitioners interviewed make use of runes,[9] using the 24-rune Elder futhark, the Norwegian, Danish, or Icelandic 16-rune younger futhark, or the Anglo-Saxon 33-rune futhorc. Reconstructionist books on runes usually begin with some account of their history, with reference to academic works such as that of Elliott (1959). Not all Ásatrúar (Ásatrú practitioner) use runes for divination; some maintain that there is no historical evidence for their use in this manner. Many do use runes, however, maintaining that a reconstructionist religion must adapt to the present day, and that the insights of its members, as long as they are identified as such, form an important part of their practices.

Nuallë (personal communication, February 5, 1996) another Ásatrúar, explains what it means to her to be a reconstructionist:

By "reconstructionist" I mean that I try by scholarly study to put together an understanding of the ways that those who historically worshipped the gods I worship lived and practiced their worship. I then try to live and practice in the same ways, so far as that is possible and/or feasible while living in the real near-21st-century-CE world.

Although a decade ago the overwhelming majority of Ásatrúar were male, an increasing number of women appear to be attracted to this set of practices and beliefs. The image of Ásatrú as the religion of male "Vikings" who were raiders and pillagers is diminishing, and although it still attracts many (men and women) as "warriors," other practitioners identify with the farmers, weavers, spinners, or poets of the past. My women informants, and some men, emphasize the importance granted women by many heathen Germanic peoples, and that several notable personages whose names have come down to us were women—for example, Queen Sigrídhr, who, after Óláf Tryggvason of Norway called her a "heathen bitch," organized the coalition that brought about his defeat and death. Books such as Gundarsson's *Our Troth* (1993) and *Teutonic Magic* (1990) emphasize that although the extant literature speaks chiefly of the deeds of the gods, according to Snorri (1987, p. 21), "No less holy are the Ásynjur, nor is their power less."

The question arises as to why people would feel drawn to a religion as obscure (in terms of the numbers of its adherents) as Ásatrú. Nuallë (personal communication, February 5, 1996) addresses the point of what her religion and spirituality does for her as an individual and as a member of a spiritual community:

> They (religion and spirituality) provide me a context in which I can deal in the universe with a set of spiritual paradigms that fit me, with gods and wights [other beings] who can do things I cannot— and also with needs that I am better suited than they to fill. They provide a framework in which I feel I am free and encouraged to develop into *myself*, rather than expected to conform to some "objective ideal." My religion provides me with several other people with whom I can share ideas and experiences, debate points of cosmology, and otherwise build a social and intellectual life, based on spiritual principles the same or much similar to my own.

For a more elaborate answer, and for a consideration of the gods and how they appear within this religion, I present a detailed consideration of one interview that was conducted at a festival held in Kansas at midsummer.

The Religion of One Reconstructionist

Winifred is a biologist, specifically an ecologist, who vowed herself to the service of the earth while, as she states, she was still Christian. Religion has always been important to her, and for a long time she was a devout Christian, training as an oblate at an Anglican monastery. She became increasingly dissatisfied, however, with certain philosophical principles and particularly with a lack of female influences or deities with whom to identify. She left Christianity, returned to it again, and then experimented with many different religious philosophies before finding Heathenism (her favored term), although, somewhat atypically, she did not espouse any other pagan religions before Heathenism. Winifred describes her religion as "The basic, um, description of following the gods and goddesses of, the Ases and the Wanes [the Old Gods of northern Europe], along with a whole cultural and philosophical context that goes with it."

Her religion provides her with community: a sense of belonging. She sees family and community at the heart of Heathenism in the old days and potentially also in the present. She had previously had experience entering into a close-knit community through marriage into a Greek family. She stated,

I lived 17 years in Greece, and was married to a Greek man and brought my children up there. And being part of a Greek tribe, a large tribe of people, I'm very much still with a tribal culture in mind, which I think was a very good preparation for plunging right into Heathen, uh, philosophy about the meaningfulness of tribes and kinships and so on. I mean coming as a foreigner into there was very much like . . . women of ancient times would have gone into strange kindreds and having to adjust to their ways and having to . . . and willingly so, except that no matter what frictions and disagreements might come about between me and individual members of my in-laws, nevertheless we were committed to one another, we belonged to one another, and my children belong to them as much as they belong to me. And that's a philosophy that as I say that I've carried over to Heathenism and I feel that I perhaps that I have more of a chance to live it than many Americans have. So that's very valuable.

Indeed, one strand to Winifred's move to Heathenism comes from her feeling of belonging, of having cultural roots, which was not recognized by Christianity:

> In fact it was something that a Jewish friend said to me, because he was describing a trip to the holy land, and he said, he said "This will really interest you, to tell you about what I saw in Jerusalem," and so forth. And I remember looking at him in a very startled way and thinking, "Why would he think that would interest me?" And then realizing, oh of course he would think so, I'm a Christian and he thought I would like to hear about that. And so that led me to question myself. Oh, if I don't feel any connection with the holy land, what is it that's important to me about Christianity? And I realized that all the images I had and that I related to were of northern Europe, of monasteries and traditions and customs and everything, and that the more I looked into all of those things the more I realized then they had Heathen roots.

An even stronger strand, however, came from philosophical approaches, her religious studies,

> and also the wish to move into a polytheistic religion, because I have always had trouble with the idea of monotheistic religions. I think polytheistic is much closer to reality as I see it anyway, and then of course that made room for the feminine principle that I was looking for also. But I still didn't know at that point that there were modern Heathens, that gathered, but fortunately I was able to find some of these books that came out in the late 80s and early 90s, um, and was very impressed and was definitely seriously considering it, but what finally tipped the balance was reading Bauschatz' *The Well and the Tree*, and his explication of the philosophy of how reality with the, with Wyrd, you know, coming out of the layers of the well, coming up into the tree, dripping down after life, life had formed the deeds. . . . I mean I've studied I think all of the major religious and philosophical systems with, with great interest and having learned and gained from doing so, but none of them did I feel really described reality the way I see it. And this did.

Winifred speaks of seeing the world and its Wyrd or fate in terms of complexity and in terms of different levels of being, which for her stem from the well of Wyrd. The tree she speaks of is the World Tree, Yggdrasil, on whose branches the various worlds have their being and whose roots dip into the well. The Old Gods, in this formulation, are themselves subject to Wyrd, or fate, and yet at times appear to be manipulating it or setting it in motion. She repeatedly returns in her talk to images of complexity:

> Again, I think, first of all I see, I see, by reality I mean everything that, that exists and not just physical, physical reality. I see it, um, as something very complex, with many layers. Other times I see it as like a fractal image, where whether you look at a large piece or a small piece the pattern's the same, and yet there's uniquenesses about each one of those. So that um, and I think these layers or patterns can easily contradict and conflict with one another, and yet they're all true. But they're true at different levels, and in order to understand, to understand that . . .
>
> It's essential when judging rightness and wrongness, goodness and badness, wisdom and lack of wisdom, whatever, to find the right layers, and there may be several of them that one has to look at, and that somehow integrate the knowledge that one finds in, and that's where the image of the well and the tree comes in, as being so useful. And why I was so thrilled to find a philosophy that allowed for that, because all the other philosophies it seemed as though there was a single truth and that the task of philosophy was to find this single truth.

Winifred is a practitioner of spae working, also known as oracular seidhr, in which a seeress enters a trance state to draw on "the well" to explore possibilities. In this state, she speaks with spirits and deities, although usually, she says, she does not hear words directly, dealing rather with images, emotions, and sensations:

> In my spae work and my images of a cosmos and how it functions, I see a well with layers in it and again I often use the images of fractals and I sometimes use pictures of those as religious, not so much religious but again contexts, in which to think about all of these things.

Winifred's Narratives of the Elder Gods

Many followers of Ásatrú ground their concepts of deity in the old literature, the Icelandic Eddas and sagas. Others prefer to rely on their intuitions, on what "comes to them," although usually they specify that these are personal and pertain only to themselves. Nonetheless, most follow similar patterns of ritual, and most will, if pushed, seek to trace back their practices to eddas and sagas. Several practitioners, including Winifred, seek to further knowledge of the older practices, and adapt them to the present day, by expanding them through knowledge gained through meditation, trance, spae working, and other "journeying." Winifred speaks of her deities as beings who engage in interactions and form relationships, as do people, with whom she has acquaintance and whose wishes she endeavors to interpret.

Throughout her discourse, Winifred makes reference to the Old Gods of northern Europe, the Ases and Wanes (Aesir and Vanir). She speaks of being particularly close to three of them: Frige (Frigga), Thunor (Thor) and Ing Frea (Freyr). She prefers the Old English form of their names; she speaks Old English and uses this language in her ritual work and in some of the poetry and songs she writes. She speaks of her deities as powerful beings who can help her and whom she in turn can assist. She addresses them in ritual work and in spae workings. She makes it known, however, that religion and spirituality are not set apart from the rest of her life:

> It runs a spectrum between, from applying part of my mind and soul to that while I'm doing something else in an effort to bring the spiritual dimension into the work that I'm doing, all the way to, you know, totally immersing myself in the spirituality, and everything in between there. . . . And before I sleep at night, and . . . when I wake up in the morning, again I don't do any rituals or anything but I just try to put my mind and heart with, with the gods and goddesses . . . poetic prayers rather than a ritual or a symbol. . . . I don't really differentiate well now I'm being spiritual and now I'm not being spiritual.

She sees each deity as having her or his own area of influence or attributes but with some overlap. These are complex entities, described by other Ásatrúar as "elder kin" rather than archetypes. Winifred states,

> Frige, it seems while there's love and warmth between us and I've had very spiritual experiences with her, on the whole our relationship is almost one of a business partnership. She has work she wants me to do, she is very clear about it, very definite, and she, uh, gives me the resources to get it done.
>
> So, so Frige is really my Lady in a sense of being sworn to her service, although I have not taken any oaths to her specifically, because I feel that with her and with any of the gods and goddesses that it may very well be that at different parts in my life I will be called by different gods to their service . . . she has my love and my work, but there's no reason I might not turn at a later time to another, and serve them in the same way.
>
> With Ing Frea . . . he asks very little from me, and instead he gives me, he gives me love and peace and companionship and he's, he's who I go to . . . to get away from everything and be renewed and refreshed and reminded about [laughs] what life is like when you're not busy all the time . . . and a lot of my music, my songs are for him, even if they're not about him they're gifts to him.
>
> And then Thunor . . . after his offering of gifts to Frigga's Web, in a sense he offered the same, the same thing to me, he offered to husband me, not in the sense of, of the full relationship of a husband, but rather the sense of husbanding your resources, and he said that he could help me use all of my strength, and abilities wisely, and not overuse them or put them in directions that would be less fruitful than other directions. And it had never occurred to me until he offered that, that I might need such a thing or might want to have it offered to me. And, but I could tell by how deeply I was moved on receiving that offer that, that I guess I did need it and I didn't realize, didn't realize it. And I feel different now, I feel that I have um, I have someone standing behind me, in the place that was empty before. . . . And also this offering put him in a new light to me, because I had not thought of him before as a husband-man, but as the supporter of farmers, and I mean that's what they do, that's what they have to do and they have to husband their resources wisely, and so forth, so it's opened up a new door into who, who Thunor is and what his powers are. That I think is very special, and that connects with Frige because I see her also as the patron of managers and administrators and government officials

and so on because of her excellent organizational abilities. And Thunor pointed out that he and Frige are sisters, are siblings through their mother, and that he supports her work, she is his queen and he defends her and her work.

The mother of both Thunor and Frige is earth, and Winifred points out that her chosen deities are earth deities, which fits with her work as an ecologist and her sense of herself as one who defends earth. In her discourse, the gods of the Elder Troth have distinct, many-faceted personalities. Her concepts of them come from mythology and folklore and also from her own trance visions.

Presenting Ásatrú:
Problems of Voice and "Truth"

So far, I have attempted to present Ásatrú by briefly examining some components of its discourse and narrative and giving examples from the talk of participants, notably Winifred. One way to analyze this material is by adopting a narrative perspective. Some interesting strands emerge within this talk, public narratives within the community, that can be described as follows:

1. References are made to myths and stories of the Aesir and Vanir, for instance, to explain the characteristics or personalities of the gods. Winifred, and other followers of Ásatrú, indexes specific pieces of what is referred to as "the lore." Knowledge of this material forms a backdrop to ritual and other events and to discussion.

2. There is a concept of polytheism (as distinct from monotheism or duotheism or a Jungian discussion of "archetypes"). The gods are, in Winifred's formulation and that of other followers of Ásatrú I have met, real entities, separate and distinct, with rounded personalities and are different from, for instance, Celtic, Greek, or Native American beings or deities.

3. There is a sense of cultural specificity. Blot and Sumbel, the ritual forms of Ásatrú, are spoken of as suitable ways to worship or honor the Aesir and Vanir and as distinct in kind from, for example, a wiccan circle. Again, they are drawn from the lore.

4. There is a possibility of direct communication with these beings, to both speak with them and gain various forms of knowledge.

5. There is manipulation of consciousness or "reality" by them or through magic inspired by them—in Winifred's case, approaching them through spae working or "seidhr." Not all Ásatrú folk practice seidhr or attend sessions, but it is growing in its following. The practice of spaecraft is referenced in the lore, for instance, in the saga of Eirik the Red. More Ásatrú folk engage in rune divination or rune magic.

6. There is a sense that spirituality is not separate from everyday life but rather informs it. Many Ásatrú folk place a high value on skills of daily living that are mentioned in the lore or known from archeology or from later folk practices—for example, woodcraft, fibercrafts, smithcrafts, and brewing. A craft fair is an important part of an Ásatrú gathering, and Winifred is a skilled craftswoman who also brings her spirituality to her paid employment as a government biologist.

7. There is a sense of individual merit combined with community worth. This goes hand in hand with an elaborate concept of "soul" and "self," which is currently being explored by some Ásatrú researchers—with reference, once again, to the lore.

By examining these strands within the discourse of individual Ásatrú practitioners, we can see how a collective process of identity construction is at work. People interpret their experiences discursively, creating definitions of experience and self. Empowerment results from Winifred's self-definition as Ásatrú, as a strong woman, and as one who will act to defend earth.

We can, however, raise a further set of questions as to the experiences that are interpreted. In a conference discussion I recently attended,[10] a participant spoke of Christian women she had studied as being in "dialogue with God." This led to disagreement among members as to whether they were "truly" describing "dialogue," which, after all, requires two participants. Some members considered these women to be participating in reflective processes but not engaged in dialogue. My interviews with Ásatrú practitioners, however, indicated that the practitioners considered that they were indeed in communication with beings, spirits, or energy forms who were distinct from themselves, although some practitioners admitted to having Western "rationalist" doubts about this.

Both anthropologists and the general public have exhibited a curious double standard about explanations of nonordinary phenomena. An account by Roderick Wilson (1994) provides an example. He tells how he had arranged for "a spiritually active young Cree" to speak to one of his classes, addressing basic concepts of Cree religion, meanings, and symbols. Later, Wilson used this talk

> as a springboard for analytic comment. One of my major points was that such belief systems are not static because practices such as shamanic healing have a pragmatic, experiential base. That is, the shaman does not blindly follow a predetermined formula, but continues to do that which works, and rejects or modifies that which does not work. At this point, most of the class (which had given the Cree lecturer rapt attention) registered widespread disbelief. They simply were not willing to accept shamanism as having any kind of even quasi-experimental or semiscientific basis. (p. 201)

When a belief or experience appears as the product of a "traditional" culture, many people will respect it—not as truth but as a cultural production, often seen as exotic and interesting. When the Western, or Westernized, professor produces similar arguments, these are irrational. Wilson (1994, p. 201) stated, "This 'respect' is frequently the product of a relativism rooted in ethnocentrism: 'I can respect your beliefs and practices because they are totally other, and so do not touch me and my experience.' "

Ásatrú perceptions and experiences may not be accorded the same validity, in the eyes of the public, as those coming from Aboriginal informants. Ásatrú practitioners are, after all, mainly of European descent and should accordingly follow the dictates of Western rationalism, according to this double standard. In the words of a student–journalist who recorded a blot I attended, they run the risk of being viewed by the general public as "a little bit, well, hokey." She was speaking merely of the concept of addressing deities (other, that was, than Judeo–Christian deities) in ritual. Although this is as far as many people's practices go, others, as mentioned previously, venture further from rationalism through meditation, journeying, or spae working.

Watching Winifred, and others, perform spae working is an extraordinary experience.[11] First, there is scene setting—drawing a circle, calling for its protection by Landspirits and other entities, or, as in the first session I observed, chanting the runes of the elder futhark—followed by invocation of those deities who themselves perform spae working. When these preliminaries are finished, the leader creates, through singing, drumming, and guided meditation, a state in which all present enter a light trance. The seeress, however, goes further, entering realms where the others do not follow, to seek answers to their questions. The questioning takes a form found in the Eddic poem Völuspé:

> . . . through worlds have I wandered,
> seeking the seeress whom now I summon . . .
> Cease not seeress, 'till said thou hast,
> answer the asker 'till all (s)he knows . . .

Within this highly charged setting, the seer or seeress indeed produces answers that do make sense to the questioners. According to experienced spae workers, the accuracy or precision of the answer is directly proportional to the emotional involvement of the one who asks a question. For those who do this work, the experience can be very special. In the following, Winifred describes the first time she did spae working:

> The moment when I stepped up to the high seat for the first time and sat down in it and put the veil over my head and they started singing for me, what I felt then was that I had been walking my entire life to reach that one moment. So it was like, it's really like a vocation for me, that's calling me. And all the different paths have come together in that.

She speaks of it as being her contribution to the Ásatrú community—a way that she can assist her deities and her people. Those who have derived the modern practice of spae working from old accounts have also drawn on present-day shamanic practices of

Aboriginal religions. Writer Diana Paxson, who has done consider-able work in this area and derived much of the form most often used for oracular seidhr, described the following key event, occurring within nonordinary reality, during a shamanic workshop run by Michael Harner:[12]

> *I am walking through a gray land . . . a world of gray mist that swirls among mighty stones. The raven flies ahead of me, not dear . . . but bril-liant as the image of the sun against closed eyelids, bright/dark/bright wings against the shadowed stones.*
>
> *"Where are you taking me?" I ask, and try to go faster.*[13]
>
> *I was aware of faint sounds from the world that I had left behind me, but wrapped in my gray cloak, I was insulated from both the noises and the chill of the building where the workshop was being held. Long practice helped me control my breathing and sink back into trance, to trust myself to Michael Harner's steady drumming and let it thrust me into the vision again.*
>
> *The stones stand like pylons to either side, their rough surfaces in-scribed with scratches whose meaning has been worn away by the winds of countless years. The raven alights on one of them, wings twitching impatiently. Clearly, she considers me rather stupid, but so far she has always waited for me to catch up again.*
>
> *"You asked for a teacher" she tells me. "That's where I'm taking you."*
>
> *I don't argue. I would never have dared to claim a raven as an ally. Especially not this one, this grandmother of ravens, whose tongue is as sharp as her pointed beak. But I thought that she was going to teach me what I want to know.*

Ms. Paxson adds, in her commentary, that she analyzed the process even as she experienced this shamanic "journey." As a westerner, she had learned to separate personal experience from scientific "textbook knowledge" and to discount the former. She was also suspicious because of her knowledge of ravens in both Native and European mythology and what they implied. She stated,

> When I sought a power animal in the underworld, I understood the significance of the raven who came to me. But just because I recog-nized her, it was easy to suspect myself of wishful thinking. . . . If I had been inventing an ally for a character in one of my novels, I might have chosen a raven. That too, was a reason to doubt what I

was hearing. I know that I can make up stories. Was I inventing this one now?

"Did anybody ever tell you that you think too much? Shut up and come along!"

The dilemma faced by sociologists and anthropologists in presenting and analyzing this material is not unlike Ms. Paxson's own. If we put the experience down to "invention," we immediately declare ourselves on the side of the rationalists, and by so doing limit the analytical possibilities open to us and the ways we can understand how informants and practitioners of alternative spiritualities interact with their world.

Goulet and Young (1994) speak of such extraordinary experiences in terms of multiple realities. Within one reality mode, so to speak, we construct experience and meaning by attending to sets of symbols and sensations that within another reality mode would go unchecked. As we shift modes, new possibilities become apparent, and old ones disappear. Ms. Paxson's commentary on her experience illustrates this point. By her account, she had to work rather hard to prevent her rationalist preconceptions from disrupting her journey; and the subsequent events involving finding her teacher led her to consider that she was not simply inventing a scenario.

Goulet and Young (1994) emphasize the need to take seriously the accounts of informants. To describe processes of construction of identity, as I am attempting to do, this is essential. This does not necessarily involve presenting the emic, or subjective insider account, and theorizing of practitioners as the only or literal truth. Most readers of this chapter are probably not Ásatrúar, although some may be. The need is for an account that readers will find interesting and that will assist them to follow my theorizing of discourse and identity. As a research fieldworker, I become a broker, attempting to create understandings between cultures or subcultures, even as I attempt to find ways of understanding identity formation. This task of brokering forms part of the research, a necessary component in attempting to represent "insider" meanings and translate these into a discourse that "outsiders" will find acceptable or comprehensible, and hence is concomitant to making a contribution to any theoretical discussion of identity formation.

In current social science, it is becoming more acceptable to present aspects of the world in ways that do not lay claim to "Truth." Postmodernist rejection of metanarrative opens possibilities for multiple analyses, in which contradiction does not invalidate insight. In other words, the ethnographer need not attempt to force observation into a single, scientific explanatory framework. The experience of seidhr is made comprehensible, for participants, by drawing on an Ásatrú worldview. Rather than attempt to rationalize the explanation, my preference is to examine its discursive construction and to pose questions about how engaging with this practice forms part of identity, in the knowledge that (a) participants themselves view identity as a complex matter and "self" as requiring both spiritual and sociopsychological theorizing and (b) the tradition of rejecting definitions of ultimate Truth is an honorable, although minority, one within the social sciences. The goal of research within interpretative and hermeneutic perspectives, as indicated by Winch (1958) and Taylor (1971/1982), has been not simply explanation but also understanding of meanings and how these form part of an individual's apparatus of perception of the social world. Recently, followers of social constructionist and narrative approaches, drawing on discourse theory, have begun to speak of competing discourses to understand not only individuals' construction of meaning and identity but also the social nature of self-perception and self-construction and how these in turn form part of the constitution of social relations within today's multicultural, multiethnic, and multifaith societies.

This concept of society as a series of complex interdependencies is reflected in the interviews themselves, and so I will leave the last word in this chapter to my chief informant, Winifred:

> I can't see where there's a single truth, I don't think . . . and it would bother me if that turned out to be [laughs] the way it really was. So in my spae work and my images of a cosmos and how it functions, I see a well with layers in it. . . . And weaving is another image of that too, creating the pattern out of empty space, brings it all together. And in terms of how the world began, you know I'm familiar with, with the myths, and . . . I don't feel that I have to pass judgment as to whether I literally believe them or not . . . so I'm just willing to let them be, be what they are and not, not decide literally

what happened. So I have those little images and those seem real to me. But I don't feel I need a consistent story about when did this start and exactly how did it happen and who did what, and what happened next. Um, it's fine to have this jumble, jumbled mess of pieces, out of which I pick meaningful pieces when I need that kind of knowledge, or whatever, and otherwise leave it be.

Notes

1. Examples include the *Mabinogi* or the Icelandic *Eddas*. The *Mabinogi* (or *Mabinogion*) is a collection of mythological stories from Wales, preserved in a medieval manuscript. The word *Edda* is used to refer to both the "Prose *Edda*" of Snorri Sturlusson, written approximately in the year 1200 and giving an account of the mythology of northern Europe, and the "Poetic *Edda*," a collection of poems made around the same time that incorporates older material. The two *Eddas* together form the basis of what is known about Norse mythology and cosmology.

2. In actuality, not all members of earth-centered religions use magic. They give reasons for their use or nonuse, and these vary with the faith or tradition and with the person's own perception of themselves. Magic, however, is defined by users in ways very different from the public perception of *Sabrina the Teenage Witch*—for instance, as attempts to concentrate thoroughly on what is important to the magic workers or as lining up one's conscious awareness with the natural world.

3. For the purpose of this chapter, these are the gods of the Celtic and Germanic peoples of Europe.

4. As with all categories of neopagans, acquiring numbers is an impractical task.

5. For example, much can be conjectured from the cyclical rhythms of the year.

6. Many people within the Heathen community choose names that reflect their spirituality. Several interviewees asked for their Heathen names to be used in publications resulting from this research project. Others are referred to by pseudonyms.

7. The Icelandic sagas are stories—part fiction and part history—of the early settlers of Iceland. *Eyrbyggja Saga* purports to trace the lives of settlers of a particular region from the late ninth to the early eleventh centuries. It was written approximately in the mid- to late thirteenth century, and so is itself a reconstruction (from a Christianized perspective) of earlier Heathen practices. It has the only account of a Heathen "Hof," or temple, although it is impossible to know the accuracy of this account or how much it reflected Christian imaginings of the older religion and its practices.

8. Although many use the term *Ásatrú*, some prefer other words, such as *Heathenry* or *Heathenism*, and others speak of the *Elder Troth*. In this chapter, these terms are used interchangeably.

9. Runes are letters or staves of any of the futharks (runic alphabets) used in northern Europe prior to the adoption of Latin script and chiefly found in inscriptions in Scandinavia, Orkney, and so on. For an account of the history and development of runic alphabets, see Elliott (1959). The most accessible introduction to their use in Ásatrú magic or religion is given by Gundarsson (1990). The word futhark means the same as alphabet and is derived from the sounds of the first six runic letters and their

representation by the present-day f-u-th-a-r-k. In the Anglo-Saxon runic alphabet, sound shifts and changes in letters have altered this to f-u-th-o-r-c.

10. This was at the Kentucky International Conference on Narrative, October 1996, where the talk forming the basis of the first part of this chapter was presented. The session referred to was a general discussion on theory of narrative.

11. I use these words deliberately and in the sense in which Young and Goulet (1994) subtitled their book *The Anthropology of Extraordinary Experience.*

12. Harner is the author of *The Way of the Shaman* (1982) and founder of the Institute for Shamanic Studies.

13. These extracts are from an essay on this experience that Ms. Paxson sent me in response to a request for information. The account, with its commentary, was prepared in 1989 for the magazine *Shaman's Drum.* Used with permission.

References

Blain, J. (1996, March). *Witchcraft, magic and religion: Some discursive reconstructions of belief and practice.* Paper presented at The Middle Ages in Contemporary Popular Culture, McMaster University, Hamilton, Ontario, Canada.

Bloch, J. P. (1994). Coherence strategies in spiritual life stories of countercultural spiritualists. In J. Knuf (Ed.), *Texts and identities; The third Kentucky conference on narrative: Studies on language and narrative* (pp. 62-74). Lexington: University of Kentucky Press.

Elliott, R. W. V. (1959). *Runes.* Manchester, UK: Manchester University Press.

Ellis, H. R. (1968). *The road to hel: A study of the conception of the dead in old Norse literature.* New York: Greenwood.

Finley, N. J. (1991). Political activism and feminist spirituality. *Sociological Analysis, 52,* 349-362.

Ford, P. (1977). *The Mabinogi.* Berkeley: University of California Press.

Goulet, J. G., & Young, D. (1994). Theoretical and methodological issues. In D. E. Young & J. G. Goulet (Eds.), *Being changed by cross-cultural encounters: The anthropology of extraordinary experience.* Peterborough, Ontario, Canada: Broadview.

Griffin, W. (1995). The embodied goddess: Feminist witchcraft and female divinity. *Sociology of Religion, 56,* 35-48.

Grundy, S. S. (1995). *The cult of Óðhinn, God of Death.* Unpublished PhD thesis, University of Cambridge, Cambridge, UK.

Gundarsson, K. (1990). *Teutonic magic.* St. Paul, MN: Llewellyn.

Gundarsson, K. (1993). *Our troth* (R. Hagan, Ed.). Seattle: The Ring of Troth.

Harner, M. (1982). *The way of the shaman.* New York: Bantam.

Harvey, G. (Ed.). (1996). *Paganism today.* London: Thorsons.

Lozano, W. G., & Foltz, T. G. (1990). Into the darkness: An ethnographic study of witchcraft and death. *Qualitative Sociology, 13,* 211-234.

Luff, T. L. (1990). Wicce: Adding a spiritual dimension to feminism. *Berkeley Journal of Sociology, 35,* 91-105.

Luhrmann, T. M. (1989). *Persuasions of the witch's craft: Ritual magic in contemporary England.* Cambridge, MA: Harvard University Press.

Luhrmann, T. M. (1993). Resurgence of romanticism: Contemporary neo-paganism, feminist spirituality and the divinity of nature. In K. Milton (Ed.), *Environmentalism: The view from anthropology* (pp. 219-232). London: Routledge.

Neitz, M. J. (1994). Quasi-religions and cultural movements: Contemporary witchcraft as a churchless religion. In A. L. Greil & T. Robbins (Ed.), *Religion and the social order* (pp. 127-149). London: Association for the Study of Religion.

Schutz, A. (1967). *The phenomenology of the social world* (G. Walsh & F. Lehnert, Trans. & Eds.). Evanston, IL: Northwestern University Press.

Smith, D. E. (1987). *The everyday world as problematic.* Toronto: University of Toronto Press.

Snorri Sturluson. (1987). *Edda* (A. Faulkes, Trans.). London: Everyman.

Tambiah, S. J. (1990). *Magic, science, religion, and the scope of rationality. The Lewis Henry Morgan lectures.* Cambridge, UK: Cambridge University Press.

Taylor, C. (1982). Interpretation and the sciences of man. In E. Bredo & W. Feinberg (Eds.), *Knowledge and values in social and educational research.* Philadelphia: Temple University Press. (Original work published 1971)

Turville-Petre, E. O. G. (1975). *Myth and religion of the north.* Westport, CT: Greenwood.

Venn, C. (1984). The subject of psychology. In J. Henriques, et al. (Eds.), *Changing the subject.* London: Methuen.

Wilson, R. C. (1994). Seeing they see not. In D. E. Young, J. G. Goulet, J. Henriques, W. Hollway, C. Urwin, C. Venn, & V. Walkerdine (Eds.), *Being changed by cross-cultural encounters: The anthropology of extraordinary experience* (pp. 16-38). Peterborough, Ontario, Canada: Broadview.

Winch, P. (1958). *The idea of a social science.* London: Routledge Kegan Paul.

Young, D. E., & Goulet, J. G. (Eds.). (1994). *Being changed by cross-cultural encounters: The anthropology of extraordinary experience.* Peterborough, Ontario, Canada: Broadview.

12

Telling Tales and Writing Stories[1]

Postmodernist Visions and Realist Images in Ethnographic Writing

RICHARD G. MITCHELL, JR.
KATHY CHARMAZ

This chapter is a conversation between two authors concerned with writing ethnographic tales in interesting ways. Ambivalence, multivocality, and give-and-take of perspectives are intended parts of this discussion. To begin, Richard Mitchell writes of his experiences in the field and as an ethnographic storyteller. Then Kathy Charmaz writes about the analysis of stories, beginning with Richard's account and generalizing to other ethnographic tales. Richard responds with an addendum to Kathy's analysis, stressing writing as an experience in its own right. We conclude where we began, in the field, with a second look at phenomena, storytelling, and authorship.

Ethnographers and writers in other genres rely on similar techniques (e.g., Bickham, 1994; Golightly, 1970; James, 1989; Krieger, 1984; Noble, 1994; Oates, 1970; Provost, 1980; Wright, 1989; Yolen, 1989). They employ five basic strategies: (a) pulling the reader into

AUTHORS' NOTE: Richard Mitchell thanks "John Huntley" for speaking his mind and for his timely gift. Kathy Charmaz thanks Gerald Rosen, David Bromige, and William De Ritter from whom she may have learned more than any of us realized. We both appreciate the comments of Norman K. Denzin, Mitchell Duneier, Lyn H. Lofland, Laurel Richardson, and the editor of this volume. Portions of this chapter were presented at the 1995 meeting of the American Sociological Association during the session on qualitative methodology.

the story, (b) re-creating experiential moods within the writing, (c) adding elements of surprise, (d) reconstructing the experience through written images, and (e) creating closure on the story while simultaneously recognizing it as part of an ongoing process.[2] Good writing reflects these strategies: They unify a work and move it toward its conclusion. That is part of our message. The other part is a caveat. Good writing transcends technique. These strategies are sensitizing and not prescriptive. Concern for technique alone does not help us understand writing, good or bad. Writing, like all forms of knowledge, is ultimately intuitive, not methodical (Sartre, 1953/ 1966, p. 240). Consider the following example, "The First Interview," an excerpt from the beginning of Richard's 12 years of study among survivalists. Survivalists are people who take seriously the possibility of imminent social disruption—economic collapse, foreign invasion, and even antigovernment violence and internal race war.

The First Interview

Recalling that first interview brings immediately to mind the March 1983 issue of the white supremacist publication *The National Vanguard*. It was a gift from my first informant. It came at exactly the right moment.

I had just finished reading "Survival Treasure Chest: Today's Pieces of Eight Make Sterling Investment" (Kogelschatz, 1983) in *Survive* magazine, to which I had recently subscribed. Gold and silver were the things to have in times of crisis, the article advised. No survivalist should be without a good supply. If this were the case, I reasoned, then my hometown precious metals dealer, John Huntley,[3] might be in contact with local area survivalists and, therefore, his shop would perhaps be a good place to start my research. I called him for an appointment. As it turned out, I was right and I was wrong. Huntley knew about survivalists but not the ones who hoard gold and silver.

I armed myself with a notebook and a list of naive questions ("How many survivalists would you say visit your shop in a typical week?" "Approximately what proportion are males or females?" "What would you estimate the average age of these survivalists to be?"). Feeling a bit insecure about my reception, I concealed my already running tape recorder in a light fabric bag. I had 45 minutes before the recorder would reveal itself by a loud end-of-tape click. I walked into Huntley's shop, shook his hand, and accepted the chair he offered at one side of his desk. After arranging my papers, and setting the concealed tape recorder on the desktop, I was ready to begin.

I introduced myself. I explained that I was a sociologist working on a book about survivalism and would like his help. I showed him the *Survive* article on investments. He had never seen the magazine before. After looking it over he opined, without much interest, that to his knowledge no survivalists of the sort the article described came to his shop. Fifteen minutes passed in unfocused talk. It seemed Huntley thought little of gold and silver stockpiling as a survival strategy, or of my writing project.

Then the conversation took an unexpected turn. Our roles reversed. Huntley began to ask me questions about myself, my wife, and the nationality of our parents and grandparents. When he learned my wife and I were both university faculty, and of German and Norwegian descent, he grew excited. "You talk about survival," he said, "I've made an in-depth study of that. . . . You and your wife would be prime candidates to be taught the realities of the last hundred years of United States civilization, and what's going to happen to us if we don't wake up!" Huntley had his own apocalyptic vision. And he had something else I just then noticed. On the desktop to his right, partially covered by a few sheets of paper, lay a .38-caliber revolver pointed my way.

The future looks grim, Huntley asserted. "We are living in a collapsing civilization. It's like an implosion." The cause of this failure? "The cultural bearing stock, the Anglo-Saxons and northern Europeans that are the problem-solving peoples of our civilization are being displaced." The presumed best of this lot, the Nordics who "fought the Mongol hordes in Europe . . . [and later] got in covered wagons and came west and survived in the wilderness" are at special risk. According to Huntley's reading of census publications, "Nordics are only having about 1.2 children per family." He added, "White people instinctively know things are wrong, particularly the Nordic because he is very sensitive to his surroundings. Even though he may not be able to verbalize this distinctive feeling, he stops reproducing, especially in the big cities. It was the Nordics that built New York City, but it's a fact that the ones who live there now have literally stopped having children." His prognosis: "If you project over a 150-year period in the United States, the Nordic will be extinct!" And elsewhere, "It's worse, it's worse in Sweden, Luxembourg, in France, even Russia and the white Communist countries, Poland, Czechoslovakia, Hungary." Other hazards are more immediate than extinction, Huntley warned. "We were 90% of the population up until the Civil War, now we are probably only 60%. When we become less than 50% of the population, then, living in a democracy, the other groups are going to completely dispossess us. We will be the dispossessed minority."

Huntley added details, examples, and citations from Charles Darwin, George Orwell, from Marx and Hitler. The tone of the conversation changed again. He began to speak of "us" versus "them"—to include my wife and me in his cause. He moved his chair closer, leaned forward. His tone became conspiratorial, as if secrets were being shared. "I'm not interested in giving you this information just so you can write a book," he clarified, "but for your own information. Then you can do with it what you will, because you might become a recruit. Then you will go out and want to proselytize." He seemed anxious to incorporate me into this hypothetical fate and to stress the personal seriousness and urgency of the Aryan's problem. At that moment I faced another problem, also serious and urgent. I glanced at my watch. In 9 minutes, more or less, Huntley would discover I had been tape-recording this conversation. The trust he seemed to imagine existed between us might suddenly end.

Right then I wished I had known more about the man. A few things were apparent: his clear blue-gray eyes, thick dark hair, athletic build, and clean, delicate hands. Some facts about him, had I known them at the time, might have put me at ease. He was 44, married, and had two teenage children. He held BA and MA degrees in music and had done some work toward a PhD. He had been a schoolteacher, and was once an unsuccessful congressional candidate. However, other information, also obtained later, would probably have made me even less comfortable.

As it turned out, Huntley was well-known to area journalists and local government officials for his frequent, unsolicited essays, phone calls, letters to the editor, and speeches at public meetings.[4] The timing of these expressions of opinion was unpredictable, but the themes were consistent: international Jewish conspiracy, growing government repression, and impending "patriotic" rebellion. Huntley was on record as having claimed, among other things, that "The Illuminati hired Marx to write the *Communist Manifesto*"; the United States military is preparing to quell a "nationwide tax rebellion of six million people, maybe more, who aren't even filing any tax returns"; the government has readied Operation Cable Splicer, which will "isolate various areas of the country [by creating] power blackouts and various communications breakdowns, then move the military in, . . . [confiscate guns and property and] arrest those people they consider dangerous—like myself." But "when they try it," Huntley bragged, "we will kick their butts right out of the country. I don't know what's going to happen but there's going to be bloodshed!"

Huntley predicted that at the head of this "patriotic rebellion" will be the Posse Comitatus, in which he had long been active. The Posse Comitatus, I was to learn, advocates armed resistance to what they view as illegitimate taxation based on personal income or property, or to any governmental authority superordinate to the county sheriff. In retrospect, this would have been relevant background material and certainly would have helped me understand what was going on, but I knew nothing of it at the time. Instead, I could only continue to listen, unsure of the interview's course or outcome. The tape recorder kept running.

From a file cabinet next to his desk, Huntley brought out the then latest edition of *The National Vanguard*. He was quiet for a moment, glancing through the issue as if to remind himself of its contents. Then placing the magazine on the desk between us, he continued,

"They talk about racism," he said. "Well, I'm a racist. I believe in preserving all the races, but not mixing them together." Huntley believed some social science, wittingly or not, contributes to the denigration of racial purity.

He continued: "One of the great misconceptions that the American civilization has been under since World War I has been the egalitarian or the equalitarian philosophy which is spread through the Franz Boaz and Margaret Mead school of anthropology. . . .

When he [Boaz] came to the United States, he was thoroughly imbued with Marxism, and the whole basis of Marxism is egalitarianism. In other words, you cannot admit to racial or individual differences if you are a Communist."

Huntley argued that this ideology of egalitarianism, while not part of the Constitution, has come to permeate educational curricula and governmental policy. "What you have here is Marxism. It goes from the very highest echelons of our federal establishment right into the school system." Marxism is only a symptom; it is not an end in itself, Huntley explained, but the means by which international Jewry seek to gain control. "What the Jews want to do is reduce us to the lowest common denominator, not just socially but biologically. They want to destroy the cultural bearing stock." Current social policies further this end, Huntley argued. "That's what integration does, it mixes the gene pool. It destroys the cultural bearing stock. And look at the manipulation in this zero population growth. The only people that have cut back on their population are the Europeans, especially the Nordics. Your Blacks and Mexicans and Vietnamese and other ethnic groups keep right on breeding."

Both Huntley and I had become agitated. Huntley seemed to care very much about the issues at hand. As he had told an earlier interviewer, "Once you get into this, if it piques your interest, you'll never get out of it. You just dig and dig and dig until it consumes you."[5] But Huntley seemed to be enjoying himself. Here he had, at once, an apparently receptive audience, perhaps a potential recruit, and the chance to unveil what he saw as a fundamental but overlooked principle of social science to a credentialed sociologist. In contrast, I felt confused and disoriented. Huntley was an obviously intelligent, widely read, articulate individual, a resident of my own community, yet he espoused racism of a sort I believed would be found only among bucolic bumpkins or the genuinely demented. The interview had drifted far from my intentions or control, my liberal sentiments had been summarily rejected, and my ability to withhold judgment was growing frail. Fieldwork was proving more than I was prepared for. In my uncertainty, I said little. While Huntley was anxious to reveal what he knew, I was trying to keep a secret. And frankly, I was frightened. If another's ideas could be so contrary to my expectations, what then of his behavior? How would my dishonesty regarding the tape-recording be received? As

Huntley spoke, I thought of the time, and of his impending discovery, now no more than a minute or two away. Huntley grew even more animated. Leaning forward again, forearms on the desk, his right hand strayed toward the revolver, brushing the papers away. Like an engrossed thinker stroking his chin, he began idly to rub his palm back and forth across the gun's cylinder. A sliver of afternoon sunlight breached the shutters and glinted off the gently swaying barrel. From my muzzle-on vantage point, and in the direct light, I could see the chambered bullets were a copper-jacketed, hollow-point design.

It ended as T. S. Eliot predicted the world will, not with a bang, but a whimper. As a final punctuation to his discourse on yet another topic, the misrepresentations of "Black History Month," Huntley picked up *The National Vanguard*. "If you want to find out what is really going on, read this!" he enthused, slapping the publication down on top of the concealed recorder. The "whap" of the descending magazine and the "click" of the ending tape coincided. The whimper was mine, a partially suppressed, involuntary cry of fear and relief. Puzzled by my utterance, Huntley offered reassurance. "You can keep it if you want," he said, tapping the journal. I thanked him, assured him I would look it over carefully and consider what he had said, and gathered my things to leave. The first survivalist interview was over. I had come confident of my will and skill to "win" respect and "acquire" information (these were the terms I used in preparatory notes to myself). My presented self, or so I imagined, was that of the competent, objective, purpose-filled researcher. I left in ambivalent confusion—titillated by flirting with apparent danger, befuddled by my naïveté, and frightened by my potential new identity, by what I had been taken for, and might become, if this study continued—a racist.

Kathy Charmaz's Writing Critique

What can we learn about writing ethnographic tales from Richard's story? Through studying his story, I offer some practical guidelines for turning research tales into written stories. These guidelines are for qualitative researchers to consider, to play with, and, perhaps, to adopt or revise. Analyzing a story reveals most clearly how the guidelines work. However, they can be used to enliven less dramatic ethnographic description and more explicitly analytic works (Charmaz, 1991). Although my analysis emphasizes finished stories, I recommend adopting these guidelines as observational and writing strategies from the beginning of the research process. The guidelines are tools. Nothing more, or less. They may help us observe more closely, write more gracefully, and, thus, state our ideas more artfully.

Pulling the Reader In

What induces us to read a story, article, or book? The opening paragraphs or the opening chapter should pull us into the story and convince us to continue. Hence, the writer invites, entices, and involves the reader to stay with the story and to remain in the scene (Hubbard, 1988; Noble, 1994). In order to bring us into the story, the writer needs to provide its context, or to imply what might follow. Often qualitative researchers use a telling anecdote, case material, or interview excerpt to do just that. A telling opener piques our interest and curiosity. In my own writing, I often focus on a concrete person or specific incident to stimulate reader involvement in more general themes. A carefully selected opener allows the writer to make implicit or explicit claims from the beginning. Writers who retell their intense experience, rather than recount someone else's, re-create its power through their written images. In more formal writing, I look for a clear, spare opener in the first paragraph or two that states concretely and specifically what research or analytic "story" this work will tell. When the author's thesis is general, the problem common, or the argument unclear, I lose interest. You probably do too.

In "The First Interview," Richard accomplishes four writer's objectives in the first short paragraph. He (a) identifies the viewpoint of the story, (b) persuades the reader to become intrigued and emotionally involved, (c) sets the mood, and (d) hints of suspense and conflict. From the start, we know that the story proceeds from his viewpoint. Told from any other viewpoint, it would not be the same story. Richard brings his readers, especially other social scientists, right into the scene with images of the white supremacist magazine. By mentioning that it was a gift from his first informant, he taps others' images and memories of initiating fieldwork. Thus, he establishes a common ground with us, his readers. But he pulls readers into the story and keeps them reading and wanting to know more when he states (about the magazine): "It came at exactly the right moment." Why was it the right moment? In this brief cue, Richard sets the stage for telling his tale. Similarly, he develops the scene when he talks about starting his research and making contact with Huntley. He arouses our curiosity further when he says, "As it turned out, I was right and I was wrong." What happened next? How did being wrong shape later events?

We want to know what happened. Richard's writing style establishes a personal connection with us.[6] Through his use of language, imagery, rhythm, order, and authentic voice, we imagine a whole human being who lived the story, rather than hear an anonymous report of it. His informal style and judicious self-disclosure allow our intimacy with him to grow. I say "judicious self-disclosure" intentionally.[7] Otherwise, the writer intrudes and the writing grates. Neither gratuitous inclusion nor intentional omission of the writer's presence (as the positivists would have it) leads to good writing. I find a built-in tension here: The writer is at once the source of meaning and the source of its obfuscation. The extent to which the writer's presence should be central and explicit depends on the nature of the research tale. Ultimately, the effectiveness of the writing partly turns on how the writer handles this tension.

Richard's story presents an interesting case of the writer's subjectivity because he is central to the drama. Yet his voice in telling the tale allows us to understand the emerging events. As Richard tells us what he thinks, feels, and does, he brings us into a jointly felt scene and prompts us to empathize with him (see Nash, 1989). Even though the story is Richard's tale, he does not dominate it unnecessarily. He brings himself into the story when needed to move the story along.

Richard's place in the story becomes layered and complex. More than being the narrator who provides the viewpoint, he acts within the scene. He becomes the narrator with a secret, the actor who takes his readers into the plot.[8] Two sharp edges frame this plot: his precipitous plunge into an unexpected scrape and his expected downfall on discovery of the tape recorder. Richard's immersion in the story fits the tale told.

Re-creating Experiential Mood

Re-creating the mood of an experience through the writing keeps the reader engaged. In addition, it unifies the scene and tightens the story. Cheney (1983) describes a pure scene as all action with minimal distractions. Only those narrative details are included that enliven the scene.

As a writer, I think about what kind of mood an experience, event, or encounter reflects and then I write it into the description. If I'm working with a more abstract idea, I ponder how I want to cast it within the analysis. When writing a story, a unified portrayal of characters similarly furthers re-creating the mood of the experience and lessens distractions. To do so, a writer may sacrifice efficient writing, that is, narrative description, for an effective story. Thus, Richard uses direct quotes from Huntley's diatribe, offers his internal monologue, and provides reflections about the scene while in it.

Richard takes us through the shifts in mood as the story progresses. Our involvement intensifies and our suspense increases. His imagery and candor place us in the scene with him. "I armed myself with a notebook and a list of naive questions." We can all imagine doing this. We identify with Richard as he sets out to play the role of social scientist to a respondent in an unfamiliar setting from whom he expects only preliminary information. As events proceed, we sense growing ambiguity and his waning morale. "Feeling a bit insecure about my reception, I concealed my already running tape recorder in a light fabric bag." The mood deepens. We feel Richard losing ground: "Fifteen minutes passed in unfocused talk. It seemed Huntley thought little of gold and silver stockpiling as a survival strategy, or of my writing project."

The mood shifts ominously as Huntley takes control of the interview and Richard notices the gun. Huntley's excitement quickens. We feel it in the short, stark sentences. Tension builds through Richard's comments, not solely through the Huntley excerpts: "However, other information, also obtained later, would probably have made me even less comfortable." Richard's hint makes Huntley more menacing. The twists and turns in the encounter keep us riveted. "Huntley seemed to be enjoying himself. . . . In contrast, I felt confused and disoriented." Urgency mounts as Richard fears he cannot escape before the tape clicks off. "Fieldwork was proving more than I was prepared for. In my uncertainty, I said little. While Huntley was anxious to reveal what he knew, I was trying to keep a secret. And frankly, I was frightened."

Adding Surprise

Throughout the story, unforeseen events pile swiftly on each other. We enter a scene with Richard where ordinary rules and values are discarded. Expectations dissolve. Uncertainty increases. Roles reverse. Stereotypes collapse. Potential threat heightens . . . fear escalates. Richard's initial insecurity sets the mood for his later predicament. The story begins with an ambiguous scene with an unexpected opportunity to probe an unknown character's views. Yet the story does not dissolve into a routine event or a mundane tale of the field. The formidable topic, Richard's apprehensiveness, and Huntley's astonishing adeptness in controlling the interview all preclude that. The momentum quickens, suspense thickens. Early in the tale, Richard warns us of dangers to come: "Huntley had his own apocalyptic vision. And he had something else I just then noticed. On the desktop to his right, partially covered by a few sheets of paper, lay a .38-caliber revolver pointed my way."

Consistent with principles of writing fiction (Carroll, 1990; Frank & Wall, 1994; Giovannoni, 1972; Provost, 1980), Richard creates tension and adds surprise by recounting a predicament. In less gripping ethnographic stories, we add elements of surprise by revealing implicit meanings and rules, showing taken-for-granted assumptions, defining worldviews, and explicating hidden processes. In Richard's story, the tape recorder, an instrument for enhancing interview recall and, by extension, the thoroughness of the report, paradoxically is transformed into an obstacle and a liability, threatening to destroy trust, create enmity, diminish access to other respondents, and even damage professional prestige. Already Richard feels uneasy and stuck in an alarming encounter. Then, beyond that, Huntley's imminent discovery of the hidden tape recorder spells disaster. Richard works the drama of his tale deep into his sentences: "At that moment I faced another problem, also serious and urgent. I glanced at my watch. In 9 minutes, more or less, Huntley would discover I had been tape-recording this conversation." The tape recorder turns into a time bomb ticking toward an explosive confrontation.

Like most writers, Richard does not allow the events to be a total surprise. He foreshadows the surprises. Foreshadowing limits the surprise and defines the obstacle to overcome. "The conversation took an unexpected turn." Richard warns us here that the predictable interviewer and respondent roles had changed. Writers also foreshadow and limit surprises by planting questions. "If another's ideas could be so contrary to my expectations, what then of his behavior? How would my dishonesty regarding the tape-recording be received?"

Reconstructing Ethnographic Experience

Why should readers accept the writer's viewpoint? What prompts anyone to trust an ethnographer's rendering of an experience? I contend the writer's presented images must resemble the experience. Though only evocative of the shared experience, ethnographers must strive to represent their subjects' understandings as well as their own (Mitchell, 1993, pp. 41, 54-55; Prus, 1996). Richard's tale may portray an extraordinary experience, a world alien to his readers. Other works address experiences that readers may share (Charmaz, 1991; Denzin, 1987a, 1987b). Readers will compare their experiences to the ethnographer's portrayed images. What helps writers to create works that seem real and true? How can we reconstruct and represent lived experience through our written images of it? We must show our readers what we want them to know. We cannot simply tell them. Nor can we persuade through mere assertion. Richard shows his readers what's happening. Showing our readers is the first rule of good writing (Carroll, 1990; Provost, 1980). Richard shows us Huntley's character as well as his own. He produces Huntley as he forms the tale. Huntley's identity emerges through using his statements such as "[The government will] arrest those people they consider dangerous—like myself." But " 'when they try it,' Huntley bragged, 'we will kick their butts right out of the country.' " Quoting Huntley reveals his viewpoint, builds another narrative voice into the story, and, simultaneously, dramatizes Richard's predicament. Richard's statements about Huntley further reveal Huntley's character. He reports that Huntley "bragged." Huntley did not state, suggest, or hope—he bragged. Richard underscores Huntley's agenda when he writes, "He moved his chair closer, leaned forward. His tone became conspiratorial, as if secrets were being shared." Richard also produces Huntley's emerging identity as he simultaneously chronicles the unfolding events. "Like an engrossed thinker stroking his chin, he began idly to rub his palm back and forth across the gun's cylinder." The blend of ethnographic commentary and direct statements all contribute to the veracity of the scene. Everything in the story serves a purpose.

Throughout the tale, Richard's tone is consistent. His words and images fit the story. We can imagine the scene. He provides sufficient description for us to surmise his predicament and to feel his trepidation. Richard builds on his vulnerability, the uncertainty, the growing ominousness—his urgency. Like a creative writer, he puts feelings together, rather than taking them apart. As Hale (1972) observes, the writer's feeling is a method of perceiving. It renders the writer open to his or her subjectivity. Feeling is concerned with secrets, hiding places, and imagined scenes. Richard's feeling forecasts his precarious position and foreshadows the emerging drama. Even his description fits the twists and turns in mood and thus makes the story powerful. No discrepancies in tone exist. He has calibrated his tone and shaped images to mirror the unfolding events.

Effective word choice contributes to Richard's presented image resembling his experience. His writing gives the impression of natural speech (Packer & Timpane, 1986; Provost, 1980). It is only an impression, an image. Richard talks with us—so it seems. He reproduces the informality and intimacy of natural speech. He does so through describing actors and events in a conversational style. He also reveals his thoughts and feelings: "The whimper was mine, a partially suppressed, involuntary cry of fear and relief." Richard describes the moment as though recounting it to a close friend. He does not replicate natural speech with all its hesitancy, irrelevancy, redundancy, and inadequacy, yet his words read as if spoken. Giving the impression of natural speech echoes the experience and imbues it with verisimilitude.

Richard's interview excerpts are pointed; they distill the experience. We certainly do not receive 45 minutes of dialogue in this story. Nor do we view all the images that Richard saw during his foreboding encounter. He creates a painting for us, rather than a photograph (Charmaz, 1995). Writers need to give us the shape, color, tone, order, and form of their stories; they do not need to provide the entire experience. Instead, they stress some events, minimize others, and ignore still others. Extraneous detail clutters the story and obscures the point. Writers supply sufficient content in distilled form to make their intentions and interpretations understandable and persuasive. Then readers can imagine the action and, likely, empathize with the writer or main character, but they may not be persuaded. To persuade, writers have to offer sufficient evidence to support the credibility of their claims. The best writers balance the least content with the most powerful persuasion.

The rhythm of the words should be consistent with the described experience. Richard's images are lucid and forceful. For example, he creates emphasis and rhythm through the parallel construction of "titillated by flirting with apparent danger, befuddled by my naïveté, and frightened by my potential new identity." Throughout his tale, the flow of sentences echoes the progression of events. The words sound right. Their length, sound, and cadence create movement and forewarn of impending action:

> As Huntley spoke, I thought of the time and of his impending discovery, now no more than an minute or two away. Huntley grew even more animated. Leaning forward again, forearms on the desk, his right hand strayed toward the revolver, brushing the papers away.

Creating Closure

Richard's ending is at once compelling and haunting. He does not offer the standard closure. There is no resolution of the conflict. No heroic overcoming of the obstacle. No ingenious solution to the predicament. Rather, a fortuitous coincidence allowed him to leave unscathed. The coincidence stops the immediate suspense but does not end the story. Instead, Richard's reflection closes this story forcefully—the entire piece coheres. His final revelation opens the possibility of another more powerful drama. This tale is but one chapter in a evolving saga (Ellis, 1995). Like a novel, Richard's closure is implicit from the beginning. He hints. He reconstructs the foreboding mood. He juxtaposes Huntley's expanding persona against his own shrinking identity. His style, imagery, and voice all move us toward the conclusion.

The meaning of the tale comes through in the last twist, the final surprise: We ourselves are vulnerable to the worlds we enter.[9]

Richard Mitchell's Addendum

There you have it. A story, and a story about storytelling, both neat, pat, finished, and quite misleading if taken at face value. Let's consider the development of "The First Interview." It was certainly not begun as a project intended to illustrate principles of writing. I knew little or nothing of the succinct and useful writing guidelines Kathy pointed out and explained with such care in the preceding paragraphs. Had I known of them in advance, Huntley's story might have taken other forms. Instead, the Huntley tale began, like most other ethnographic writing, as a mundane list of observations and notes, nearly formless, entirely fragmented. For direction I had only a vague personal sense of the word, tone, and cadence it would be nice but not necessary to achieve. Drama did not assert itself from the field but was sifted, organized, and built up out of a confused mass of quotidian detail and ambiguous feelings over successive drafts and considerable time.

Feelings have been mentioned, and writing is an affect-filled experience to be sure. As a would-be author, I had feelings in these times. But far from fear, trepidation, and existential angst, this writing period was one of growing personal satisfaction, reassurance, and fulfillment. The memory of clumsy, faltering fieldwork was set aside and in its place came the adventure of tale telling. Quiet, safe at my desk or in my favorite seat at the local coffee house, I luxuriated in creating with words and re-creating in fantasy my own dual characters, the clever writer and the fieldworker to whom exciting things might happen. I reveled in temporary enchantments. Life was mine to transform, idealize, simplify. My pen drew imaginary sides, set rules, and made action consequent and lasting. At the heart of writing experience are moments of the intense imaginative actualization I've elsewhere called "flow" (Mitchell, 1983, pp. 153-192). Fleetingly, action and awareness merge, the spontaneous "I" joins the socialized "me" in concerted and complimentary effort. Like mountain climbing, chess competition, delicate surgery, and other forms of cathected action, writing at its best demands the full focus of our creativity and skill. In return, we get what we give. Unequivocal commitment yields a full measure of intrinsic reward.

In these comments, neither Kathy nor I imply support for a distinction between so-called realist and impressionist reportage. There is none. No worthy author's writings derive entirely from empirically ungrounded figments of fantasy. All ethnographic stories are stories of some portion of human lived experience, experience that is eminently real, immediate, concrete, and meaningful to those who live it. Sartre put it bluntly: Human lived experience "is, it is what it is, and it is as it is" (as quoted in Solomon, 1988, p. 180). That's clear enough. All ethnographic stories, too, are stories, more or less imaginative, nuanced, and stylistic interpretations of the worlds we study. Quibbles over the ontological status of the truly true and debates over the primacy of one discourse over another serve no useful purpose. The problem of perception, of obtaining consciousness of the world, is not an issue here. Our concern is finding ways for individual consciousness to join the intersubjective, ways to report experience to others and to ourselves. All stories including accounts of scientific knowledge are relative and provisional. All are but temporary way points in the ongoing construction of meaning. William Pierce, the editor of *The National Vanguard*, publishes facts of human character and history on which Huntley performs his own analysis. Huntley's account of history and current events is the grist of Mitchell's storytelling. Mitchell's tale provides Charmaz with material on which yet other sorts of analyses are performed. And so it goes. Facts call out interpretations; interpretations become facts. Realities and impressions answer each other, reciprocate. The last one up claims expertise, authorship, but only until the next telling.

However crafty and complete our stories are, they can be no more than tentative offerings, possible ways of telling from among many. In the field, the people we study talk back, resist, bend, reinterpret, and even reject the images, pictures, and conceptions we and others create of them. We can, of course, insulate our accounts from the risk of empirical disconfirmation. We can shift our studies away from the holistic complexity of human social life to the analysis of symptoms and parts—rate-data, written texts, audio- or video-tapes, and other ephemera. These stand-ins do not talk back but obligingly lend themselves to passive and noncontradictory analysis. Simplifications of this sort may be done in the name of dispassionate reason, as with uncritical positivism, as ungrounded literary or cultural criticism, as ameliorative moral projects such as found in soul-saving rescue ethnography from the mission station or soup kitchen, or as urged by so-called standpoint epistemologies. In all cases, the yeasty, ambivalent, amorphous experience of social life is set straight, held at arm's length, narrowed, and sanitized in the names of procedural or political propriety.

Postmodernism's strength is the encouragement it lends to varieties of aesthetic and critical writings that together may add usefully to the social sciences. But merely claiming postmodern allegiance is not enough. We must rid ourselves at once of the intellectual sclerosis of positivism and works in the name of science that are merely methodical in other ways, that are without art or craft. To borrow from Feyerabend, we do not wish to exchange the professional incompetence of modernism for an equally inconsequential incompetent professionalism, a self-satisfied postmodernism without human roots.

Epilogue

A few weeks before sending this article to press, I visited Huntley again. This time, the advantage of surprise was mine. I used a different magazine to start our conversation. After neutral greetings, I gave him a copy of the lead article from the May 1995 issue of *Atlantic Monthly*—"The Diversity Myth: America's Leading Export." There was a message in this gift: I was not an ordinary coin shop customer. He could tell I knew something about him, but what? Was I friend or foe? (I was not sure either.) The 12 years had dimmed recollections for both of us. As Huntley leafed through the article, he probed, "Uh, do you live around here? Have we talked before?" I affirmed both questions with a few details and, like the proud parent I am, I showed him a picture of my blond, blue-eyed, smiling 3½-year-old daughter. That was enough. Friend.

Huntley became amiable and, as before, instructive. The years had done nothing to diminish his eclectic literacy and eccentric zeal. He was soon launched into an impromptu lecture full of new facts and familiar themes. He warned again of the Franz Boaz legacy and the "spreading tentacles" of egalitarianism. He spoke of Shakespeare's disdainful view of blacks, of the "abhorred union" of Othello and Desdemona, the ineptness of Portia's one black suitor in *The Merchant of Venice,* and the villainy of Aaron from *Titus Andronicus,* the Bard's "Devil incarnate." Next, Huntley turned to the Rockefeller dynasty, starting with the patriarch, John D.'s father, "a bigamist and a charlatan," who traveled the byways of Pennsylvania and the East "fathering at least ten illegitimate children" and peddling raw petroleum as an elixir. The Rockefellers' interest in oil had its roots in this crude patent medicine, he told me, for "this stuff was just bubbling out of the ground . . . and nobody knew what to do with it . . . so they developed pharmaceuticals" and, as a result, "ninety percent of pharmaceuticals are petro-based." He spoke of recent scholarship, of Edward O. Wilson's work in sociobiology, of *The Bell Curve,* and even of a recent article from *Society* titled "The Seeds of Racial Explosion," by USC economics professor Timur Kuran. Huntley continued for 10 more minutes. As before, he seemed enthused by his topics and pleased with his audience.

There was something different about this visit. I felt more at ease, in control. Huntley's ideas were indeed strange but not unprecedented. In the past dozen years, I had heard the likes of them more than once. I was on familiar ground. Half attention was all I needed to follow his arguments. I listened, but also looked around the shop. Things had changed. A few years ago, Huntley had moved his business downtown, across from the county courthouse where he could "keep an eye on things better." (The police chief later told me this surveillance works both ways.) Huntley was visibly older. His hair was still thick but near white. His waist was still thin, but now so were his arms. The furniture had been rearranged. Huntley's desk—and his gun—were now in an adjacent room, nearly out of sight, nearly out of reach. We talked standing at the counter this time, and I noticed I was three or four inches taller than he. Judging from the posters on the walls and windows, Huntley is more active in community theater and music than politics these days.

It was late afternoon, time to close. The comforting institutional shadow of the courthouse crept up Huntley's storefront. Bidding him goodbye, I walked toward home, calm and satisfied with the results of the day. All had gone well. I found new data and no real danger. Yet my composure was not full depth. It never is these days. Then and now, I wonder about the other ways this interview might have gone. I've been face to face with a good deal of extremism in the past 12 years—at meetings of the Klan and the Aryan Nations, at clandestine training camps and public conferences, among anti-government militias, messianic zealots, and would-be revolutionaries. Not all these encounters have been so serene or civil, but I'm always lucky, I tell myself. Just be prepared and know what to expect—that's how to stay out of trouble. I was not surprised by Alan Berg's assassination or the Oklahoma City bombing. I've heard plans for similar events being discussed often enough. Mostly talk, I tell myself. Lately, however, I've grown uncertain, apprehensive. I wonder, have I done everything necessary for the next interview? New tape recorders run silently. And with a permit, I could carry a gun.

Notes

1. This chapter is reprinted with permission from Mitchell and Charmaz.

2. In keeping with grounded theory methods, Kathy Charmaz developed these guidelines before reviewing the literature on fiction writing. They derive from her earlier work but strikingly echo strategies of fiction writers (see especially Carroll, 1990; Frank & Wall, 1994; Giovannoni, 1972; Hale, 1972; Noble, 1994).

3. Huntley is a pseudonym. All quoted material in this discussion of the first interview, unless otherwise identified, is from transcripts.

4. The sources of material attributed to Huntley in this paragraph are intentionally omitted. They derive from public documents that identify Huntley by his proper name.

5. The source of these comments is deliberately omitted.

6. Style means the presence of the writer in the writing and reflects how the writer conveys his or her thoughts (Barzun, 1975; Lambuth, 1976; Strunk & White, 1959). Tone, an element of style, reveals ambiance and the writer's attitude (Packer & Timpane, 1986).

7. Postmodernist writers can err by attending too much to themselves and too little to their collective stories. Gary Provost (1980) contends that writer intrusion works only when the writer was a participant or possesses special expertise. Writer intrusion differs from voice. The writer's voice lets the reader imagine him or her

speaking. A writer creates a voice by drawing on his or her perspective, vision, sentiments, and humor.

8. Richard's narrative distance fits his story. Narrative distance is not merely a ploy to gain or to claim objectivity; rather, the relative degree of narrative distance should fit the story and, in turn, fit the experience. Richard's telling of the tale brings him deep into the narrative. My involvement is in putting the analysis together, not in the story itself, and fosters much more narrative distance (Atkinson, 1992; Lofland & Lofland, 1994; Richardson, 1990; Wolcott, 1990).

9. Michael Agar (1990) argues that creative nonfiction techniques in ethnographic writing can lead to reshaping the research process to fit the text. That is possible if we put the story before the experienced process. If, however, we put the process first, with all its nebulousness and stickiness, then we can use fiction techniques for purposes consistent with Agar.

References

Agar, M. (1990). Text and fieldwork: Exploring the excluded middle. *Journal of Contemporary Ethnography, 19,* 73-88.

Atkinson, P. (1992). *Understanding ethnographic texts.* Newbury Park, CA: Sage.

Barzun, J. (1975). *Simple & direct: A rhetoric for writers.* New York: Harper & Row.

Bickham, J. M. (1994). *Setting: How to create and sustain a sharp sense of time and place in your fiction.* Cincinnati, OH: Writer's Digest.

Carroll, D. L. (1990). *A manual of writer's tricks.* New York: Paragon House.

Charmaz, K. (1991). *Good days, bad days: The self in chronic illness and time.* New Brunswick, NJ: Rutgers University Press.

Charmaz, K. (1995). Between positivism and postmodernism: Implications for method. In N. K. Denzin (Ed.), *Studies in symbolic interaction* (Vol. 17, pp. 43-72). Greenwich, CT: JAI.

Cheney, T. A. R. (1983). *Getting the words right: How to rewrite, edit & revise.* Cincinnati, OH: Writer's Digest.

Denzin, N. K. (1987a). *The alcoholic self.* Newbury Park, CA: Sage.

Denzin, N. K. (1987b). *The recovering alcoholic.* Newbury Park, CA: Sage.

Ellis, C. (1995). *Final negotiations: A story of love, loss, and chronic illness.* Philadelphia: Temple University Press.

Frank, T., & Wall, D. (1994). *Finding your writer's voice: A guide to creative fiction.* New York: St. Martin's.

Giovannoni, J. O. (1972). 8 Steps to professional writing. In A. Mathieu (Ed.), *The creative writer* (pp. 31-37). Cincinnati, OH: Writer's Digest.

Golightly, B. (1970). The use of dialogue. In F. A. Dickson & S. Smythe (Eds.), *The Writer's Digest handbook of short story writing* (pp. 58-65). Cincinnati, OH: Writer's Digest.

Hale, N. (1972). A note on feeling. In A. Mathieu (Ed.), *The creative writer* (pp. 118-124). Cincinnati, OH: Writer's Digest.

Hubbard, F. A. (1988). *How writing works.* New York: St. Martin's.

James, P. D. (1989). One clue at a time. In S. K. Burack (Ed.), *The writer's handbook* (pp. 204-207). Boston: The Writer.

Kogelschatz. (1983). Survival treasure chest: Today's pieces of eight make sterling investment. *Survive, 41,* 38-39.

Krieger, S. (1984). Fiction and social science. In N. K. Denzin (Ed.), *Studies in symbolic interaction* (Vol. 5, pp. 269-287). Greenwich, CT: JAI.

Lambuth, D. (1976). *The golden book on writing.* New York: Penguin.

Lofland, J., & Lofland, L. H. (1994). *Analyzing social settings* (3rd ed.). Belmont, CA: Wadsworth.

Mitchell, R. G., Jr. (1983). *Mountain experience: The psychology and sociology of adventure.* Chicago: University of Chicago Press.

Mitchell, R. G., Jr. (1993). *Secrecy in fieldwork.* Newbury Park, CA: Sage.

Nash, W. (1989). *Rhetoric: The wit of persuasion.* Oxford, UK: Blackwell.

Noble, W. (1994). *Conflict, action & suspense: How to pull readers in and carry them along with dramatic, powerful story-telling.* Cincinnati, OH: Writer's Digest.

Oates, J. C. (1970). The nature of short fiction; Or the nature of my short fiction. In F. A. Dickson & S. Smythe (Eds.), *The Writer's Digest handbook of short story writing* (pp. xi-xviii). Cincinnati, OH: Writer's Digest.

Packer, N. H., & Timpane, J. (1986). *Writing worth reading.* New York: St. Martin's.

Provost, G. (1980). *Make every word count.* Cincinnati, OH: Writer's Digest.

Prus, R. (1996). *Symbolic interaction and ethnographic research: Intersubjectivity and the study of human lived experience.* Albany: State University of New York Press.

Richardson, L. (1990). *Writing strategies: Reaching diverse audiences.* Newbury Park, CA: Sage.

Sartre, J.-P. (1966). *Being and nothingness: An essay on phenomenological ontology* (H. Barnes, Trans.). New York: Washington Square Press. (Original work published 1953)

Solomon, R. C. (1988). *Continental philosophy since 1750: The rise and fall of the self.* Oxford, UK: Oxford University Press

Strunk, W., & White, E. B. (1959). *The elements of style.* New York: Macmillan.

Van Maanen, J. (1988). *Tales of the field.* Chicago: University of Chicago Press.

Wolcott, H. F. (1990). *Writing up qualitative research.* Newbury Park, CA: Sage.

Wright, L. R. (1989). How to keep the reader turning the pages. In S. K. Burack (Ed.), *The writer's handbook* (pp. 238-241). Boston: The Writer.

Yolen, J. (1989). Story-telling: The oldest and newest art. In S. K. Burack (Ed.), *The writer's handbook* (pp. 489-493). Boston: The Writer.

Name Index

About the Contributors

Cheryl Albas is Associate Professor of Sociology at the University of Manitoba. Her research interests are in the areas of student life, cross-cultural proxemics and family interaction.

Dan Albas is Professor of Sociology at the University of Manitoba. His theoretical areas of interest are dramaturgy, proxemics, paralanguage and symbolic interaction. His substantive publications are in the area of student life and communication via tone and voice.

Jenny Blain teaches Sociology and Anthropology at Mount Saint Vincent University in Halifax, Nova Scotia. Her areas of specialization are discourse analysis, gender, and the construction of identity. Her current research project, funded by a grant from SSHRC, is on constitution of identity and community in present-day Earth-Centred religions, with a specific focus on Ásatrú.

Richard A. Brymer is Associate Professor of Sociology at McMaster University, Hamilton, Ontario. He attended University of Texas (B.A. 1959/M.A. 1962) and Michigan State University (Ph.D. 1967). His research is in the area of evolution, deviant behavior and social problems.

Kathy Charmaz, Professor of Sociology at Sonoma State University, has written about chronic illness, self and identity, the sociology of

253

time, grief and bereavement, and qualitative methods. Her book *Good Days, Bad Days: The Self in Chronic Illness and Time* was given the Charles Horton Cooley award from the Society for the Study of Symbolic Interaction and the Distinguished Scholarship Award from the Pacific Sociological Association. Her co-edited volume with Allan Kellehear and Glynnis Howarth, *The Unknown Country: Death in Australia, Britain and the USA* was recently published. Currently, she is involved in several projects including an empirical study of the body, explications of qualitative research, and a series of works on writing social science.

Kerry Daly received a Ph.D. from McMaster University in Sociology, and is currently Professor in the Department of Family Studies at the University of Guelph. He has several areas of research interest including adoption, fatherhood, and the phenomenological experience of time in families. Although his research involves the use of both quantitative and qualitative methods, his expertise is in the use of qualitative methods. He is co-editor of *Qualitative Methods in Family Research* (1992), which is now in its fourth printing. He is author of *Families and Time: Keeping Pace in a Hurried Culture* (1996) and co-author (with Michael Sobol) of *A National Study of Adoption Issues* (1993).

Anna Dienhart has come to academic research after spending 15 years as a consultant and economic advisor to large corporations. After receiving her Ph.D. in Family Relations and Human Development at the University of Guelph in 1995, she now brings her many years as a researcher to new questions concerning the family. Publications from her recent research projects include articles on looking at family therapy practices to effectively engage men in family change, using narrative family therapy to engage fathers in responsible parenting of their children, a critique of cultural practices that may limit men's involvement in fathering their children, and collaborative parenting partnerships as an alternative to gender stereotyped roles for mothers and fathers. Her recent research has won an award from the National Council on Family Relations.

Scott Grills (Ph.D., McMaster University) is Associate Professor of sociology at Augustana University College, Camrose, Alberta. His research focuses on generic social process through attending to deviance as a feature of everyday activities, and he has published articles on political activity, recruitment, and deviance designation. Formerly an editor with the journal *Dianoia*, this is his first edited volume.

Leslie Irvine earned her Ph.D. at the State University of New York at Stony Brook. At the time of this writing, she teaches sociology at Wesleyan University in Middletown, Connecticut. Her research interests include selfhood, the emotions, gender, medicine, and popular culture. The research referred to in her chapter is from her dissertation, titled *Romancing the Self: Codependency and the American Quest for Fulfillment*. In 1997, she was awarded the Herbert Blumer Award from the Society for the Study of Symbolic Interaction.

Richard G. Mitchell, Jr. is Associate Professor of Sociology at Oregon State University. He is an ethnographer with interests in qualitative methodology, avocational risk-adventure, professional ethics, and separatist, segregationist and millennial social movements.

Robert Prus (University of Waterloo), an interactionist working in the Chicago-school tradition, has recently completed the volume *Subcultural Mosaics and Intersubjective Realities* (1997) and is presently working on *Beyond the Power Mystique* (1998). Both books are informed by his ethnographic work on the marketplace.

Clinton R. Sanders is Professor of Sociology at the University of Connecticut. He is the author of *Customizing the Body: The Art and Culture of Tattooing* (1989), the editor of *Marginal Conventions: Popular Culture, Mass Media and Social Deviance* (1990), and co-editor (with Jeff Ferrell) of *Cultural Criminology* (1995). Sanders' major area of concentration is the connection between social deviance and popular culture. He has done research on various drug using subcultures and conflictual interactions in public settings. Sanders' current research is focused on human relationships with companion animals. His most recent book, *Regarding Animals* (with Arnold Arluke, 1996), was awarded the 1997 Charles Horton Cooley award by the Society for the Study of Symbolic Interaction.

William Shaffir (Ph.D., McGill University) is Professor of Sociology at McMaster University, Hamilton, Ontario. His research has been in

the areas of hassidic communities, qualitative methodology, professional socialization, and religious defection. He continues to study
hassidic Jews and has recently published on the messianic revivalism
among the Lubavitcher hassidim. Research plans include studies of
deviance among haredi—ultra-Orthodox—Jews, and ex-politicians.

Robert A. Stebbins received his Ph.D. in sociology in 1964 from the
University of Minnesota. He is Professor of Sociology at the University of Calgary, where he conducts qualitative research on serious
leisure and North American Francophones living as a linguistic minority. He is also the editor (with William Shaffir) of *Experiencing
Fieldwork* and the author of several articles on exploratory research.